HUGH GOLDIE

# THIS HUMAN NATURE

THE THINKER'S LIBRARY—No. 64

# THIS HUMAN NATURE

## A HISTORY, A COMMENTARY,
## AN EXPOSITION

BY

## CHARLES DUFF

"The history of those animals with which
we are best acquainted, forms the first
object of our chiefest curiosity."
*Goldsmith.*

*Definitive Edition*

LONDON
WATTS & CO.
5 & 6 JOHNSON'S COURT, FLEET STREET, E.C.4

*First published (Humphrey Toulmin), 1930*
*Cheap Edition, 1935*
*First issued in the Thinker's Library*
*(revised and abridged), 1937*
*Definitive Edition (Thinker's Library), 1950*

*Printed in Great Britain by Richard Clay and Company, Ltd.,*
*Bungay, Suffolk, and published by C. A. Watts & Co. Ltd.,*
*5 & 6 Johnson's Court, Fleet Street, London, E.C.4*

# CONTENTS

## BOOK I

### A PREFACE TO ALL HISTORY

## BOOK II

### THE TAMING AND SOPHISTICATION OF HUMAN NATURE

## BOOK III

### ROMAN MATERIALISM AND INSTITUTIONALIZED CHRISTIANITY

# BOOK IV

### WAYWARD PROGRESSION OF HUMAN NATURE

# BOOK V

### HUMAN NATURE TODAY AND TOMORROW

# Book I: A PREFACE TO ALL HISTORY

## § 1

## WHYS AND WHEREFORES, IF ANY

VERY little is known of human nature, and one reason for this is that man has always made great efforts to hide his true nature. We do not know the origin of mankind; and talk of man's " destiny " is mostly balderdash. Researches into the antiquity of our remote ancestors have covered a limited geographical area: a few parts of Europe, one or two districts in Northern Africa, and certain spots in Western Asia and North America have been superficially investigated and have even been made to yield a few elementary but as yet futile secrets. We are here because we are here; and no man that has ever lived can give a better reason. To some people it may appear pitiable that we mortals should not know whence we came, where we go—if " go " is the right word—when we die; or why. We are never sure of the reasons why we behave as we do while we are here, and one of the most difficult problems to decide is which is the wise man and which is the fool. By modern " boost " standards, a film star, a successful stockbroking racketeer, a power-politics gangster, or the man who can cure halitosis is great, and Socrates a perverse old blatherskite who never did a useful hand's turn in his life, but rather wasted his own and other men's time by poking an inquisitive nose in the direction of mere

1

ideas. Man's short and conceited strut on this earth hardly gives him time to realize his utter insignificance in the " Space-Time-Continuum " in which this alleged globe spins its mystical little part. For all that, we are living matter: as we can prove to ourselves (but not necessarily to others) by sitting on a red-hot cinder. In history, nations appear and disappear like colonies of ants; and for almost the same reasons. A casual glance through a telescope may show us what looks to be a world similar to our own smashed to smithereens in a collision with a silly wandering comet. Astronomers assure us that this is not likely to happen to us; but in nature the unexpected is not uncommon; and astronomers are not infallible. In history, the lives of the greatest men when closely examined show them to be human beings not greatly dissimilar from ourselves. Their story is often little better than a tale told by idiots.

Now we have reached the twentieth century of the Christian era, and in it life differs from life in the past only in that it is more complex and faster. But beneath this speeding up, which as yet devastates only limited areas of the earth's surface, there is the old and elemental product: human nature. And this human nature is not uninteresting to observe; it may even be amusing. Man is still by far the most interesting animal, and the term also includes woman. His place in the universal order of things lies somewhere between devil and deity, on which side is sometimes difficult to determine. The first study of man must always be man, and in such a study a little science may be useful. But let us be frank in regard to this:

science contains much which, for want of a better word, we may put under that broad heading of rubbish. Psychology, for example, flounders in a sea of pawky contradictions so absurd that were we to take them seriously they would deprive us of mind. Anthropologists may give us the dimensions of the caveman's brainbox, and yet neither they nor any other scientists can tell us the meaning of laughter. Nor can they tell why a mere idea (or even a tone of voice) may produce important chemical changes in our blood, or emotions which may cause us to writhe or groan.

We are still swayed by the heritage of the past: at least 400,000 years of quasi-animal existence; 100,000 years or thereabouts as a hunting animal, following who knows how long as a hunted animal; 25,000 years as a social being, of which period there are records going back 10,000 years. In this period of 10,000 years at least four great civilizations have passed through their spring, summer, autumn, and winter; their infancy, youth, prime, and old age; in Egypt, in China, on the shores of the Mediterranean, and in Arabia. To these may be added a fifth, which for convenience we call Western Civilization, and it includes America. Its springtime began a thousand years ago among Western European nations, and already the older peoples in it can feel the first blasts which mark the beginning of winter.

We see around us men and women at their best and at their worst, and the hum-drum of life provides us with a mean or norm. A definite standard or " yard-stick " is hardly possible or even necessary in assessing human nature, which is nakedly exposed only during stress or emergency or by pure accident. A king or president, prime minister or bishop or great financier, who dared expose his real nature to the world would be ruined. But mostly the mass is so blind, apathetic, ignorant, or helpless, that a great rascal, with the aid of bounce, bluff, and a working knowledge of human nature, may stalk brazenly through life, loudly advertising hoof and horns. The ordinary man is so frightened when other men begin to know his true nature that he hastens to disguise it as quickly as possible: by dissimulation, mystification, hocus-pocus, exaggeration, romance, and rationalization—not to mention a host of other very human tricks, far too familiar to the reader to be worthy of mention here.

A swift survey of recorded history shows us that in the mass human nature has changed very little. The great religions *assume* that there is never any change. Possibly if any great change ever occurred it was during those hundreds of thousands of years from which no record has survived. Manners and customs (or as some insist on calling them, morals) may have become more cruel in their mental as opposed to physical effects; or more refined in their cruelty. But, as regards the basic instincts and emotions, one human being is still much the same as another.

The peoples of the chief civilized nations of the world have not recovered from the second of the two most devastating and cruel wars of which we know, but they must needs prepare for another. Europe has now many millions more men under arms than she had in 1914, and the U.S.A. do not neglect measures of defence and preparations for the bigger and better slaughter of the millions of enemies which their worldly success has created. All this demonstrates in a practical and easily comprehensible manner the effect which the Sermon on the Mount has had upon the better side of human nature. Atomic bombs or the prosaic cloud of bacteria replace the more picturesque cloud of arrows, showing our superiority over primitive men and the generations that come between us and them. Are not the users of high explosives spiritually superior to the wielders of clubs and battle-axes? Is not the aerial incendiary bomb, which grills the sleeping infant, a clear indication of the tender hearts which beat among leaders of our higher modern races? Could anything be pleasanter to contemplate than the fact that during the 1914–18 war it was not uncommon on both sides for guns to be blessed before an action began? I can assure the pious reader from personal observation that, on at least one occasion, the results were in every way satisfactory to my side.

## ¶ *A Bungled Job?*

Nobody knows whether there is life in any of the planetary systems: but there seems to be no reason why life in a form beyond our comprehension should not exist in other parts of the universe, especially as we do not understand that form of it with which we are acquainted here. Nor is there any reason to suppose that, if there is life in other worlds, it reaches its highest point in beings resembling our friends and neighbours. The probabilities are against it. It is only modern man who has regarded the world as anything but the centre of the known universe, and himself as anything but the highest and most important form of life that has ever existed, or could possibly exist. But, if science now teaches us otherwise as regards the universe, we know by looking round our narrow circle of acquaintances, by considering some of the greatest figures in history, their lives and habits, and then by thinking of ourselves, that, if there is no higher form of life than man, there has surely been a piece of bungling somewhere.

¶ *The Proud Protozoon*

Let us go back as close to the beginning as is practical, and take a cursory glance at that now famous ancestor of ours, the unpleasant blob of animate jelly which the text-books call protozoon. How did it deport itself and habitually behave towards its fellow protozoon in those remote days (so remote that there is no record of them except in human imagination) before it succeeded in achieving the dignity and status of the walking ape which, " by the grace of God," became man?

The spiritual side of the protozoon's nature consisted chiefly of pride in itself, and so proud was it that its chief desires were divided between self-preservation and self-reproduction. It had no sex to speak of, and therefore experienced neither joy nor grief in the process of multiplication; indeed, it must have had a dull, miserable existence. Its courtship, like that of a religious ascetic, was of itself; its wooing was eating and drinking. Then, at maturity, it would break up into *nuclei*, round which portions of simple living matter remained or gathered to grow into baby protozoa: replicas of their principal or creator. They in turn became other protozoa, and such was the simple cycle of primitive life: *pride in self* provided the motive of life, the *élan vital* of Bergson. From this we may argue that SELFISHNESS was the driving force of primeval organic life.

It is nevertheless true that this love-of-self, pride-in-self, selfishness—call it what you will—manifests itself in a myriad forms. But it is not a rule that the more complex forms of life must necessarily have it in a complex form, though the tendency is that way. The form in which selfishness occurs differs in individual animals and men, differs from age to age, from country to country, race to race, and often from time to time in the life of the same person in different circumstances. Selfishness works in a thousand disguises. Who suspects of selfishness the dear old lady who seeks out the blind beggar to give him a shilling? But does she not do this for the sake of a very self-satisfying thrill, even when pity or bad conscience is in the background? A horrid thought.

I am informed that to contemplate the origin of our race in a speck of jelly, and our progressive development through an elaborate ancestry of sponges, worms, clams, centipedes, sharks, snakes, lizards, sloths and monkeys, is distressing to many good people. It is a shock to those sacred religious beliefs which they have learned from their parents and teachers. Let them think for one moment of the truth behind the stork story: that they have themselves a germinal origin and a humiliating embryonic development, as every schoolgirl now knows; and then let them consider seriously the prospect presented in the other theory; and there is really very little in it to which exception may be taken.

¶ *Enmity Based on the Desire for Life*

In the protozoon there was that strange spark which, for want of a better word, we call *life*. It was essentially a *craving to live*, and this craving manifests itself everywhere throughout the plant, animal, and human world. Basically it is primitive feeling, and throughout every phase of existence retains at all times its principal features. An old proverb says: " Self-preservation is the first law of nature," and this is a scientific truth. It is only when human beings lose normal reason and reach the highest pinnacles of humanity that they deny the truth in this idea. Self-sacrifice may be the highest form of morality and suicide may be logical: but both are nearly always anti-biological. When the protozoon ran short of his accustomed diet, he overcame hunger by consuming one, or a part of one, of his own race. He would eat his own parent or brother. The widespread growth of cannibalism among those unpleasant ancestors of ours was responsible for the beginning and rapid growth of self-defence, growing out of fear, based on self-interest, and ultimately springing from pride and the craving for self-continuation and perpetuation. Thus the spirit of *enmity* arose and flourished. Eaters were considered enemies by the possible meals; and vice versa. Hence the origin of an ineradicable habit common to all life: War. So long as protozoa are hungry they will fight to exist. It is the simple law of all life. It applies equally in the jungle and among civilized nations. So long as there are so many people that the existing food supply is insufficient, there is one way out: destruction, usually in the form of war. There are, of course, other causes of war. It has been made into an amusement at different times in the world's history. There have been wars for which the only reason was the whim or fancy of a ruler. There have been wars regarding Invisible and Intangible Things, such as the Supreme Being, Hell, or the Devil. There have been purely grabbing wars, not prompted by sheer hunger, but by greed. The history of colonization provides endless examples of this. And there have been wars, such as the First and Second World Wars, for which no set of satisfactory reasons has yet been found, but which may be blamed upon what are called " power-politics." The social and spiritual changes in mankind that have resulted from war are without number.

¶ *The Dominant Law of Human Nature*

The antagonism which springs from selfishness exists throughout all nature, often with very beneficial results. Is not " Competition is the soul of trade " a maxim of modern Capitalism? Two firms produce or sell similar articles, and in order to attract customers they must attempt to surpass one another, if not in the quality or fine price-cutting of the goods, then in advertising or telling lies about the goods. In advertising it is seldom necessary to tell the truth; there are on record cases where the plain truth was told with disastrous results (as many men of business may whisper in your ear).

As a result of cannibalism and fighting, the protozoon developed new qualities and, indeed, evolved into entirely different forms of life. These forms might differ in outward appearance, but they all retained the original characteristics of pride-in-existence and selfishness, though often certain favoured creatures would be able to conceal them. A million new creatures came into being, encouraged their own existence by every trick and craftiness imaginable; and they preyed upon one another. The highest form of life which sprang from primeval mud was man, who became Lord of Creation because he had more pride in his existence, more craving for life, more ingenuity, and more selfishness than any other beast of the field.

That is a brief account of the dominant law of human nature; the law of selfishness.

¶ *Impossible to Love one's Neighbour as one's Self*

This law has innumerable corollaries, one of which is that the unselfish creature is either killed or eaten—often swallowed alive—or otherwise extinguished until its species disappears. The selfish animal may develop its selfishness into a form of cunning called intelligence, and this, with an assortment of related qualities, may enable it to draw many advantages from other animals less intelligent than itself. I should perhaps mention that this theory of pride-in-self is by no means new. Nor is it always considered a high motive for existence. Twice at least, as we shall see later, it has been challenged: by the Indian mystic and teacher, Gautama Buddha, who taught the complete elimination of self; and again by the Jewish realist, Jesus of Nazareth, who, following the idea propounded by the Chinese philosopher, Lao Tsu, of six hundred years earlier, said: " *Love thy neighbour as thyself.*" Both ideas have from time to time caught, held, and even inflamed the imaginations of many good men. Large bodies of mankind have rendered them lip-service, but very few who lived or live in the hurly-burly of life have ever attempted to put them into practice. There are others who make a spare-time amusement of playing with the precepts of moralists for an hour or so every week. In the twentieth century there is among ourselves a tacit acknowledgment of the impracticability of Christianity, the real reason being that to take it seriously always means the suffering of sheer physical discomfort. And man, like all other animals, prefers comfort to discomfort; more so now than ever before in the course of his existence.

This theory of pride is worth a little thought. It explains many otherwise obscure problems of life. It helps us, for example, to realize why man made God in his own image. It also explains why the fully developed type of higher man has often been driven by pride to master the technique of selfishness, and hence to form great empires; or to constitute himself a high priest of religion, a dictator, a prime minister, a mathematician, or a great creative artist in literature or one of the arts; or to turn himself into a hard-boiled millionaire. Pride, says G. K. Chesterton, consists in a man making his personality the only test, instead of making the truth the test; and cheek or brazenness is not an assertion of superiority, but rather a bold attempt to balance inferiority. He goes even further, and states that all evil began with some attempt at superiority. We are able to prove the truth of this Catholic thought by the example of the protozoon continuing its existence and proving its superiority over a brother by virtue of having eaten him.

The rich man in modern capitalist society does precisely the same with the poor.

## § 2

## SELFISHNESS: AND THE SEXUAL ORIGIN OF SOCIETY

We have already seen that self-regard is the primary quality of living matter, whether this be in the form of protozoa, insects, or animals, including apes and men. This self-regard or selfishness is the fount of a great diversity of characteristics, some of which, such as memory, hunger, power of adjustment to environment, and power of growth, are inherent; while others are acquired or secondary characteristics, such as fear. The sexual qualities (of these I shall have something to say later), which spring from the desire for self-perpetuation, are of great importance and give rise to a host of secondary qualities upon which society is based. Indeed, the sexual qualities are partly responsible for the present organization of society. In primitive society the first ties between human beings were the sexual, and out of this bond grew the habit of association. At first man was a solitary animal which wandered about in search of food, avoiding all others of its kind, excepting females. Over one or more of these he exercised an uncontrolled despotism and, although he permitted his mates to have no rights, he was prepared if need be to fight for them. In the " lower " strata of society this is still so. In the East End of London a man will still fight for his mate if another threatens to run off with her; in the West (and more aristocratic) End he lets her go: perhaps with a philosophic sigh of relief. This is a slight change in human nature, though an unimportant one.

A strange compound of intense individualism and the sexual instinct, blossoming into fear or hate (they are almost the same thing) and jealousy, was responsible for the family tie.

On this foundation all human institutions are based.

¶ *Pen-picture of Adam*

That fallen angel, the father of humanity, was in many ways a better man than we think he was. Nobody knows exactly what he was like, but, following the deductions of scientists, we may draw our own conclusions as to his nature and appearance. In stature he was low and thick-set, with thin legs that were inclined to be bandy; a shaggy creature of dirty yellow or brownish colour, with an undershot jaw and strong, yellow teeth, the canines projecting slightly over thick, sensuous lips. Some say he had a dash of the ape in him. When angry—which might be at any moment—he bellowed, gnashing his molars; and tears of rage often filled his fierce little eyes. When pleased he threw back his head and showed the whole of his dental equipment, puckering cheek and jowl as a dog does. Restless, bright eyes glowered from under a low, beetle brow. His appetite was voracious and he fed upon almost anything edible, from the lean, raw flesh of his kith and kin to the roots and fruits of the forest. Nor was he above devouring carrion in seasons of necessity; for there were times when long enforced fasts made him the complete animal. The outside of his dwelling is described by a most eminent writer as a garbage-heap consisting of decayed and decaying remnants of meals. It was only with difficulty that primitive man restrained his offspring from picking over this garbage-heap, because he was not convinced in his own mind that to eat from it was either unhealthy or unpleasant. Man even now often eats putrid food, in the form of game and cheese, as a delicacy. In China he eats old eggs.

Primitive man was incapable of sustained effort in anything except flight from his enemies. He never expended energy methodically, or knew method in anything. But, like most lazy animals, he was capable of great physical exertion in emergency; and his robust constitution could bear severe pain and offer resistance to inclement climatic conditions. The nature of early man was mercurial: quick changes from joy to sorrow, from mirth to anger, and from placidity to excitement were his wont. At one moment he would beat his wife (or wives) unmercifully, and the next he would grunt loving nothings into her (or their) not too clean ears; and perhaps playfully turn a female over to work off a short stiff spasm of remorse or emotional reaction. Mere trifles annoyed, angered, or amused our primitive. He took little heed for the morrow, leaving that to his female housekeepers, who were also his beasts of burden—and incidentally the animals upon which he most often vented his spleen. His intellect was of the imitative sort, and its development was entirely due to a terrible struggle for existence. Early man was a *hunted* as well as a hunting animal, and fearful were the monsters he had to encounter. Before at last holding his own against the huge beasts and reptiles that surrounded him, he was driven from post to pillar, from cave to tree-top, from one garbage-heap to another; it was in this process of being hunted that he developed most of that cunning which later became known as intellect.

## ¶ *The Bludgeon, Man's first Invention*

Early man could mimic cleverly the shriek of the hawk, the howl of the wolf, the meeow of the scented polecat, the deep bellow of the buffalo; these mimickings were his first articulations, the beginnings of language. The track of beast or fowl was an open book which he read as he ran in a crouching attitude, mostly on all fours, standing upright only to peer into the jungle. One man of a scientific turn of mind and of superior intelligence invented a useful household utensil: the bludgeon. With it he could not only silence a nagging wife, but he could also more easily defend himself against other men or animals. The bludgeon evolved into a sort of missile; and another genius invented the spear. The knife used was a sharp shell, and it was an ingenious fellow who thought of tying this to the end of a casting-stick. These simple weapons were used with formidable strength and skill, and the power they gave to primitive men merely whetted their appetite for more. Then came the mighty genius who, by a divine stroke of wit, invented the bow capable of sending a suitably-modified spear on an errand of destruction. Yet another man of genius came forward with poison for the end of the arrow; and in this manner was evolved the weapon which very largely helped to change man from a hunted into a hunting animal.

¶ *Origin of Language*

In the early days of humanity those who were not of the same flesh and blood were enemies, to be exterminated by any trick or trap. Man asked for no quarter and expected none. He demanded no explanation of the universe and was not troubled by abstractions other than vague, nightmarish imaginings of the " Great Unknown "—intellectual contact had not yet been established with either God or Devil. A lazy, unprogressive brute he was, whose life was eating, drinking, sleeping, and occasionally fighting; his intellectual development, as in the case of most modern men, ceased shortly after the attainment of puberty. Communication with other members of the race was achieved by an uncouth chattering and gesticulation, like that of apes. It was in this communing that our primitive ancestor showed his greatest originality: talking was his favourite pastime, just as it is among men today. An instinctive prompting caused the formulation of simple language. We do not know whether it was man or woman who first used language: but man has always used it with greatest effect in dealing with numbers of his fellow men, and woman has always used it with greatest effect in dealing with individuals. The nagging wife of the primitive had an immense influence upon the development of language; for the male was often compelled to ransack his imagination for words to reply to feminine shrewishness. Many of those early words had sounds indicative of their meaning: " bow-wow," " pooh-pooh," " tut-tut," the more sophisticated word " borborygmus," and so forth are survivals to our own times. In our own age children say " puff-puff " for locomotive. It is also probable that conversation was interspersed with clickings of the tongue, gutturals, glottal stops, sniffs, snorts, and wheezings; as well as gestures and signs like those used by the deaf and dumb. Vocabulary was limited to essentials: the chase and the needs of the home. The physically lazier men remained near the home and became more subtle intellectually than those who went a-hunting.

It may be interesting for us to consider for the moment the mentality of this primitive man. Probably the greatest authority on the subject is Lévy-Bruhl. He shows us that primitive man's mentality was, and is, extremely different from our own. Everything which happened around primitive man, and was not immediately explicable or very obviously a simple occurrence, was connected with occult or mystic powers. These mystic forces, which he treats as first causes, remain invisible and intangible to his ordinary means of perception. The connection and effect are immediate; they do not admit of intermediate links, or at least if they recognize them they regard them as negligible. Primitive mentality is thus indifferent to secondary causes, and it is in this that we find the greatest difference between early human nature and our own. The savage mind is so absorbed and distracted by the occult and mystic first cause that what is to us the intermediate chain of causes disappears entirely from his vision. Thus even today, among primitives, if a crocodile devours a man, or if he is killed by having eaten an unknown poisonous plant, the mind of the primitive leaps immediately to magic or witchcraft of a sorcerer as the true cause, and attaches no importance whatever to the crocodile or the poison.

## ¶ Primitive Men of Genius

Notwithstanding the above important difference between the outlook of the primitive and our own, Lévy-Bruhl has given us a mass of evidence to show that the intellect of our early ancestor *can hardly have been inferior in capacity to our own.* It is certainly not to be viewed as a rudimentary form of ours, as infantile and almost pathological. If there is one way in which man differs from brute creation, it is in the marvellous powers of imagination which he possesses, even in his very primitive state. The peculiar quality of human imagination is its power (varying to an amazing extent among individuals) to visualize phenomena and their interconnections wholly within the mind. It was this imaginative activity of mind which produced the supreme genius who discovered how to create fire; the genius who invented the wheel; the genius who saw the incalculable possibilities in cereal plants; the genius who first mounted a horse; the genius who first tamed a dog; and the genius who first domesticated the cow, the goat, and the sheep. It is this same quality of imagination— we see it in every age of recorded history—which accounts for all discoveries, inventions, creations, and great scientific systems of thought, such as

Darwinism and Marxism. It was the same power of imagination which created a whole series of morbid and other illusions which persist to this very day. "The idea of unseen power in indefinable and intangible things was, as we shall see later, a tremendously weighty discovery . . . from the point of view of its subsequent importance for most modern religion and science." [1] Its earliest expression was of the simple and concrete character of the present-day West African fetish, to which the native ascribes a power to bring him luck, or of the floating tree-trunk in the river, which by its mysterious appearances and disappearances still gives the Fijian hill tribes or the Ten'a Indians the impression of a mystical power. In modern times we have in the world many primitive tribes, but the spread of "civilized" ideas has in some way or other affected them, generally for the worse. A great link with the primitive past was severed in 1877 when the last member of the Tasmanian race died. The Tasmanians were in almost every sense of the word thorough-going primitives, and it is from close observation of their life and habits that we are able to make many reasonable deductions regarding our ancestors.

¶ *Unknown Origin of the " God " Idea*

There is still some doubt in the minds of even the most confident students of religion and anthropology as to the origin of the " God " idea. We may speculate that it began in the animistic tendency of primitive minds reading into surrounding nature, as

[1] Lévy-Bruhl.

in the case of the crocodile or the tree-trunk cited above. But that primitive man sat on his tail thinking hard for hour after hour, after the manner of an Einstein, as to the origin of his existence, and then, in a flash, solved the mystery by attributing life to Gods or a God (for the idea of *one universal God* is fairly modern) is an absurd proposition. Primitive man, in the early stages, was so lacking in inductive intelligence that he often failed during the summer to lay in a store for the wants of an inevitable winter. It is therefore most unlikely that he should have had the particular form of intellectual acumen necessary to evolve an idea of God very quickly, when he had scarcely got beyond eating carrion and bludgeoning a neighbour who interfered with his promiscuity.

¶ *The Importance of Fear*

Fear has been both the saviour and, in a sense, often the destroyer of human nature. We have seen that all life is based on selfishness and the will to live, but with this always goes the fear of pain or death. Fear is both an instinct and an emotion. "The fear of the Lord is the beginning of wisdom." If we substitute the word Unknown for Lord— although there is no need for us moderns to do so— we find the wisdom which provides impetus to our natural craving for life. Fear is a necessary characteristic in the preservation of personality. We are afraid to do this, that, or the other thing, lest those around us obtain a view of our lives different from that which we wish to convey. It is a favourite ingredient in drama, and it is because of it that the religious spirit has persisted. Abolish fear, and you remove much of the driving force of many great actions. From my own personal experience, I am inclined to believe that nine-tenths of the courage so widely manifested in the European War was the result of fear. Men were afraid to be afraid. To create this fear of being afraid, a thousand and one tricks and devices were necessary, in the form of propaganda, social taboos, ignominy, and even the threat of execution. A man at the front was presented with two alternatives. The first, to face the enemy with a sporting chance of survival, and perhaps of promotion or decoration for some act conspicuously useful to his side. The second, court-martial by a group of men armed with powers of life and death, and brutalized by the modern system of military training which, to be effective, must be as cruel as that of the jungle, though pretending otherwise.

We meet many types of fear. There is women's fear of mice or spiders, which, considering the bravery with which they face, for example, a heavy operation, is something inexplicable. Then there are physical and moral fear, as well as physical and moral bravery. Demosthenes, the Greek orator, who displayed supreme moral courage at a time of crisis in his city, was nevertheless so subject to physical fear that, when he fell against a bush in a military retreat, he is said to have grovelled before it, asking it for mercy. It is, perhaps, during an earthquake or a shipwreck that human beings are most likely to show their courage or their fear. The truly moral man will not pillage during an earthquake, nor will he fight in a shipwreck, crushing beneath him women and children in an endeavour to find a seat in a lifeboat. On the other hand, we hear from time to time even now prophecies to the effect that the world will end on such and such a date. Some years ago there was a scare to this effect, and in various parts of the world, but particularly in U.S.A., there were thousands of people who went to church and prayed ardently in a manner never before their custom, that they might be saved from the catastrophe. Fear is, after all, merely one of the forms of the selfishness which keeps us alive. Fear and worry regarding his destiny are two of the chief causes for man's progressive theology. The worship of ghosts—figments of a terrified imagination—afterwards supplanted by the pagan deities, and then by the single God, are the stepping-stones of this progress.

¶ *Man's Greatest Discovery*

We may now consider a few of those momentous discoveries which have led to changes in human nature since the days of the primitives. Of these the most important was certainly the discovery of fire. It is almost impossible for us to think of man without fire, but how he discovered it is still a mystery. A jungle or prairie conflagration which left behind it roast pork or roast goose and baked roots, may have suggested the idea of cooking; and it may have been this which prompted men to take advantage of opportunities for nursing the spontaneous combustion of decaying vegetation, or the flames left behind in a shrub or tree struck by lightning. One can visualize a primitive housewife, jealously fanning a heap of such matter into flame. Indeed, it is not unlikely that fire was first so produced by a woman who employed it in a manner that showed man how useful it could be. He or she who first produced fire by mechanical means was not only the supreme genius of antiquity, but also the greatest benefactor of the human race. In all history no person was responsible for greater subsequent changes in human nature. The forest and the jungle, with their dangerous diseases, their poisonous reptiles and insects, fierce beasts and destructive fowls, could be cleared by fire. It is also possible that life itself was prolonged by the ability to cook food or preserve it for future use by drying or smoking. With fire it was possible for man to smile at the vagaries of climate. Greatest factor of all, it caused our ancestors to develop the wandering spirit. It was by wandering, by the culture of foreign travel, as it were, that man first set out on the quest which has never ended, and which is the chief cause of civilization—namely, the quest for greater comforts in life. The use of fire is the dividing line which separates human from purely animal nature. Man is the only fire-making animal.

It is a long way from the first discovery of fire to the steam engine and steamboat of the nineteenth century. A greater distance in progress separates man without fire from the fire-maker. Gunpowder, with the many gentle uses to which it has been put, is an outcome of fire. There is still, I believe, or was until quite recently, a race which could not kindle fire, but knew how to preserve it—the Andamanese. Fire has played an immense part in both political and religious progress. In China, for instance, at the coronation of an emperor, the royal procession was permitted to move through the distance between palace and temple only during the burning of a joss-stick of prescribed length. In the simplest form of Christian worship from which all symbolism is eliminated the word fire is used figuratively, in allusion to ancient altars. From this poetic allusion it is not difficult, by means of symbolism, to trace the road back to fire-worship, when sacrifices were made to gods by burning humans on a fire. The anger of our own God was placated during the Inquisition by the incineration of obstinate heretics. In the 1914–18 War the palm for philosophic destruction must be given to the Germans for their ingenious invention of the *Flammenwerfer*, the Flame-Thrower, which could project a jet of blazing oil to a distance of about three hundred yards. I have a horrible recollection of a soldier friend who was hosed, as it were, with burning oil and left only with sufficient tissue to constitute life.

The face of the earth was altered by fire, and in that struggle between man and animal which was largely responsible for the formation of human nature, and of which we shall hear more later, it played a foremost part. Fire was responsible for pottery, the beginning of the first plastic art. But most of all it was used as a weapon to subdue Nature: to burn down forests, to make new pasture land, to harden the points of weapons used in attacking the mammoth or the mastodon: for the manufacture of flaming arrows or of fiery javelins to be hurled against the foe; in the preparation of vegetable poison, which in itself was a great advance in the art of warfare.

¶ *Effect of Externals*

Fire-producing man, confident in his new powers, wandered over the face of the globe. In Mesopotamia, between the Tigris and the Euphrates, he discovered a spot where flourished a plant that could be made into a convenient and palatable food. He noticed that, where the ears of this plant fell at the end of a season, a fresh crop would appear. By planting ears of wheat he learned to provide himself with as much as he required, and this wheat could be made into a nourishing food. From Mesopotamia restless wanderers carried with them ears of wheat in their quest for favourable climates and comfortable territories in which to live: to the valleys of the great rivers, the Nile, the Ganges, the Yangtze Kiang, the Hwang-Ho; across the steppes of Siberia, and round the edges of the Black Sea. The discovery of oats and rye followed: these two plants were found to flourish in climates unfavourable to wheat, and thus the range of man's wanderings and possibilities was further extended. Bread, milling, elaborate pottery, and many of the commonplaces of life may be attributed to the use of fire with which is coupled the utilization of the cereals. The first man to use fire gained immense prestige, and he who first made use of a cereal must have gained no less. They became magicians, forerunners of kings, priests, and doctors; and, like them, the terror of the countryside. Families or clans began to be formed, grouping themselves around those with the mystic knowledge of fire and cereal. To fire and wheat may be attributed the responsibility for turning man from utter savagery.

A few isolated groups of human beings, mellowed by the benevolence of warmth and bread, aided by the natural configuration of the country in which they settled, and the favourable climatic conditions, became the torch-bearers of civilization and culture. That is an example of the effect of externals upon human nature.

## § 3

## FROM EARLY BREAD-EATING TO MODERN CANNIBALISM

Men congregate where food is easy to obtain. The fact that in Mesopotamia a nourishing foodstuff could be obtained without great exertion was attractive to nomadic tribes that had hitherto moved from one pasture to another in accordance with the seasons of the year. Here many of the more intelligent and perhaps lazier wanderers found that they could live without further wandering. So comfortable a prospect influenced them to settle, just as within the last two hundred years European settlers in the United States fell upon and exploited those areas which offered the quickest and most promising returns. In the course of time, as man was cultivating the wild wheat between Tigris and Euphrates, those tribes that continued to wander, or were unable to impose their will on the inhabitants thereabouts, brought the grains of wheat to the East. At least ten thousand years ago it became the staff of life of the hundreds of races living between the Atlantic and the Pacific.

Henceforward, man need no longer spend all his time hunting for the wherewithal of existence. He need travel no more unless he desired to do so for pleasure or for profit. He could work quietly during seed-time and harvest and settle down to a life of comparative laziness during one half of the year. This ability to be lazy was the beginning of contemplative thought and the origin of all philosophy. Restlessness or hustle kills thought. Only a man of leisure can think, is the rule of life; there are exceptions, but they are few and unimportant. This ability to be lazy was also the beginning of vice, for the hunter had little time for genuine evil.

> Satan finds some mischief still
> For idle hands to do.

—an old tag with some truth in it. The wealth of those peoples who had found the value of wheat caused no little envy and jealousy among less fortunate people. Hence there were raids for plunder, the beginnings of organized primitive warfare. War is still made for plunder, but not in the form of wheat. It is now made for markets and the ability to collect tokens whereby comforts and luxuries may be purchased, as financiers will perhaps tell you. The fact that wheat was so valuable and so convenient a form of sustenance and enabled men to have leisure also influenced the development of art, which had begun with the making of weapons, tools, and household utensils. Given a fair amount of leisure, almost any race of human beings will produce works of art, in the form of pottery or painting or sculpture. Remove the opportunity provided by leisure—both art and philosophy vanish. Bearing this in mind, one can check active periods of history and indicate those of peace and prosperity; unless prosperity has become

B

a sole mass-ideal, as for instance, in the United States today, where most art is crude and vigorous, but with little æsthetic appeal to those not born in the atmosphere.

¶ *Origin of Diplomacy*

Although a form of unleavened bread had long existed in Mesopotamia, a Chinese gentleman named Ching-Nung is reputed to have been the first person who taught the making of bread as we understand it nowadays; but he made a far more profound discovery, the story goes. In that memorable year 1998 B.C. he learned to make wine from rice, a discovery the effects of which may still be seen in any bar. It was probably as a result of bread- and wine-making that dumb barter arose. Those settlements of men which had the ability to make bread and wine found themselves favourably situated in regard to their ignorant neighbours. The latter coveted the bread and wine and were willing to exchange their meat, milk, fish, or wool for the valuable life-giving products. But men were even then suspicious of one another, and the system of credit (or of credit tokens, which we call money) had not yet been invented. The method of exchange was somewhat as follows. The tribe with bread would deposit a pile of loaves at a given spot between their territory and that of their neighbours. These would come, take the bread, and deposit what they were prepared to give in exchange for it, a matter no doubt settled by the exchange of plenipotentiaries, forerunners of modern diplomats. Thus trade began, and it was trade more than anything else, with the possible exception of war, which caused the intercommunication of races, leading to a mixing of blood and leaving most of the earth with a population of mongrels.

At this stage man had become a comparatively tame animal. In the thousands of years which intervened between utter savagery and the state of tameness outlined above, he had passed, as we have seen, through two phases, both of which profoundly altered his nature. At first he was a hunted animal. On all sides we see him surrounded by fearsome beasts which were ready to devour him without a moment's notice. He therefore developed all the characteristics of the hunted animal, including the bravery which a rat shows when it is cornered. He became mean and cunning, quarrelsome and fierce. From day to day his energy and ingenuity were devoted to schemes for avoiding his relentless enemies of the animal world. It was a phase of continual warfare in which the animal world yielded step by step, not so much to the physical strength of man as to the increasing cunning of his mind. Man was at first a slayer. He killed animals mostly for self-protection, and was thus provided with a surfeit of fresh meat. There are men of science today who affirm that primitive man was a vegetarian, but this seems extremely unlikely in view of the fact that in order to live he must fight and exterminate many animals which would provide him with succulent and nourishing food.

¶ *Influence of Animals*

Naturalists say that in their wild state and untouched by contact with man, most animals are harmless. Hudson declares that even the fierce puma will never attack except in self-defence. Comstock asserts that venomous reptiles, alligators, bears, skunks, and other fearful creatures are quite harmless until man comes into contact with them. The question now to be decided, not by scientists, but by philosophers, is this: did man get his ferocity from animals, or did they get theirs from him?

It is doubtful if any animal has changed human nature by aiding the progress of man in his long journey from savagery to civilization more than the horse. This animal was first domesticated in Central or Southern Asia, and no race has utilized it more than the Arabs. The religion of Mahomet depended for its widespread success almost entirely upon the horse. We shall see later how Mahomedanism affected human nature, but meanwhile let us not forget that the horse was largely responsible for it. In Arabia, as Winwood Reade has pointed out, the Arab horse lived in his master's tent, sucked from his calabash, and slept with the family. He played with the children, showing that gentleness of nature immortalized by Dean Swift; and when the time came snorted and panted excitedly and sympathetically in the war-charge. To the horse also may be attributed much of the success of Cortez in his conquest of Mexico. The mail-clad chargers of the Spaniards struck terror into the hearts of the native Aztecs and Toltecs, who thought that horse and man were one animal. It is as a result of contact with horses that man has developed many of his finer feelings. In modern times he repays this animal by using it as a beast of burden or as a means towards his amusement in the hunting field or on the racecourse; to carry shells and ammunition with which he blows to pieces other horses and men to which he is opposed in warfare; and, finally, he may eat it.

¶ *Henry Ford on Food*

Can we doubt that the food on which they lived influenced our ancestors? Modern science informs us that stature depends very largely on diet; but does a man's nature depend upon his diet, and if so, how much? The influence of nourishment upon the development of racial characteristics has been shown in a series of experiments by Japanese scientists in Tokio. To determine whether the slight stature of the Japanese depends upon their rice diet, the regular rice dinner of a group of school children was supplemented by other articles of food, such as are customary among taller races. The results of these experiments, which were extended over a period of years, showed an increase of several inches in stature and several pounds in weight. An English military physician has confirmed this by experiments with Indian races of varying stature. Sikhs and Pathans are bigger men than the Indians who use other diets; Mahomedan Sikhs consume milk, cheese, and vegetables, which the Brahmans do not. Mr. Henry Ford stated a few years ago that most active crimes are the results of wrong feeding. " If," said he, " people would only learn to eat the things they should eat, there would be less need for hospitals and prisons." There is little doubt but that food has an influence upon character; nobody but a confirmed vegetarian could have written George Bernard Shaw's plays. The good Rabelais had a philosophy of life which was " Eat, drink, and be merry, for tomorrow we die."

The coarse, sensual, and self-indulgent person will gorge himself with rich and toothsome food. Most men who have grown fat *through over-eating* are lacking in healthy decision. How good a psychologist was Shakespeare when he made Cæsar say " *Let me have men around me that are fat*," such men being more easily bent to a stronger will! It is also well known that stout men are good-tempered; but it may be that they are too timid or too lethargic or perhaps too wise to quarrel or disagree with anyone.

Is there any doubt but that meat-eating has a marked effect on character? What it comes to is this, that meat provides energy in a concentrated form and the man who eats meat ought to have much physical exercise if he is to benefit from it. If he has not this exercise, he grows bad-tempered and irritable, and may make himself a nuisance to those around him. Many thinkers dating back to Buddha and Pythagoras have advocated the simple, almost fasting diet for the contemplative existence; meat is to be eschewed. But the English philosopher, Herbert Spencer, was a believer in the meat diet. Somebody informed him that his thought would reach greater heights were he to become a vegetarian. An ambitious man—all philosophers are amazingly ambitious—he changed his habits and began to limit himself to vegetable foods. However, his work immediately began to deteriorate, and it was not long before he was back again on beef, mutton, and pork, on which he wrote the *Synthetic Philosophy*.

¶ *The Elixir of Life*

The question of man's diet is one of great interest from many points of view. The world is now worried to death to know whether it has any influence upon cancer, that scourge which, among civilized people, is responsible for one out of every eight deaths. No light has hitherto been thrown on this. An Order of Roman Catholic monks whose diet was of the simplest, and who lived on very little in the way of meat, was found to be equally susceptible to cancer with those who live a hale, hearty, and healthy existence.

We all know the phrase, "One man's meat is another's poison." Some people are poisoned by eggs, other cannot eat fish, etc. There are few people who can safely eat the general run of foodstuffs, and there are few who are not influenced in some way by a meal. When Mr. Lloyd George was Prime Minister of England, he scored many notable political triumphs and settled many disputes at his breakfast table, to which he regularly invited friends and/or opponents. A keen judge of human nature, he must have realized that one of two things would happen, either (a) his friends or opponents would be liverish and dull-witted in the morning, or (b) they would be merry and bright. If they were the first, he could corner them easily; if they were the second, he could take advantage of their good temper. He always won his points in those days. The eating and drinking bouts of our ancestors produced bards and entertainers, forerunners of Shakespeare and the modern theatrical music-hall, cinema, or cabaret performers. Ten thousand years ago the Tribal Nights' Entertainment was Dinner, Theatre, and Dance, culminating in the satisfaction of the sexual appetite, on the same lines as now in London, New York, Paris, Buenos Aires, or among the Mandingos or Bantus. The eating of meat and the drinking of strong drink exhilarate the enjoyment of such amusements, just as they often prompt men to action or stifle clear thinking.

¶ *All Men Cannibals when Necessity Drives*

There is scarcely anything that men have not eaten at different periods and among different races in the world's history. There have been root-eaters, twig-eaters, and seed-eaters. There have been and there are locust-eaters, elephant-eaters, and cannibals. Indeed, there are still a few places in which cannibalism exists. In periods of extreme necessity cannibalism may become a widespread practice among civilized races, as in China during the year 1928. In the stricken provinces of North-West China many instances of cannibalism were found among the twenty million people who were reduced by famine : a striking example of how close a highly civilized people, who have lived through a period of three thousand years of philosophy, can be to the animal.

The question often arises whether civilization is responsible for such savagery in mankind. The answer is that it is not; the tiger in man has existed from the time when he was a hunted animal and it requires extreme circumstances of hunger to show it in the broad light of day.

¶ *Sex and Salesmanship*

Other factors have had their influence on human nature : clothes and fashion, for example. We may assume that early man ran about naked, and that the first clothes were for the simple purpose of protection against the weather, and were not prompted by modesty. Indeed, in some parts of the world today the only clothing used is an ointment or sweet-smelling balsam of vegetable origin. Cleanliness is a virtue among the lower animals, so we need not pride ourselves for its existence among mankind. It is an equivalent to decoration. But the vagaries of clothing and fashion require an encyclopædia to describe. In women they are primarily the outcome of a desire to startle and attract males, or to cause anger and jealousy among other females. No woman, except the sexual pervert, wishes to attract other women. Rouge and lipstick, powder, corsets, perfumes, high heels, silk stockings, colourful dresses, beads and jewellery, furs and feathers are for a biological purpose: to attract the attention of the opposite sex. They are the equivalent of the nose-rings, nose-sticks, tattooing, and paint of the ladies of Melanesia. Fashion under capitalism has grown into a trade conspiracy to sell goods. In Europe, when short skirts became fashionable after the 1914–18 war, thousands of workers in the cloth factories were thrown out of work, and employers racked their brains for some means of inducing women to cover their knees. New fashions resulted. Women were aided in the economic revolt against the short skirt and the low neck by the highest authorities of certain religions; the Pope himself was backed by Signor Mussolini in an endeavour to persuade women to observe decorum. The Church started a " *Wear more clothes* " campaign, while cloth manufacturers joined in a religious chorus of " *Cover your knees* " and put it out that a woman's knees were not a pretty sight.

Evening dresses grew longer.  The battle is not yet over.

## ¶ *Influence of the Razor*

We may add to these frills on human nature the habit of shaving the face, as one which has had a profound influence.  Three thousand years ago, the razor was a toilet requisite for men of the " upper " classes.  Among primitives, who were naturally hairy, he who could remove the fungus from his face became awe-inspiring to his neighbours.  Hence it was that priests, kings, governors, judges, generals, and other racketeers decided they had better shave in order to add to their influence over their more weak-minded fellow-creatures.  Personal conceit was behind the desire to be clean-shaven, for most of these men believed that their faces were by nature more noble than those of the commonalty.  Alexander the Great is shown to us as a clean-shaven man, and it is stated that he set a fashion for the smooth visage. Hair was, and is, the symbol of virility; but the smooth face was, and is, the symbol of eternal youth.  Whiskers and moustaches are compromises.  The goatee beard signifies strength of character, or even pugnacity, as in the symbolical case of Captain Kettle.  The clean-shaven face now tends to be a minor symbol of civilization, except among exhibitionists, Chinese pirates, and naughty fellows in all civilized countries.

## ¶ *The Imitative Instinct*

We know that animals imitate one another, and this propensity is inherited by men, with whom it is an instinct which has not weakened with the passage of time. " Fashion " and also Politics take advantage of this imitative instinct, which is one of the strongest of human qualities. It is by virtue of imitation that men have become educated; it is by virtue of it that the landscape of the civilized world is changing into a dull uniformity. In the suburbs of London you may walk along almost any of the more prosperous roads, and you will see houses built to the same pattern, flower-gardens laid out in almost the same way, window curtains of the same material, and in the same scheme of colours; you will see standing in the road motor-cars of a few standard makes; you will see the mistress of the house possessed of whatever breed of dog happens at the moment to be fashionable, and she will wear a frock or a costume which is a uniform. Suddenly the racketeers—that is, builders, landscape gardeners, cloth manufacturers, makers of motor-cars, or dog breeders—will decide that a change would be good for business. They know that they may safely rely upon the imitative qualities of the crowds of quasi-monkeys to buy just what is put on the market. It is the desire to cater for this continual necessity for change that is responsible for the creative spirit of the modern fashion artist. That fine sounding phrase *God made all men equal* is as yet in the prophetic stage, for there still remain the few who wish to differ from their fellow creatures. But they wilt before standardization. The inward feeling of natural inequality drives men to imitate their fellows outwardly, in order that inwardly they may feel their equals. This explains what is meant by " dressing up to a social position," and why it is that,

when you meet an over-dressed man, you may
expect to find an under-dressed mind.

¶ *Women prefer Rogues*

He who will not imitate has always been considered
to be anti-social. Progress is the movement of
crowds. In order to keep up with the crowd, men
become hypocrites. The man who is born with what
we must call for want of a better phrase " anti-social
propensities " may be forced to assume the personi-
fication of righteousness. Those who are cruel will
affect kindly and philanthropic acts. The murderer
is often outwardly, and often quite sincerely, fond of
his pets. Those who assume too strong an attitude in
favour of the orthodox are suspect, and those who are
too outwardly good are inwardly bad. It is the
outward assumption of goodness, and the careful
study of its outward technique, which enable rogues
to succeed in life.

This illustrates the necessity for hypocrisy, as well
as giving an indication of what may be the origin of
manners.

The success which rogues and vagabonds have with
women is not difficult to explain. They do not possess
that lack of hypocrisy so noticeable in the honest
man; and they make a point of demonstrating to
women those sentiments which women fail to appreciate unless they be demonstrated. One of the chief
differences between the natures of English men and
women is that, whereas men generally dislike to show
their feelings, women like doing so. Hence the man
who can dissimulate skilfully persuades a woman of
his affection, even when it does not exist. This is

greatly appreciated by the woman; for women gladly suffer illusions, persuading themselves that they are not illusions, where love is concerned. If it were not so, the human species would long ago have become extinct. The man who praises a woman for those qualities which she does not possess, rather than for those which she actually does possess, is a wise man; he who omits to emphasize the intelligence of a pretty nincompoop or the physical beauty of a blue-stocking, is lacking in elementary knowledge of woman's nature.

## § 4

## MANNERS, MOBS, AND WAR

It is a matter of dispute whether manners in the twentieth century are better than those which have existed at peak points of past civilizations. The old instinct of self-preservation often provokes a man or woman to fight for a seat in a train, omnibus, or street car; and we are told that to do so is ill-mannered. Barrie tells a story of the manners observed at social functions in Scotland. It is customary there, in many families, to say grace before meals; and it is often a problem for the hostess to decide who is to say grace. If two or three clergymen are present the problem becomes acute. Which one shall have the honour of saying grace? There must be good reasons for the choice, or the feelings of the others would be lacerated. Barrie once heard a hostess decide the question off-hand, by asking in this manner: " Mr. So-and-So, will you please say grace, as you are nearest the door?" Our manners have greatly improved in the course of time, and the temper of man in ordinary circumstances nowadays would appear to be better than that of his ancestors. A good example of this may be found in the behaviour of audiences at theatres in England where there has been, unhappily for the drama, a decided decay in the old custom of booing. In Shakespeare's time, and even in the eighteenth century, a theatre was sometimes almost wrecked by a disappointed audience.

When Lamb frequented the theatre the hissing and booing had degenerated, as had also the drama itself. It is rare, in England, for an audience to hiss and boo a production, and this notwithstanding the fact that the average play is worse than it has been for a long time. If a play is bad, or unacceptable, nobody goes to it; in the great age of the drama in England everybody went to the play, and everybody execrated the authors and actors if it was bad. This salutary influence having disappeared, the public must bear with whatever is given to them, or keep away. *It is in superficialities such as this that human nature shows its greatest changes.*

## ¶ *The More Men, the Less Sense*

The imitative instinct which, as we have shown, was responsible for the beginnings of standardized thought, is also responsible for the mob mind. Crowd impulse and that inherent tendency to act in herds, or packs, have always been so widespread in their expression, that they may be regarded as a commonplace of human nature. Trotter, dealing with this undoubted instinct among animals, says: " It can scarcely be regarded as an unmeaning accident, that the dog, the horse, the ape, the elephant, and man are all social animals. The advantages of gregariousness seem actually to outweigh the most prodigious differences of structure, and we find a condition which is often thought of as a mere habit, capable of enabling the insect nervous system to compete in the complexity of its power of adaptation with that of the higher vertebrates." Manifestations of the crowd, or herd, instinct are shown in the normal man's dislike of being conspicuous, and this is also obvious in shyness and in stage-fright. From this suggestion of sensitiveness it follows that anything which associates the suggestion of leaving the herd will tend to its rejection. An imperious command from an individual known to be without authority is disregarded; whereas the same person making the same suggestion in an indirect way, so as to link it up with the voice of the herd, will meet with success. The French psychologist Le Bon shows that a crowd is not only a gathering of people but *a state of mind* representing a mental unity. In the history of human nature it is a cruel fact that *the quality of this state of mind has always gravitated towards the level of the lowest intelligence and the lowest morality of the individual unit*. This may best be exemplified in modern times by those political mass-meetings at which contemporary Cæsars bellow their emotive platitudes into microphones. Their appeal is cunningly directed to the primitive feeling among men, in which higher rational expression or intellectual protest is completely and utterly lost. The crowd revolts against the teachings of philosophers who emphasize the importance of self-analysis, and therefore disintegrate the tendency to a mass-mind. The crowd insists on compliance with those principles which are nearest to the primitive feelings of individual man, and it will tear to pieces any spirit which digresses from this fundamental law. Scarcely one great moralist or thinker in the whole of human history was popular in his own time. Many were executed for their teachings, Socrates and Jesus Christ being outstanding examples. It is only after their death that posterity renders homage, which is not always sincere, to men of high moral calibre.

¶ *Madness of Mob Mind*

If we consider with the herd instinct the reaction to authority, we have the ingredients for those widespread hysterias which have shaken the world from time to time. In the early days of the 1914–18 War a governmental edict was placarded all over the United States: " *Obey the law, and keep your mouth shut.*" And it was so, more or less. When war had progressed from the very early stage in which combats were between mere individuals, families, or small clans, and became an affair of nations, empires, or, in its recent phase, whole groups of nations on each side, we see the practical uses made by leaders of the fundamental characteristics of human nature, which have been outlined in the preceding pages. The psychologist Freud has pointed out in his own quiet but logical manner that it is not that masses of people sink very low in time of war, but that they are never in times of peace so high as they believe. In times of war the whole veneer of civilization is removed, and we see before us a ghastly spectacle such as was so vividly portrayed over the face of the world between 1914 and 1918 and from 1939 to 1945.

It is useless to argue against this. There was more sheer brutality in one day on the Western front, practised by the highest types of modern man in the First World War, than can be found among the most savage peoples of the jungle, or ever existed in the early days of human history, when, we are optimistically informed, man was merely an ape. The Italian rape of Abyssinia, the terrible Spanish War of 1936–39, and the Second World War culminating in the atomic bomb, all provide evidence of the mad cruelty.

Nor was brutality in the Great Wars of the twentieth century confined merely to combatant soldiers on both sides, men in the grip of a vast machine and driven by Fate, as it were, to commit brutal slaughter. From the pulpits of Christian churches there were preached sermons in which piety and sheer vindictiveness were blended in a diabolical mixture. The most humane and reasonable men were affected by it. Those who, in their hearts, revolted against the whole business, had either to keep their mouths shut, or they were thrown into prison, beaten, and tortured, not with the more humane physical tortures of devil-men, but with the far more cruel mental tortures of modern civilization. Passions released by war permeate every stitch of the modern social fabric. Reason is thrown overboard, and emotionalism rules the day. In the newspapers, on the stage, in the music-halls, in the schools, in the pulpits, in the homes of the people, the stupid sentimentalism of glory is paraded on every possible occasion. No lie is too great in time of war; and no measure too savage. It is a quaint fact of human nature that those who are most tame in times of peace, and who then behave in an exemplary manner, are the most likely to throw all restraint to the winds when mob emotionalism becomes epidemic. Even women, from staid mothers of families to modest country maidens, succumb to the general destruction of the moral code. In 1917 I stood on the platform of Waterloo Station in London as one of a draft of infantrymen proceeding to the front and I saw the mildest of women, sometimes with babies in their arms, kiss their men good-bye and say, " Give the Germans one for me." So far did the passions run during the war that the phrase " Gott strafe England " became a catchword in Germany; and an ingenious author wrote a " Hymn of Hate " which was sung in the Central Empires. The war was waged even against inanimate things; we were forbidden to speak the enemy language, to read his books of philosophy, or to eat foods emanating from the culinary art of the opposing forces. By burying our heads in the sand, we hoped to see less of the danger; by making a loud noise and clamour, we drowned reason; and by martial music and propaganda of hate, we stimulated our nervous systems for the fight. All this was natural and necessary.

The world talks of *the revolt against war*.

*There has always been a " revolt " against war.* There is a revolt against war in the Bible, and in Greek literature we find the same revolt. Jonathan Swift raged against the insanity of war in the eighteenth century. There have been few writers in the whole of literature who were really in favour of war, and the greatest that the world has seen have all

revolted against war, with the exception of that very
honest man Mahomet. There appears to be, deep
down in human nature, a brute-beast instinct which
favours war. For periods varying in length it is
submerged, and we occupy ourselves with the routine
of peace. The cauldron of humanity simmers for a
while, and then it boils over—often as a result of
some cosmic influence of which we have no knowledge
whatever.

And yet war has been responsible for much real
progress, and it has been responsible for many a change
in human nature. As Winwood Reade says rightly,
" By means of *War* the animated life was slowly
raised upward in the scale, and quadrupeds passed
into man. By means of War the human intelligence
was brightened, and the affections were made intense;
weapons and tools were invented; foreign wives were
captured, and the marriages of blood relations were
forbidden; prisoners were tamed, and the women set
free; prisoners were exchanged, accompanied with
presents; thus commerce was established, and thus,
by means of War, men were first brought into amicable
relations with one another. By War the tribes were
dispersed all over the world, and adopted various
pursuits according to the conditions by which they
were surrounded. By War the tribes were compressed
into the nation."

¶ *Quantity and Quality of Brains*

If we compare the present with the past, and trace
events to their causes, we shall find that we have
reached our present stage not by a series of immutable
laws, but rather by provisional expedients, and that

the principle which in one age affected the advancement of a nation, in the next age might retard the forward movement or even destroy it altogether. Even despotisms and slavery have been responsible for improvements in human nature. The history of the greatest successes in history is not a record of the triumph of great minds, but it is for the most part a chronicle of political chicanery, debauchery, and cynical exploitation, in which large masses of men have been moved to commit and submit to unutterable stupidities. Although there has been a great increase in knowledge, there has been practically no change in human *capacity*, from that far-off day in which the first genius found a method of producing fire. Past generations have handed down knowledge to us, and each generation may or may not add to the wealth of knowledge already available. There is a fair amount of evidence to show that much useful knowledge has been entirely lost at various times in our history. The destruction of the great library at Alexandria in A.D. 389 by Theophilus meant the disappearance of we know not how many advances in the province of intellect. From the excavations of the anthropologists we know that the brain capacity of primitive man was as great as our own. The Cro-Magnons of perhaps 50,000 years ago had brains which were slightly greater in weight than our own, the average weight of the male brain today being about forty-eight ounces. The heaviest known human brain belonged, as might be expected, to an Englishman. He was a bricklayer who died of tuberculosis in 1849; his brain exceeded sixty-seven ounces and was well proportioned.

As regards the purely intellectual side of man's nature, authorities maintain that *no* modern race of men is the intellectual equal of the Greeks of 2500 years ago.

Galton has drawn our attention to the fact that in the century between 530 and 430 B.C. the small country of Attica produced fourteen illustrious men —one for every 4300 of the free-born, adult population. In the two centuries from 500 to 300 B.C. this small country produced over two dozen illustrious men, whose achievements were truly amazing. The philosophers and men of science included Socrates, Aristotle, Plato, Demetrius, and Theophrastus; the orators, Demosthenes, Lysias, Æschines, and Isocrates; statesmen and commanders, Aristides, Themistocles, Pericles, Cimon, Phocion, and Militiades; the poets and dramatists, Sophocles, Euripides, Aristophanes, and Æschylus; the artists and architects, Phidias, Polygnotus, Ictinus, and Praxiteles; and the historians Xenophon and Thucydides. Galton concludes that the average ability of the Athenian race of that period was, on the lowest estimate, as much greater than that of the Anglo-Saxon race of the present date as the latter is above that of the African negro.

¶ *The Growth of the Child*

Let us turn again to our friend the protozoon, and compare with it the early stages of man's life. The newly-born child is unable to think, but its existence is made possible by the selfish primitive instincts which are exactly similar to those of the protozoon. During the first three weeks there is only the desire for food and sleep, together with a tendency to defend itself, indicated by a willingness to cling to anybody in its immediate neighbourhood. At the end of about three weeks the emotions begin to show themselves, and it is perhaps not surprising that the first of these is the ability to be afraid, and to be surprised. At the end of ten weeks we see signs of curiosity, pugnacity, and a little anger. By twelve weeks we see anger more fully developed, and with it the beginning of jealousy. Then comes the desire to play, and following this we see, in about the thirteenth week, the ability to associate ideas, which is the beginning of reason. It is only in the fourteenth week that true affection begins to show itself, and a baby is five months old before it begins to manifest any signs of sympathy. Eight months have passed before appreciation appears, and about the same time we see the budding shoots of conscious pride and resentment. By ten months the baby may suffer grief which is not the outcome of actual physical pain. At this stage hate and cruelty show themselves. The year-old child begins to use objects around it as tools, and it will open a tin or use a stick to draw something towards it. At the end of fifteen months we see the ability to suffer remorse, and it is at this late stage that the child shows for the first time any signs of deceit. But it should be noted that it is only children of high intellectual capacity who show deceit in the fifteenth month of their lives. Some anthropologists assert that the mentality reached by the modern child in fifteen months is equal to that of primitive man, but I do not believe them. It may perhaps be of interest to compare the development of the ape with

that of the child. Kohler has closely investigated
the mentality of the higher apes, and has demonstrated once and for all time that, although they may
be superior to us in morals, they are certainly inferior
to us in intellect. The most advanced among the
group of intelligent apes with which he experimented
was capable of only the most elementary acts based
upon logical reason, and then very often when some
solution of a problem was indicated.

¶ *Society has the Criminals it Deserves*

A French criminologist wittily said, " *Society pre-
pares crimes and the criminal is the instrument that
executes them.*" Another declares that social environment may be the cultivation medium of criminality;
the criminal is the microbe, an element which becomes
important only when it finds the medium which causes
it to ferment. In other words, every society has the
criminals that it deserves. Many instincts are
inherited which seem to make crime inevitable. The
acquisitive instinct, the sex instinct, the fighting
instinct—these, if unrestrained, may lead directly to
offences against law. Such instincts are inherited
by every human being; they are part of the mental
equipment of the human race. The criminal, if he
differs from the rest, differs merely because his
instincts are stronger than our own. In the hereditary equipment of the youthful criminal the most
serious handicap is not lack of morals, but lack of
education, comfort, and intelligence. Among the
juvenile delinquents in London, as many as 80 per cent
are below the average level in general ability. The
ordinary criminal, when grown up, still shows the

mental age of a boy of only ten or eleven. Most rogues are fools. Such cases as that of Leopold and Loeb are exceptional; this case sprang from sheer conceit on the part of at least one of these boys. Of all the conditions that go to the making of the youthful criminal, the most important are those that centre in the home. Improper discipline is perhaps the commonest. The discipline may be too lax or too strict; or, worst of all, it may be of the oscillating, forcible-feeble type, where the boy is one moment cuffed for making a noise, and next moment bribed with a penny to keep him quiet.

## ¶ Men of Genius may be Criminals

The late Professor Lester Ward, referring to the skilful and daring criminal in the United States, called him " the genius of the slums." By this expressive term he meant that when native talent or genius finds its birthright cheated by the blight of poverty, its course nowadays often becomes perverted by sordid surroundings and lack of constructive opportunity. To satisfy the craving for wealth, excitement, and achievement, to secure an outlet for the expression of the powerful primitive urge, it almost inevitably turns into anti-social channels, and hence we get crooks and gangsters. A poet of importance in French literature, Paul Verlaine, is an interesting example of the man of genius who was also distinctly a criminal. Verlaine was leader of the " Decadent " school of the nineteenth century. The precise rank that he will ultimately take as a poet is not clear, but must always be high; he has been both unduly neglected and unduly extolled. He excels in delicate passages of vague and mystic reverie, in sudden lines of poignant emotion. His private life was vicious, even for a poet, and he is quoted here merely to show that crime is not a question of intellect. Criminality consists in a failure to live up to the standard recognized as binding by the community. The criminal is an individual whose organization makes it difficult or impossible for him to live in accordance with this standard, and easy to risk the penalties of acting anti-socially. By some accident of development, by some defect of heredity or birth or training, he belongs to an older social state than that in which he is actually living. " Men of undoubted intellectual power are sometimes found among criminals. Villon, one of the truest, if not one of the greatest of poets, was a criminal, a man perpetually in danger of the gallows; it does not seem to me, however, by any means clear that he was what we should call an instinctive criminal. Vidocq, a clever criminal who became an equally successful police official, and wrote his interesting and instructive *Memoirs*, may not have been, as Lombroso claims, a man of genius, but he was certainly a man of great ability." [1]

¶ *Great Utility of Mendacity*

Mention should be made of the semi-criminal type known as the " pathological " liar—that is, the person who makes amusement for himself and often for others by conceits of exaggeration and stories that surprise. It is a common human weakness which has persisted throughout the centuries. The writing of " fiction " is based on the use of this

[1] Havelock Ellis, *The Criminal*.

quality. Yet, pathological liars are often dangerous when their lying takes the form of spreading stories and rumours. Others of them frequently serve a useful purpose. In the early days of the European War, for example, there was that wonderful story of the Russian troops having landed in England, to pass through it on their way to help the Allies in France. Probably it was started by a pathological liar. It was one of those lies which were pleasant and comforting in days of trial. It spread like wildfire through England, and was of great military value. A telegram from Rome was published to the effect that there was to be a concentration of a quarter of a million Russian troops in France. On September 14, 1914, the London *Daily News* published the following:

> As will be seen from the long despatch of Mr. "X.Y.Z.", our special correspondent, Russian troops are now co-operating with the Belgians. This information proves the correctness of the general impression that Russian troops have been moved through England.

Such a piece of news, at a moment of great anxiety, was just what was wanted to counter bad news that could not be suppressed. No official denial was necessary, although it was a complete falsehood.

The pathological liar is often unaware that he is lying, and pays little attention to the morality of it. His phantasy generally springs from a sense of inferiority, and the only way he can compensate for this inferiority is to indulge in dreams in which he is in a position of importance. The same phenomenon may often be observed in politicians, writers, and poets; but they occasionally turn it to good account.

Goethe admits that, in his early childhood, he felt himself developing into a pathological liar, and it was only by a great mental effort that he turned his imaginings into metaphysical speculations.

¶ *The Principles of State and Other Propaganda*

While on this subject I must mention Ponsonby's analysis of lies told by belligerents in the 1914–18 War. He says that there must have been more deliberate lying from 1914 to 1918 than in any other period of the world's history. Original lying has always been on more or less the same scale, but the telegraph, the wireless, and the printing-press have given lying an amazing fillip. I can illustrate this " golden age of lying," as Lord Ponsonby will have it, by quoting from his book.

" There are several different sorts of disguises which falsehood can take," says Ponsonby. " There is (1) the deliberate official lie, issued either to delude the people at home or to mislead the enemy abroad. As a Frenchman has said, ' As long as peoples are armed against each other, there will be lying statesmen, just as there will be cannons and machine-guns.' A circular was issued by the War Office inviting reports on war incidents from officers with regard to the enemy and stating that strict accuracy was not essential so long as there was inherent probability. (2) There is the deliberate lie concocted by an ingenious mind which may only reach a small circle, but which, if sufficiently graphic and picturesque, may be caught up and broadcast; and there is the hysterical hallucination on the part of weak-minded individuals. (3) There is the lie heard and not denied, although lacking in evidence, and then repeated or allowed to circulate. (4) There is the mistranslation, occasionally originating in a genuine mistake, but more often deliberate. Two minor instances of this may be given:

(a)

*The Times* (Agony Column), July 9, 1915:
Jack F. G.—If you are not in khaki by the 20th, I'll cut you dead.—Ethel M.

The Berlin Correspondent of the *Cologne Gazette* transmitted this:

If you are not in khaki by the 20th, hacke ich dich zu Tode (*I will hack you to death!*).

(b)

During the blockade of Germany it was suggested that the diseases from which children suffered had been called *Die englische Krankheit* (the English disease) as a permanent reflection on English inhumanity. As a matter of fact, *Die englische Krankheit* is, and always has been, the common German name for rickets.

(5) There is the general obsession, started by rumour, magnified by repetition, and elaborated by hysteria, which at last gains general acceptance. (6) There is the deliberate forgery which has to be very carefully manufactured, but serves its purpose at the moment, even though it be eventually exposed. (7) There is the omission of passages from official documents; and the 'correctness' of words and commas in parliamentary answers which conceal evasions of the truth. (8) There is the deliberate exaggeration—such, for instance, as the reports of the destruction of Louvain: 'The intellectual metropolis of the Low Countries since the fifteenth century is now no more

than a heap of ashes' (*Press Bureau*, August 29, 1914). 'Louvain has ceased to exist' (*The Times*, August 29, 1914). As a matter of fact, it was estimated that about an eighth of the town had suffered. (9) There is the concealment of truth, which has to be resorted to so as to prevent anything to the credit of the enemy reaching the public. A war correspondent who mentioned some chivalrous act that a German had done to an Englishman during an action received a rebuking telegram from his employer: 'Don't want to hear any good about Germans.' Sir Philip Gibbs, in *Realities of War*, says: 'At the close of the day the Germans acted with chivalry, which I was not allowed to tell at the time.' (10) There is the faked photograph ('the camera cannot lie'). These were more popular in France than here. *In Vienna an enterprising firm supplied atrocity photographs with blanks for the headings so that they might be used for propaganda purposes by either side.* (11) The cinema also played a very important part, especially in neutral countries, and helped in turning opinion in America in favour of the Allies. (12) There was the 'Russian scandal,' the best instance of which during the 1914–1918 War, curiously enough, was the rumour of the passage of Russian troops through Britain. Some trivial and imperfectly understood statement of fact becomes magnified into enormous proportions by constant repetition from one person to another. (13) Atrocity lies were the most popular of all, especially in England and America; no war can be without them. Slander of the enemy is a patriotic duty. An English soldier wrote (*The Times*, September 15, 1914): '*The stories in our papers are not exceptions. There are people like them in every army.'* Stories of the maltreatment of prisoners have to be circulated deliberately in order to prevent surrenders. This is done, of course, on both sides. Whereas naturally each side tries to treat its prisoners as well as possible so as to attract others. (14) The repetition of a single instance of cruelty and its exaggeration, distorted into a prevailing habit on the part of the enemy. Unconsciously each one passes it on with trimmings and yet tries to persuade himself that he is speaking the truth. (15) There are lies emanating from the inherent unreliability and fallibility of human testimony. No two people can relate the occurrence of a street accident so as to make the two stories tally. When bias and emotion are introduced, human testimony is accepted as conclusive. The scrappiest and most unreliable evidence is sufficient—' *the friend of the brother of the man who was killed,*' or, as a German investigator of his own liars put it, ' *somebody who had seen it,*' or, ' *an extremely respectable old woman.*' (16) There is pure romance. Letters of soldiers who whiled away the days and weeks of intolerable waiting by writing home thrilling descriptions of engagements and adventures which had never occurred. (17) There are evasions, concealments, and half-truths which are more subtly misleading and gradually become a governmental habit. (18) There is official secrecy, which must necessarily mislead public opinion. (19) There is sham official indignation depending on genuine popular indignation, which is a form of falsehood sometimes resorted to in an unguarded moment and subsequently regretted. The first use of gas by the Germans and the submarine warfare are good instances of this. (20) Contempt for the enemy, if illustrated, can prove to be an unwise form of falsehood. There was a time when German soldiers were popularly represented cringing, with their arms in the air and crying ' Kamerad,' until it occurred to Press and propaganda authorities that people were asking why, if this was the sort of material the Allies were fighting against, they had not wiped it off the field in a few weeks. (21) There are personal accusations and false charges made in a prejudiced war atmosphere to discredit persons who refuse to adopt the orthodox attitude towards war. (22) There are lying recriminations between one country and another. For instance, the Germans were accused of having engineered the Armenian massacres, and they, on their side, declared the Armenians, stimulated by the Russians, had killed 150,000 Mahomedans (*Germania*, October 9, 1915)."

" Other varieties of falsehood more subtle and elusive can be found, but the above pretty well cover the ground." [1] Since then, we have the radio to help.

Lord Ponsonby then goes on to expand his analysis, giving examples of each kind of the above lies used wholesale throughout the war. We may assume that his statement is correct, if incomplete. It shows in a striking manner the basic immorality of modern man, and that, given the right atmosphere, he may sink to

[1] The above " Twenty-two points of lying " are quoted from *Falsehood in War-Time*, by Arthur Ponsonby, M.P. The book is documented and worth perusal by those who are interested in the question of religious influence upon truthfulness.—C.D.

any form of lying trick, in order to thwart and deceive his fellow men.

### ¶ Does Human Nature Change?

We may now well ask ourselves the question: " *Does human nature change?* "

In view of what has already been said, a very great question mark stands vividly before our eyes. Indeed, what it all seems to amount to is this: *the superficial manners of man have changed considerably, but those fundamental instincts and emotions upon which human nature is based have undergone little real change.* In everyday life, and in what may be called the ordinary run of existence, many of these instincts and emotions are repressed. At a given moment in the life of an individual, of a nation, of a race, and nowadays of a continent, remove the lid of culture and civilization, and we see boiling in the pot the whole vile stew of the primitive. The history of human nature is the history of a gradual repression of primitive instincts and emotions, with moments and in circumscribed localities in which there is a sudden release of the repressions—during the Crusades, World Wars, the Spanish Civil War, social revolutions, and so forth. We then witness acts by individuals and by groups, by races and by nations, of a sort to show that we are, to all intents and purposes, not far above the level of jungle beasts. Such inventions as the aeroplane, wireless telegraphy, or the talking pictures do not cause great changes in our nature. They are merely externals, and are not without some slight effects. A long period of time may be necessary to cause even the slightest changes. We shall see that, in the last

two thousand years, Christianity has changed the
outlook of men, and given a great impetus to superficial humanitarianism. The same may be said of
the other great religions, and Marxism is now being
tried. But one may ask whether Christianity, which
brought in its train a whole series of terrible wars,
not to mention physical and mental torture, has really
caused anything very wonderful in the way of a
change in our natures. Marxism may go deeper.

c

# Book II: THE TAMING AND SOPHISTI-
CATION OF HUMAN NATURE

## § 1

## REAL ESTATE AND JUJU BECOME
IMPORTANT

WE have discussed the origin of fire and indicated its importance upon the development of man's nature. Of scarcely less importance was the fence, invented to separate one person's land from that of another. It seems strange to us to think that originally land was not *owned*, in the sense that real estate can be owned nowadays by an individual, a group, or a nation. There was in many places communal use of land. But one day a greedy man conceived the idea of marking off a piece for his own private use, and surrounding it by a fence to keep other men from trespassing: that was the origin of property, which has caused so much trouble in the affairs of men in all ages. Great families, tribal boundaries, and nations sprang from it; one school of thought believes it to be the pivot of human history. It seems quite simple, this fence idea, and yet its origin cannot date very far back. I do not mean the fence which primitive man might build round his cave or shelter to protect it from the attacks of wild beasts or of his fellow-men of other tribes. Probably that was the first kind of fence. But far more subtle was that idea of surrounding a piece of useful land with a hedge,

60

or a row of sticks, to mark it off from that which was occupied by a neighbour. The importance of this apparently modest idea in human affairs can scarcely be exaggerated, for was not this fence or boundary the cause of the first economic war? We see its effects on our own times. On each side of *every* fence in the world there are to be found interests which conflict with one another in some way. There appears to be little possibility of avoiding the problems which they present; they have seldom been avoided in the past. No country but possesses a property law; and there is no civilized country in which the squabbles about real estate do not bring a rich harvest to a type of human being which exists rather to sit on the fence than to live on either side of it: parasite man, in the form of lawyers, etc.

¶ *The Wheel Rounds Off Human Nature*

Man the hunted animal, man the hunter, man the fire-maker, man the agriculturist and pastoralist, man the fencemaker—these are great landmarks without ascertained dates in the history of human nature. The next landmark which we shall consider is the wheel, for it, too, has shown itself to have been a powerful influence. It is as a result of the invention of the wheel that life has been speeded up to its present pace. " In our own time the wheel has taken on a marvellous extension. It gives us electrical energy to use; it transmits power; it keeps time for us; it measures all things from a map to the speed of light; it permits our curious toys, such as moving pictures. It endows us with the special uses of the gyroscope; it drives our turbines by steam and water, and soon perhaps by air. It even aids in our vices, and by its impersonality, and exactitude, it makes our gambling reasonably impersonal." [1]   One might add that it enables us to wage war on a scale hitherto possible only to the imaginations of fiends.

¶ *The Canalization of Humanity*

It was also this simple device, the wheel, which caused man first to make a road, later a highway, and still later the network of railways to be found in civilized parts of the world and in many that are still living through their age of barbarism.

¶ *Migrant Man*

The wheel was followed by the vehicle, and the vehicle by the road, of which the importance is incalculable. The road was responsible, for example, for the military success of the Roman Empire; and it was the road which, by facilitating the spread of Christianity, as well as the influx into Rome of wealth and luxury from conquered territories, led to its decline and fall. As we have shown, primitive man became a wanderer chiefly because of the invention of a means of making fire. The habit of wandering, once acquired, was assisted by the road to develop into a nomadic tendency which man has never abandoned. At one period vast numbers of Asiatics spread westward over the plains of Eastern Europe. They were undisciplined forces, but they had with them fire and wheels, horses and grain, which they used in their settlement of Europe. Since then the wandering

[1] Hilaire Belloc: *The Highway and its Vehicles*.

spirit of man has shown itself in vast migrations; at first warlike raids, now often peaceful penetrations. In the past four hundred years, for example, the continent of America has been the goal of a migration from Europe. The results of these invasions and migrations mean an intermixture of races which seems on the face of it to be beneficial to humanity; or the resultant mixture asserts that it is. The mingling of the wise and weary with the young and powerful can produce excellent results. The interchange of ideas proceeds; and new means of comfort are discovered. Hitherto migrations and penetrations have taken place chiefly among white races, and now the white race everywhere consists of mongrels. The yellows and the blacks do not mix very much or even very well with the whites; nor are they all anxious that they should do so. In a sense, therefore, there are three kinds of human nature, outwardly indicated by the colour of the skin.

## ¶ Origin of Sport

With the aid of his fire, his wheels, and his roads, man was enabled to settle in large groups which grew into cities. He still continued to hunt; but when he was unable to do this he had to find other means of working off excess energy. Occasionally he could do so in war; but when there was no war he was driven back upon other expedients, and these were based upon a sort of instinct to *throw*, to *run*, and to *strike*, which came from hunting or war. In this we see the origin of games. Hunting changed from a serious business into a sport, and as such it has almost disappeared because of the intense development of that idea contained in the fence and the boundary. But the hunting spirit survives. Nothing can cause more excitement in the household of a highly civilized family than the hunting down of a rat or mouse or even of so beautiful an insect as a wasp. Boys still love to throw stones at cats, dogs, or birds, and must be taught that it is wrong before they will desist from this cruel amusement. In England we still hunt the hare, the fox, and the stag where these can be found. Not many of them remain, for they have very little chance against the modern hunt.

## ¶ Nightmare Origin of Religion

The origin of the religious spirit cannot be traced so successfully, although many attempts have been made to do so. The contemplative part of early man's life must have been something in the nature of a nightmare. He feared everything unfamiliar and unknown, as he still does. He developed a whole series of ideas regarding things that were forbidden or "taboo." Out of these fears and taboos was evolved a system of religion, at what date in man's history we do not know. Nor can one be sure that religion existed among all the primitive races, for even now there are races with scarcely any religion. Spencer evolved a plausible theory of the origin of religion based upon evidence furnished by the life and thought of modern savages. According to him, the primitive formed a conception of the soul from what he believed to be his experience: that after dreams or swoons the mind which had temporarily roamed away from the body was able to return. The next step is the belief that after death the soul exists for a time as a spirit; following this, in comparatively modern times—that is, in ancient Egypt—an idea of the *immortality* of the soul began to show itself. Then, again, early man blamed evil spirits for all the calamities and catastrophes of his existence. Gradually these were narrowed down to two spirits, the one representing Good (God), and the other representing Evil (Devil). These old imaginative conceptions have come down to us, and are the basis of most of the religious systems of the world. There are, however, still races which have not advanced so far as the idea of God. In Brazil the Chunchas of the Amazon valley have no religion, nor have many of the Indians of the Gran Chaco. Until quite recently, Indians and tribes that dwelt on the shores of the Hudson Bay had no worship nor any words to express the God-idea. Before the arrival of missionaries with their whisky and rum the Esquimaux did not know of good or evil spirits. Until deaf mutes (of any race) receive *education* they never formulate in their minds any idea of recognizable religion. But once religion has taken root it is not long before it shows signs of growth and expansion. It is a long way from the hazy concepts of early religion to that of Akhnaton, the Egyptian, or Judaism, in which the idea of a localized or tribal Deity was expanded into a Universal God, omnipotent and omniscient.

¶ *Influence of Things Invisible and Intangible*

The basis of the Jewish religion is the doctrine of rewards and punishment: the man who behaves in the manner decreed by God will be rewarded (by God), and he who does otherwise will be punished (by God).

Compound interest is given on good or bad deeds. The authors of the first five books of the Bible took no account of Hell, and the idea of offering rewards and punishments in the after-life is a comparatively modern idea—a few thousand years old, at most. Around the main ideas of morality of the Hebrew religion there grew an elaborate mythology which was closely connected with, and influenced by, the mythologies of preceding and contemporary people. The ethical code was savage, though a very practical one, dominated by brute-man's tribal spirit of vendetta or reprisal, by which the Almighty vented His wrath on individuals, nations, or races for failing to pay mental, moral, or monetary tax and tribute. There is no doubt that these ideas, when stripped of the symbolism and formalism added by priests and rulers, had a profound influence upon human nature. It was these *Invisible and Intangible Things* which caused the first spiritual change in our nature: they were responsible for a repression and a breaking-in or taming. The reason is obvious. Before the arrival of the God who was everywhere, was everything, and had even the hairs of human beings' heads well and truly numbered, the man who wished to do wrong, and was not immediately under the observation of his fellows, could do so almost with impunity. But now a powerful " Universal Spirit " had arrived who was *taking account of every action, even if done by stealth*. How could man, with his inheritance of fear from the days when he was a hunted animal, behave otherwise than to attempt to do that which his teachers taught him was right? It was the first blackmail on a grand scale. Almost at the same time as the Hebrew use of the Universal God (that is to say, about five thousand years B.C.) another bright idea was evolved. It happened somewhat in this manner. If the Great Universal God were omnipotent and omniscient, it was rather difficult to explain why he permitted so much evil in the world. Another God—one not so powerful, but almost—had to be invented: and so the Devil arrived among us. It would appear that the Devil-idea spread far more rapidly than that of the single God: far away to the West are to be found traces of his existence in paintings that may have been made perhaps thousands of years before our era. The true history of the Devil is now fairly well known, and his evolution from a kind of Horned God and ruler of the underworld of evil has been chronicled in terms of moderately scientific history. Let it suffice to say here that without him the success of the Universal God might not have been nearly so great as it undoubtedly was. It is an amazing commentary upon human faith and credulity that existing religious and scientific doctrines relating to the creation of the world, the tyranny over man by Invisible and Intangible Things, the control of his destiny after death, all of them resulting from the imaginative speculation of men of genius (but in no manner capable of proof in terms of reason), have swayed whole nations and governed every action in the life of masses of individuals. Rulers with their priests, supported by armies or the equivalent, have made use of religious systems to control actions not under their immediate supervision. Emperors and kings submitted to this system of spiritual government, often with beneficial results. In Western civilization today much of this completely bogus influence is disappearing, but the great trading and colonizing nations still use it as a means to keep order in less sophisticated races.

## § 2

## THE PHŒNICIANS AND OTHERS

We now come to that part of human history in which tribes and clans become nations. To trace this through every phase in its development is impossible, but it is necessary for us to give some consideration to those races and nations whose activities are known to have had a profound effect upon Western human nature. Of Assyria, Babylonia, and the early Empires of Mesopotamia little is yet known for certain. We have already seen that it was in this part of the world that man first discovered the cereal plants; and we have seen how they changed his nature. In regard to the more complex civilizations which grew out of the agricultural and pastoral existence of man in the area between the Tigris and the Euphrates, we may summarize their effect upon human nature by saying that they gave us a host of myths and legends which became interwoven with our religion and, in some cases, were responsible for great wars and rumours of wars. The Holy Trinity, for example, originated in this part of the world. Three thousand years after its discovery, it was the cause of many grave and bloody disputes among Christian Churches. But it was to two other peoples that some of the greatest changes in human nature must be attributed: the Egyptians and the Phœnicians.

¶ *Influence of the Boat*

It is perhaps necessary, first of all, to say something about the origin of the boat; for it was the boat, together with an almost equally important invention, the steering-oar, that was responsible for the success of the Phœnicians; and hence their great importance. It is possible that in very early times wanderers from the Phœnician cities of Tyre, Sidon, and Damascus may have reached Egypt and observed the boats on the great river. The possibility of trade with the West showed itself to the Phœnician wanderers who had reached the banks of the Nile. By means of shipping they could explore the Mediterranean, and their business instinct was supported by an amazing ingenuity for shipbuilding and navigation. They became explorers and navigators because they were traders. They were traders because they liked to accumulate wealth in its already very old form of gold. To the Phœnicians must be attributed the great honour of having consolidated the gold standard; although the earliest actual coinage of which we know was made by Crœsus in Lydia about 2500 years ago. The Phœnicians did most of their trading by means of gold dust, nuggets, ingots, or articles made of gold. To accumulate quantities of this substance they made long and perilous voyages, resulting in the establishment of colonies along the North African coast. Later, in 800 B.C., the colony of Carthage, founded by Tyre, became the greatest maritime power the world had hitherto seen. The original efforts of the Phœnicians to increase their trade developed in the colony of Carthage into the desire for maritime power;

in precisely the same manner as nearly two thousand years later the early British Colonial Empire and naval power grew from the desire for increasing foreign trade. The little colony of Carthage became a great city with a population of a million souls; possibly the largest single unit of humanity that had hitherto been known on earth.

## ¶ Pirates the First Navy

Carthage claimed the Western Mediterranean, and organized piratical raids on the ships of other nations, just as, in the sixteenth and seventeenth centuries, the ships of England were sent abroad to pillage the galleons of Spain or to seize what land or property they could find. One of the Carthaginian navigators, Captain Hanno, in 520 B.C., sailed out of Carthage, venturing into the unknown ocean west of the Straits of Gibraltar. Herodotus tells us that Pharaoh Necho commissioned in 609 B.C. a group of Phœnician navigators to attempt the circumnavigation of Africa. The story is that they succeeded, taking nearly three years on their voyage; an astounding achievement for that age, if true.

## ¶ The Semitic Sense of Equivalents

Although trade existed in many parts of the world before the days of the Phœnicians—we know of a Sumerian trade of some importance in ancient Babylonia—the palm for ability in trade at that period must be given to this race or people. They were a branch of the Semitic race; a kind of Jews. To the Semitic race must also be given the palm for accountancy, measuring, and weighing. It was they who first showed that very strong sense for *Equivalents* which is mostly responsible for their material success in the world. The Jew still attaches a sentimental value to a bargain; and he prefers to do business with little profit rather than remain idle. Business for business's sake is the spirit in which the Jew has treated his occupation on this earth. To him it is almost an art for art's sake. The Jews are sentimentalists and one of the wisest races on earth. Jewish thought has in some matters reached farther than the thought of other human beings, and this is because they are continually meditating on the unknown or some practical equivalent for it. Jews discovered sin and God; a Jew evolved the theory of Relativity. Many of the most beautiful flights of mathematics and science are the work of Jews, and by obtaining control of those fictitious tokens called money, they have achieved a power in the world which has often made governments bow before them. The Jews have reduced doubt in the minds of men on subjects as widely different as the existence of God, the value of money, and the constitution of the atom.

¶ *Human Standard of Living Raised*

The importance of the Phœnicians in human history is briefly this: *They raised the standard of living over the greater part of the known world.* They encouraged the desire for comfort and luxury. They spread a knowledge of their alphabet, one of the finest achievements of the human mind. They taught our ancestors book-keeping, accountancy, the use of money, and equivalents. They invented credit. They worked out the principles of trade and infused a new ideal into the minds of men. They set up the God of Commerce and made a code of commercial morality. Being a materialistic, energetic race with a genius for navigation, they did not hesitate to explore unknown regions. Their talent for commercial enterprise was so advantageous to other peoples that for a long time they did not need to wage war. It will be noticed that the Phœnician contribution to human history has had lasting and far-reaching effects. From their time to the present day, commercial enterprise has never ceased; it is even extending.

## ¶ Sad End of the Phœnicians

But the Greeks supplanted them. The Phœnicians found it cheaper to pay tribute than to go to war, and submitted to the Emperor of Syria, sending their money with equal indifference to Nineveh or Memphis. When the empire was disputed they were compelled to choose a side. They chose the wrong one, and Tyre and Jerusalem were demolished. Phœnicia declined in the East, Carthage was rising in the West. We shall see later the part that Carthage was destined to play; but in the meantime let it not be forgotten that this city, which later all but caused the downfall of Rome, was the child of Phœnicia, the motherland which had succumbed to the warriors from the East. The Phœnicians, having made the fatal mistake of trusting too far to the peacefulness of men, paid the inevitable penalty of downfall.

## ¶ Invention of Writing

By this time one more weighty factor is added to those which influenced the development and changes in human nature from the primitive to modern man.

Above all those qualities which were engendered by the commercial activities of the Phœnicians, there stands out one of paramount importance. It is fairly modern in the sense that it occurred within the last five thousand years; its influence has extended from that day to the present, and is not yet by any means ended. I refer to writing.[1] We may abandon to the experts the decision as to whether writing was first actually invented by the Chinese, the Sumerians, or the Egyptians. For practical purposes we must attach ourselves to that form of writing which we know came to Phœnicia from Sumeria. In this part of the world learned men had evolved a system of perpetuating their ideas by a form of picture-writing upon slabs of clay which were afterwards baked hard. Originally they wrote with " styles," which, by a process of evolution and for purposes of speed, became wedge-shaped. They used pictographs or a form of picture-writing similar to that found among tribes of Red Indians on the American continent. They also used ideograms, a pictorial representation of an object to convey another idea, as we ourselves use the word " tongue " to express " language " or " dialect." The evolution of graphic symbolism began. In ideogrammatic writing, language or dialect might be expressed by a pictorial representation of a tongue. The Sumerians also used phonograms, a more complex idea. One sign would be used as a basis for a number of ideas, each of which would be distinguished from the others by some slight or even diminutive modification of the basic sign. The Sumerians must have been a people of amazing

[1] See H. G. Wells, *The Outline of History*.

ingenuity, for, in using these three methods of reducing ideas to permanent records, they covered practically the whole of human thought concerning writing. They went further, for they evolved from pictograms, ideograms, and phonograms a further development which is called syllable writing—that is, the representation graphically of a spoken syllable. This form of writing is still used in Japan, in conjunction with and parallel to the Chinese method. The system of writing thus evolved by the Sumerians spread over the whole of the Near East—Assyria, Chaldea, Babylonia. And then the Semitic race of Phœnicians in their travels eastward, first for purposes of trade, and then, in the manner of the later Carthaginians, for purposes of conquest, took over what must have appeared to them to be a marvellously useful system of recording business transactions.

## ¶ The Fixation of Tradition

They, in turn, set their ingenuity to work, and now we meet with another of those unknown men of genius whose work has affected the whole history of the world, and been responsible for a considerable development of the human mind. This unnamed genius was the Phœnician merchant-scholar who conceived the idea of *alphabetic* writing. Among the earliest records of this convenient alphabetic writing are to be found accounts, business letters, itineraries, lists of customers for business transactions, and handy medical prescriptions for the cure of those common ailments which follow the human animal everywhere and at all times. Henceforward verbal tradition began to be fixed: thoughts could be communicated over unlimited distances; and henceforward increasing numbers of human beings were able to share the best and the worst of such knowledge as existed. It was the beginning of standardized thinking. This was a momentous event in the history of human nature.

## ¶ First Great Code of Laws

Although writing was first used for commonplace affairs of life, for business transactions, medical prescriptions, and so forth, it was also used in the formulation of the first legal systems. Law, originating in custom based upon the convenience and comfort of the tribe, had existed from the times of the primitive. With the development of the road and the growth of cities and commerce it became more complex; and was an essential in the preservation of order, the repression of masses to strengthen the authority of kings and priests. It was therefore well mixed with religion and, although it often courted those Invisible and Intangible Things which have shown themselves to have had so great an influence, it has always remained fairly close to the soil, materialistic and realistic, with the chameleon-like quality of changing its colour to suit the background of power. As we shall see later, Roman law, upheld by the legions of the Emperors, was the chain which bound the world for many hundreds of years.

Thanks to writing, we are able to tell more or less the habits of the men and women who lived under the old Babylonian Empire of nearly five thousand years ago. A block of black diorite nearly eight feet high, discovered by the French archæologist de Morgan in 1902, contains the oldest known code of laws in the world; the Code of Hammurabi. With the exception of a number of clauses pertaining to Invisible and Intangible Things, it is remarkably modern in its tone; so much so that it raises once more in our minds that great question as to whether there has really been any considerable change in human nature. The code, it is believed, antedated that of the Pentateuch by at least a thousand years, and formed the basis of Babylonian legislation under a king whose rule extended from the Tigris to the Mediterranean. This code of laws is the starting-point of all classified and regulated legislation known in history. It begins with the same formula which precedes nearly all legislation: a preamble, glorifying the ruler or supreme authority, verging into a description of the general purpose for which the law is conceived, and giving a brief outline of its contents. The idea of " *An eye for an eye and a tooth for a tooth*," the chief principle of all Jewish law, was practised to its logical extreme. Punishment was made to balance crime to such an extent that if the ceiling of a jerry-built house collapsed and injured the owner, the builder received an equivalent punishment. If the owner was killed, the builder was put to death; if the owner's son was killed or injured, the builder's son received his proportion of punishment, or was executed. Furthermore, " a woman who wanted a divorce, if she could show fault in her husband, might take her marriage portion and go home; but if the fault were hers, she was thrown into the water." There are regulations concerning slaves which were *far more humane* than the regulations regarding slaves in the Christian eighteenth and nineteenth centuries. There are elaborate provisions for the protection of honest debtors, such as may well make modern legislators feel ashamed.

¶ *How Writing may Imprison the Mind*

From writing to the provision of a means of preserving the ideas of writers is not a great step. About three thousand years ago there was a standard dictionary of the Chinese language containing about forty thousand characters. That dictionary was largely responsible for the astonishing conservatism shown by the Chinese throughout history. The complexity of the Chinese language, due mostly to the lack of that originality which we have noted among the Sumerians, coupled with its fixation in an elaborate dictionary, and afterwards perpetuated in the classical literature, were responsible for an imprisonment of the Chinese mind. No nation on earth has changed less in the nature of its individuals than the Chinese. Reading and writing became a privilege to be gained only by long study and limited to a special class. At a time when the Near East and Europe in the West were being tamed, chiefly by the spread of knowledge through the written word, the masses of Chinese depended entirely upon oral tradition, springing from the teachings of a few philosophers who had mastered the intricate art of reading and writing their complex script.

§ 3

# THE EGYPTIANS

Reference has already been made to the influence of the surface configuration of the earth upon human nature. It would be impossible to give all the instances there are of this fact. We have in the history of Egypt one of the finest examples of what a river can be to the rise, progress, and even decline of a whole people. Old Egypt was a somewhat secluded country. It lies almost across one of the highways of the modern world—that leading from England to India and the East. But we first see Egypt on the dim horizon of history hidden and encircled by mountains, deserts, and the Mediterranean Sea, all of which were avoided by contemporary peoples. A country so shut off from the rest of the world became for many hundreds, even thousands, of years impervious to outside influences. Down the centre of this secluded land, of which the climate was and is perhaps the most perfect on earth, there runs the great River Nile. In this singular river-valley it was easier for men to live and thrive than in almost any other part of the world. One cannot think of Egypt without at the same time thinking of the river which makes it. Every year the Nile overflowed its banks, fertilizing the fields, and so the Egyptian, by virtue of his climate, the nature of his soil, and, above all, because of his river, became a settled husbandman and agriculturist. He was spared the disquietude and hardships of a hunting existence. Not only was there no need for him to be a nomad, but he had every inducement to remain where he was. And it so happened that the early men who found themselves in Egypt—whence they came we do not know more than that it was probably from Asia, perhaps from the Gobi—became rooted in their land. Life was so easy that they had not only an abundance of wealth from little effort, but also a great deal of spare time on their hands. Hence it was that they were able to think, to give time to the development of the arts and sciences, to evolve theories regarding the hereafter and regarding the nature, habits, and influences of a host of gods and devils. From the very earliest time from which records or legends survive, when Egyptian husband-men went about naked and painted their bodies with green pigment, they possessed kings and priests, noblemen who controlled the land by a system not unlike feudalism. In the centre of every village there stood one hut larger than all the others, with wattled walls and an elaborately adorned entrance. Inside there was an image in wood of the god most favoured by that particular neighbourhood, and there would always be a man of superior intelligence to tend the god and opportunely to interpret his wise edicts to the silly common people. Those spiritual leaders of the old Egyptians, six or seven thousand years before the Christian era, were already cynically enlightened. They divided their country into two kingdoms, which were united by the political astute-ness of King Menes about six thousand five hundred years ago.

¶ *The Material Value of Mystical Knowledge*

In those early periods of Egyptian history the priests laboured unceasingly on behalf of their people. They investigated problems of science, and in 4366 B.C. an important work on anatomy was said to have been written by Teta. They made religion not only mysterious, but *magnificent*—an amazingly astute move. They were keen students of astronomy, and in the course of centuries they mapped out the heavens. By means of this knowledge of astronomy, of which the masses of the people knew nothing, and were permitted to know nothing, the priests could foretell eclipses of the moon and the risings of the tide. They gained immense prestige from knowing the precise hour at which Mother Nile would overflow her banks. By a careful observation of meteorological facts they could give a very good idea of the weather—maybe as good as our Meteorological Office can give today. All the learning of Egypt reposed in this priestly class, which became more powerful from day to day, until eventually they and the government were one. It was to the priests also that came the idea of writing, and they were responsible for a system of hieroglyphics capable of expressing subtle, abstract ideas. It was the priests also who thought out a system of government which would keep the labouring classes in a state of utter subjection and at the same time stimulate them to work diligently for the benefit of king and state. We find their sound ideas echoing down the ages, even to those inspiring and beautiful words which, in the Book of Common Prayer of the State Church in England, tell me (and you)—

> "To honour and obey the King and all that are put in authority under him : to submit myself to all my governours, teachers, spiritual pastors, and masters : to order myself lowly and reverently to all my betters . . . and . . . to learn and labour truly to get mine own living, and to do my duty in that state of life, unto which it shall please God to call me."

These doctrines, inspired by the Invisible and Intangible, and backed by prisons, thumbscrews, blud-
geons, truncheons, machine-guns, poison gas, hang-
men, soldiers, police, law and magnificence, pomp
and ceremony, dignity and piety, have helped in the
enslavement of the masses from time immemorial.
They represent the best-paying racket ever devised
by the mind of man.

¶ *Beginning of Organized War*

The old kingdom disintegrated and collapsed, but
in the third millennium B.C. Egypt became once more
united under a single sovereign; and it was the
Middle Kingdom, as it is called, which became the
great period in Egyptian history and the one which
showed most effect upon, and indeed some changes
in, human nature. It was during this period that the
ennobling influence of WAR, in the modern sense
of the word, showed itself. This is not to say that
war had never before existed; but it was a small
affair of families or tribes against other small groups
of more or less the same size. Now we see for the
first time a well-organized army, officered by men of
an educated and aristocratic type, and working out
its plans scientifically. Tactics and strategy entered
into higher education. Egyptian arms now flowed
into remote lands: Nubia was turned into a vassal
province, and the gold of its desert swept into the
coffers of the Pharaohs. A busy commerce began
with the Mediterranean countries and with the
Phœnicians. For two hundred years great progress
was made in the arts and sciences; this was the
classic period of Egyptian literature. As inevitably

happens when a nation grows rich (and indeed it often happens also to the individual), a period of laziness followed. A decadence and degeneration set in, and we must move ahead for fifteen hundred years—that is, until about three thousand five hundred years ago—before we find Egypt again a really prosperous kingdom. The art of war was again developed, and in 1530 B.C. we come across, for the first time in history, an idea which has remained down to this twentieth century: the idea of conquest and *world power*. The reign of Thothimes III was notable for a vast development in the two sister arts which we find so often walking sweetly hand in hand— War and Religion. Great territories in Asia were subdued, and the first Great Empire of the world came into existence. It was now that the soul of man was first found to be immortal; it was now that an ingenious priestly explorer discovered Hell. No earlier mention of these two factors in human nature can be found anywhere in history. To the Egyptians must be given the honours for these two great discoveries, the influence of which upon the trend of events and the nature of man is to be found in almost every part of the world. At this period the most powerful section of the community was the priesthood, which included not only the ministers of religion, but also the civil service and liberal professions. Priests were chroniclers, keepers of records, engravers of inscriptions, physicians of the sick, embalmers of the dead, lawyers and law-givers, sculptors and musicians. Labour was under their control; in their hands were factories and public works. Key posts in the army—that is, all those requiring higher education—were filled by them. The clergy preserved the monopoly of the arts which they had invented; the whole intellectual life of Egypt was in them. It was they who judged the living and the dead, enacted laws which extended beyond the grave, issued passports to the place above or to the place below.

Under the admirable instruction of those enlightened men, the Egyptians became a prosperous and a moral people. Monumental paintings reveal their whole life, but we see in them no brutal or licentious scenes, because they well knew what ideas to perpetuate and what to suppress.

## ¶ Influence of the Hereafter on the Here

Here may have arisen that system of morality based upon rewards and punishments in the Hereafter which spread itself eastward and profoundly affected the laws and religion of the Jewish races, the chief concepts of the Christian and other religions: Be good here and you will be well treated after death; do evil here and you will have a hot time. In order that full weight might be given to the system, and that there should exist powers and authorities capable of fulfilling it, it was necessary for the Egyptian priests to invent a number of symbols representing the powers of the unseen world of the day. They had a multiplicity of gods. Wonderful and mystic ceremonies and " High Masses " were performed in the temples: Egyptian magic became famous throughout the known world, and its influence lasted long, as we see in our temples today. The good Egyptian priests pointed out to their clients that it was then (as it is now) a fearful thing to fall into the hands of the living God. " He shall pour down rain upon the sinners, snares, fire and brimstone, storm and tempest; this shall be their portion to drink. . . . O terrible voice of most just judgment, which be pronounced upon them, when it shall be said unto them, Go, ye cursed, into the fire everlasting, which is prepared for the devil and his angels." And so on.

## ¶ *Akhnaton Discovers* our *God*

It is to an Egyptian king who lived from 1375 to 1358 B.C. that we must give the honour for what was long considered to be the greatest discovery in the history of the world. For religion consisting in the superstitious worship of crocodiles, parrots, etc., this king substituted the worship of Aton, the god of the Solar Disc. The temples of all the other gods were closed, and the very names of the gods obliterated. Amenhotep IV, or Akhnaton as this important king was afterwards called, conceived the god Aton as a kind father to all, to be worshipped at sunrise and sunset; a more refined and philosophical worship was introduced. The milder and more human aspect of the sun was stressed and cruelty was concealed. The number of priests was reduced and religious ceremonies simplified; psalm-singing and prayer became the order of the day. No graven image of Aton was permitted to be made. The new god was formless, a divine *Essence* permeating space, with only a benevolent mission and influence. Flinders Petrie says, " How much Akhnaton understood we cannot say, but he had certainly bounded forward in his views and symbolism to a position which we cannot logically improve upon at the present day." We have already seen that the Egyptians were responsible some time about 1530 for the discovery (*a*) of the Immortality of the Soul, (*b*) of Hell; and now we may add (*c*) the discovery of our own God, the date of the last-named very important discovery being round about 1370 B.C.

¶ *Our Debt to Egypt*

What is our debt to the Egyptians? The discovery of the Immortality of the Soul, the discovery of Hell, the formalization of God. Are there three ideas which have more influenced the lives of men in the last three thousand years, the period of the world with which we are best acquainted? Have these ideas changed human nature? To these doctrines others were added, the result being first the development of Judaism, then Buddhism, then Christianity, then Mahomedanism; in the Far East we shall see the rise and spread of another set of ideas, originally shorn of the concept of life after death, the Immortality of the Soul, and so forth. From Egypt also there spread by way of the Phœnician traders to Greece the same ideas; they attached themselves to Greek philosophy, and were again the subject of endless debate and responsible for the works of some of the greatest philosophers. The humanitarian ideas of Akhnaton trickled through the darkness, transmitted here and there by an intelligent, contemplative Phœnician trader, until we get God the Father of the Book of Genesis, as well as the possibly older gods of Babylon and Assyria. Christianity and Mahomedanism spring from precisely the same ideas as those of the old Egyptian religion: Immortality in

Heaven or Hell, with either rewards or punishments hereafter, but with a difference in Mahomedanism, which conceived it necessary to cater for the stronger sexual impulse of the Near Easterners. This religion provides for men a paradise of chorus-girls with dark eyes, beautiful lips, and curves pleasing to the eye: and a paradise of handsome, warm, brave, strong, and generous sheiks for the benefit hereafter of those women who observe its laws, and who themselves thus share in the reward for observing God's laws on earth.

## § 4

## THE TAMING OF EASTERN MAN

About the founder of Buddhism much is known: concerning his existence there is a mass of legend even greater than that which surrounds the origin of other great teachers. He was born towards the end of the sixth century B.C. in a small tribal community in Nepal. His father was a member of an important clan called Sakya, and the child was named Siddhattha Gautama. According to legend his conception was immaculate, but of this we Westerners cannot (as we can in the case of Jesus) be sure. There is nothing to distinguish the first twenty-eight years of his life from the same period in that of other young men who were sons of minor chiefs. Indians call him " Prince," and he was a prince if the ruler of a clan may be called a king. Be this as it may, in his twenty-ninth year our young man turned his thoughts to the study of religion and philosophy.

¶ *Buddha Meets God and Devil*

We are informed that the Deity appeared to him in four visions: in the form of a man broken by age, then of a sick man, then of a putrefying corpse, and finally of a dignified hermit. Regarding each one of the first three, his cheery companion said to him, " To this we must all come," but when the fourth appeared Gautama saw a possibility of avoiding the mental evils that are associated with the first three. A desire to become a hermit and to live a life of meditation seized upon Gautama. He returned to inform his parents and fellow-clansmen, who received the news with great rejoicing. Gautama soon after that settled in the jungle to a life of fasting and penance. It would appear that illumination came to him in a series of flashes of vision. The great question which he attempted to answer was: *Why was he not completely happy?* He concentrated upon self-analysis. We have seen in an earlier part of this book that selfishness is the motive force which drives humanity to nearly all its actions. No man discerned this fact more clearly than Gautama. He evolved a fundamental maxim to the effect that *All suffering and all unhappiness are due entirely to the selfishness of the individual.* " Let us endeavour," said he, " to abolish selfishness; and good must inevitably follow." The Four Great Truths of Buddhism are these: (1) The undoubted existence of suffering or sorrow in this world. (2) The cause of this suffering is the action of the outside world on the senses, exciting a craving for something to satisfy them, something to meet greed, avarice, and innate desire. (3) The necessity for causing this sorrow to cease, by a complete conquest and destruction of the lust for life and inborn selfishness of men. (4) Only a life of virtue based upon an " Eight-fold Path " can be the cure for the unhappiness and sorrows of this life.

## ¶ The Eight-fold Path to Bliss

The Noble Eight-fold Path propounded by Buddha depended upon a strict observance of Right Belief, Right Aims, Right Speech, Right Actions, Right Means of Livelihood, Right Endeavour, Right Mindfulness, and Right Meditation, in accordance with his definitions of these factors. Gautama set forth on a missionary journey to tell the world. His was a revolutionary doctrine, which cut to the root of Brahmanism, the orthodox religion of India at that time. He became Gautama the Buddha, or teacher, the founder of a great religion and subtle philosophy; indeed, one more subtle than any which had existed before, or which has been conceived since. He himself possessed a mind of very high order. With regard to the origin of man, the Buddha began by saying, " Please do not waste time on this problem. It is really of no importance to your present existence. Nor need you worry about the hereafter; for that also is of no concern to us, there being no knowledge of it except in abstract speculation; and such speculation is a waste of time. Our concern is with our life here, and Heaven knows it presents a big enough problem! Let us concentrate on it and see if we cannot make for ourselves, all of us, a world of peace and happiness, in which cruel struggles, war, killing, greed, jealousies, and indeed all those things which we know to be evil, shall be eliminated. The only way to do this is, in the first instance, by the *complete abolition of selfishness*, and a general purification of the mind." Thus, Buddhism was in the first instance an intellectual religion: it was not an appeal to the emotions: and it held out no bribe in the form of reward in the hereafter nor any threat for a neglect of its precepts, other than a continuation of unhappiness. It was an appeal to reason, and it was as such that it pleased and still pleases many men of intelligence. It is perhaps necessary to note that India was a country in which even at that time the affairs of the mind were admired and respected before all else. Hence the Buddha was not persecuted as Christ was by his contemporaries, but rather hailed as a philosopher bringing a new and reasonable code of behaviour into the world. To follow it there was not any need for a man to leave his business, no need for penances, for fasting, or for waste of time in the self-hypnosis and mental masturbation of prayer. Naturally, those who wished to become teachers of the new philosophy must train themselves thoroughly, and for them a special course of teaching was devised by the leader.

In a few years the gospel of Buddha had spread itself over a great part of India, and in the course of time it reached south as far as Ceylon, and later spread eastward and northward, to the Malay Peninsula, to Tibet, China, Mongolia, Manchuria, and even to Japan. Originally a pure doctrine, it became, after the death of its founder (as has happened to all other religious systems), a prey to the worldly. It developed a priesthood and a series of complex excrescences in precisely the same manner as Christianity, Taoism, and Confucianism. It became the religion of bishops, priests, deacons, and what-not. Nevertheless, the fundamental teachings remain for those who would have them, just as the fundamentals of Christianity (as outlined in the Sermon on the Mount) exist for those who care to take them seriously. There must be about five hundred million Buddhists in the world today, and although it is in essentials much too subtle for the ordinary man to grasp, Buddhism has an intellectual appeal such as is not to be found in any of the other great religions. It is perhaps no mere accident that the great teachings of Jesus should be a reflection of some of the chief precepts of the Buddha, of which the following are but a few examples: " Blessed is he who does no harm to his fellow beings." " Blessed is he who overcomes wrong and is free from passion." " To the highest bliss has he attained who has conquered all selfishness and vanity." (Compare Matthew v, 3 to 11.)

This great religion was to Eastern peoples what Christianity has been to Europe and America. It was the first great challenge to the conscience of men, in which it caused a quickening and a generous appeal to unselfishness.

¶ *Chief Justice Confucius on Punishment*

Let us now move farther east and see what was happening in regard to human nature at a period almost contemporary with that of the Buddha in India. Three great Chinese teachers appeared within a very few years of one another; and they in their turn did for China what Buddhism did for India and what Christianity afterwards did for the West. Kong-fu-tsi, or Confucius as we call him, was born in 551 B.C. His father was governor of a district in the present province of Shantung. He entered the Civil Service, but did not find in a government office sufficient spare time in which to pursue his studies, whereupon he resigned and turned to teaching. When he began to teach, his fame soon spread throughout China. By way of reward he was appointed a town magistrate, and in the course of time became Minister of Justice and chief judge in his own province of Lŭ. Judge Confucius became renowned for the dispensation of a remarkably even and equitable system of justice, and legend informs us that so good was his influence that crime almost disappeared. He believed in *reformation* rather than punishment; and he was against the infliction of the death penalty upon those whom the State had failed to instruct. Confucius considered it a tyranny to execute a person brought up in darkness and ignorance of moral virtues. Jealousy at his unorthodox reforms caused neighbouring feudal lords to scheme for his removal, and this excellent man was led eventually to retire in disgust with his fellows. At last he was permitted to return to stand behind ministers, a sage to be consulted in cases of emergency. The remaining five years of his life were spent in literary pursuits, and in the compilation of his celebrated *Analects*, which were to become the Bible of a great part of China.

¶ *Excellent Manners of the Chinese*

Confucius was responsible for the introduction of a new idea. It was that man should strive by gentle

D

and well-mannered behaviour in this life to become a sort of superior being; a peaceful, benevolent aristocrat. Everybody should be, like the late Lord Curzon, a superior person. Confucius attached supreme importance to the moral behaviour of the State, his idea being that, if rulers and administrators achieve a noble ideal of kindly and well-mannered behaviour, such an influence must trickle through and ultimately affect every department of life. This attitude of mind explains his objection to the capital punishment of undesirables; he regarded it as *setting a bad example* in manners. He preached stern self-discipline, punctilious observance of politeness, and absolute justice in affairs. All these, one should note, are intellectual attainments. His teaching comes roughly under five heads, each of which elaborates itself into a system which is really very simple and capable of being understood by any person. Moral excellence of any kind he called *virtue*. Intellectual attainments must be controlled always by *humaneness*. *Righteousness* is merely fair and honourable dealing, and an observance of *duty*, " *To know what is right, and not to do it, is sheer cowardice.*" All men must show confidence, trustworthiness, and sincerity. With these forms of virtue men must observe earnestness, bravery, and perseverance; children must show the highest respect for their parents. Such, in brief, is the simple, straightforward teaching of the realistic Confucius. Almost on a level with Confucius, we must mention Lao-Tsu, the author of the Tao Te Ching, the Bible of another great Chinese religion: Taoism. Lao-Tsu was a librarian, who preached a *blasé* indifference to the powers and pleasures of this world; and emphasized the necessity for a return to the simple life of the past, to the state of natural man in the " Golden Age " of which there is conjectural record.

¶ *Constant Knowledge of Lao-Tsu*

His book is full of statements and precepts which either stagger the Western mind or merely cause a smile : " *Attain complete vacuity, and sedulously preserve a state of repose* "—a precept no doubt admirable, but hardly capable of comprehension in the Western world today. His book is full of riddles, but nevertheless contains much real wisdom. For example : " *Requite injury with kindness* " and " *Do good to the evil ones in order that they may become good.*" The above examples do not indicate the full teachings of this philosopher, which are on the whole extremely mystical, and, where comprehensible at all by the Westerner, show the best policy of life to be : *Keep your hair on, look after Number One, and do not be discontented.*" During his lifetime his teaching had little success ; but, because of its obscurity and paradoxical wisdom, it was seized upon by men of satirical temperament, who turned it into a great religion. The religion thus founded has many millions of adherents.

¶ *Mo-Ti's Doctrine of Mutual Love*

There arose in China yet another great teacher, Mo-Ti, who lived in the fourth century B.C., after the doctrines of Confucius and Lao-Tsu had been established in China and before the arrival of the Buddhist teachers in that country. As Wells and others have pointed out, Mo-Ti's doctrine bears an extraordinary resemblance to the teaching of Jesus Christ, in political terms. It was, as it were, the forerunner of the new gospel. " The mutual attacks of state on state; the mutual usurpations of family on family; the mutual robberies of man on man; the want of kindness on the part of the sovereign, and of loyalty on the part of the minister; the want of tenderness and filial duty between father and son—these, and such as these, are the things injurious to the empire. All this has arisen from want of mutual love. If but that one virtue could be made universal, the princes, loving one another, would have no battle-fields, the chiefs of families would attempt no usurpations; men would commit no robberies; rulers and ministers would be gracious and loyal; fathers and sons would be kind and filial; brothers would be harmonious and easily reconciled. Men in general loving one another, the strong would not make prey of the weak; the many would not plunder the few, the rich would not insult the poor, the noble would not be insolent to the mean; and the deceitful would not impose upon the simple."

¶ *Inevitability of Morality and Inventions*

As may be imagined, Mo-Ti was a little before his time in morality. But he outlined in the above passage one of the essential claims of the Christian religion: the doctrine of mutual love. It seems as if morality, as well as inventive thought, ripens slowly in the human mind and everywhere suddenly bursts forth to fruition. There is an *inevitability* about it: for otherwise why should thoughts such as those recorded in this section and those which we shall indicate as characteristic of the age of philosophy in Greece (almost contemporary in time), and then but a little later the teachings of Christ—why should all these come to the world within the very short space of a few hundred years? There is a parallel in modern times, and it is in the realms of mechanical and scientific thought. A long series of inventions and scientific discoveries have been achieved almost at the same time by different men often working in different parts of the world. Perhaps the most striking of these was the working out of the theory of natural selection and variation in the same year (1858) by Darwin and Wallace. There was also the discovery which led to the use of internal-combustion engines in motor-cars, made by three separate investigators, working independently in three different countries at the same time. One may well ask the question: *Is a development of morality inevitable?*

§ 5

## LIBERATION OF THE MIND BY THE GREEKS

We shall now briefly consider what the Greeks contributed: for Greek civilization and Greek influence, diffused mainly by the wars of Alexander of Macedon in his selfish quest for power and glory, were responsible for a profound change in human thought and in the spiritual side of men's natures over the most important part of the globe. No doubt I shall by many be considered misguided if, having indicated the great achievement of the Greeks, I go on to say that much of it was negatived by the bludgeon rule of

materialistic Rome; and that what was not completely extinguished by Roman rule was suffocated
by institutionalized Christianity.

Only once in history did we mortals come within
measurable distance of what seems like mental sanity
in comparison with what preceded and what came
after. Only once did a whole nation almost reach
ideal, healthy, balanced minds in the healthy bodies of
its individual citizens. It was a brief episode, but a
glorious one; the closest approach to human perfection on a considerable scale of which there is record.
Notwithstanding the bad turn of events which for
practical purposes wiped out the Greeks, one is forced
to the conclusion that their influence upon the
development of the nature of Western man has been
greater than all other influences, Christianity itself
included. " Without what we call our debt to Greece
we should have neither our religion nor our philosophy
nor our science nor our literature nor our education
nor our politics." [1] It is a dismal reflection upon
man's intelligence that he has never had the wisdom
to take full advantage of the immense intellectual
heritage left to him by this small country of big minds.

The Greek world was composed of city groups of
" Aristocrats," with farms in the immediate neighbourhood and having all their manual and a part of
their intellectual drudgery done for them by slaves.
The gentry had nothing to do but to cultivate their
bodies and their minds, and this no doubt explains
their rapid development. They lived mostly out of
doors, while their wives remained in the home. A
woman who entered society and mixed with men,

[1] Livingstone's *The Legacy of Greece* (1921).

forfeited her title to respect or lost her heart to one or
more handsome athletes. It was almost inevitable.
Little money was spent on wives, houses, or food;
rich men were expected to give dramatic entertain-
ments and to contribute a company or a ship for the
protection of the city. The market-place was a
general club. "There the merchants talked their
business: the labours of the desk were then unknown." Again I quote the picturesque Reade:
"The philosopher instructed his pupils under the
shade of a plane tree, or strolling up and down a
garden path. Mingling with the song of the cicada
from the boughs, might be heard the chipping of the
chisel from the workshop of the sculptor, and the
laughter and shouts from the gymnasium. And sometimes the tinkle of a harp would be heard; a crowd
would be collected; and a rhapsodist would recite a
scene from the *Iliad*, every word of which his audience
knew by heart, as an audience at Naples or Milan
know every bar of the opera which is about to be performed. Sometimes a citizen would announce that
his guest, who had just arrived from the sea of Azov
or the Pillars of Hercules, would read a paper on the
manners and customs of the barbarians. It was in the
city that the book was first read and the statue exhi-
bited—the rehearsal and the private view; it was in
Olympia that they were published to the nation.
When the public murmured in delight around a picture
of Zeuxis or a statue by Praxiteles, when they thun-
dered in applause to an ode by Pindar or a lecture by
Herodotus, how many hundreds of young men must
have gone home with burning brows and throbbing
hearts, devoured by the love of Fame. Education

in Greece was not a monopoly; it was the precious privilege of *all the free*. The business of religion was divided among three classes. *The priests were merely the sacrificers and guardians of the sanctuary; they were elected, like the mayors of our market towns, by their fellow-citizens, for a limited time only*, and without their being withdrawn from the business of ordinary life. The Poets revealed the nature, portrayed the character, and related the biography of the gods. *The Philosophers undertook the education of the young; and were also the teachers and preachers of morality.* If a man wished to obtain a favour of the gods, or to take divine advice, he went to a priest: if he desired to turn his mind to another, though scarcely a better world, he took up his Homer or his Hesiod: and if he suffered from mental affliction or sickness, he sent for a Philosopher." (The italics are mine.)

¶ *The First Confidence in Reason*

Professor Lowie says that we may liken the progress of mankind to that of a man a hundred years old, who dawdles through kindergarten for eighty-five years of his life, takes ten years to go through the primary grades, then rushes with lightning rapidity through grammar school and college. Culture, it seems, is a matter of exceedingly slow growth until a certain " threshold " is passed, when it darts forward, gathering momentum at an unexpected rate. So it was in Greece; so it is in Russia in the twentieth century. It is no exaggeration to state that never before and never since was such attention given to a discussion of intellectual problems. The result was the *creation of confidence in reason*, in which five words

I would summarize the Greek contribution to the development of human nature. Before this, prejudices tend to vanish, and no problem in religion, philosophy, or morals need be shirked. The attainment of Truth and Beauty was the ideal; it overshadowed all else. The Greeks and many of their ideas became dispersed over Asia, and such was the influence of their superiority that countries in which they had no political power adopted much of their culture and their manners. They also surpassed the foreigners—" barbarians "—as much in the arts of war as in those of peace. Fifty years after the end of the Peloponnesian war, in 359 B.C., Philip, King of the country called Macedonia, which lies to the north (the Scotland of Greece, as it were), conceived the idea which ultimately led to the undoing of much of the practical good that Greek philosophy was achieving in the mental liberation and true spiritual education of mankind.

## ¶ The Beginning of Militarism

Philip had the soldier's mind, and he dreamed of a consolidation of his own country with the Greek States into a strong military union which might set about the conquest of Asia. He invented the packed mass of infantry—the phalanx—and also the mobile cavalry formation; and he trained large bodies of infantry and cavalry to collaborate in attack and defence. He systematized this branch of warfare, evolving new tactics for his novel army. The battle of Chaeronia, 338 B.C., was one of the most important in history, not because of its magnitude, but because of its effect upon the subsequent trend of political events. By this victory Greece was now at his mercy: a Græco-Macedonian confederacy was formed. Plans were laid for an onslaught on Persia, to be interrupted momentarily by the assassination of Philip by one of his first wife's satellites. But they were afterwards put into practice by Alexander his son. At the age of twenty this young man found himself in command of an excellent army. Having inherited his father's ability (which was further strengthened by tuition under the philosopher Aristotle), Alexander proceeded to what must be regarded as one of the two supreme military adventures in world history. For a period of two years he occupied himself in dealing with subversive movements among those Greeks who thought that such a mere boy could not possibly take the place of old Philip, either in leading them to conquest or in keeping them in some sort of order. He succeeded in subduing those Greeks who from their education aspired to liberty; and when this was completed he conceived his great scheme for a military conquest of the East. From the memorable day on which he crossed the Hellespont in the spring of the year 334 B.C. to his death at Babylon in the summer of 323 B.C., a period of just over eleven years, his life was spent in ever-growing conquest. Science and philosophy as well as the political life of Greece itself were brought to a standstill during the busy period of the Macedonian adventurer. It was this amazing military adventure of the Macedonian which was responsible for the widespread, superficial diffusion of Greek ideas: from the borders of Illyria through Asia Minor, Mesopotamia, Persia, Baluchistan, and Afghanistan, a part of India, not to mention Syria,

Egypt, and a part of the Mediterranean shores—all this vast territory, the most sensitive in the world to ideas, received its superficial leaven of Greek culture.

¶ *Is Man a Determining Agent?*

It is difficult to form any sort of reasonable estimate of the personality of this man.  His ambition was to conquer the whole habitable globe as it was then known, and Grote thought that he might have accomplished it " had God spared him ";  for he was not only the first scientific military organizer, but also one of the best.  Alexander was courageous in the military sense of the word;  he was also violent, ungovernable, and cruel;  and, like Herr Hitler, Signor Mussolini, and lesser modern dictators, could stand no contradiction or criticism;  only subservience and adulation were acceptable.  He had little sense of culture, but was not without political ideas and ideals;  for he wished to amalgamate Greeks and Persians and to make Greece a world-wide power in which the people would live on terms of comparative equality and without the old, smug division into Greeks and barbarians.  There is no doubt but that Fortune served him remarkably well, and that he took full advantage of every opportunity she offered.  " The extent," says Ogburn, " to which man is a freely determining agent in directing social evolution is one of the fundamental questions in sociology.  This question is very similar to the old philosophical question of freedom of the will.  It is also at the root of the question of the influence of the great man in history." [1]  Elliot Smith declares:  " Sir Charles

[1] William Fielding Ogburn, *Social Change.*

Oman calls attention to the patent fact that history is cataclysmic. The career of mankind has not been the inevitable result of the action of natural causes; but has in large measure been shaped by accidents and catastrophes, by the actions of dominating personalities who have deliberately provoked great movements, peaceful and warlike, which have shaped the destiny of the world." [1] It is a matter of dispute whether any one man has had greater influence than Alexander upon the subsequent results of the great age of Greek culture which had preceded him. Although his armies had a backbone of Macedonians, the brains were very often Greek; and nothing could prevent the widespread dissemination of the culture which was carried everywhere by Greek members of his forces. Wheeler aptly sums it up thus: " Man as a base line for measuring the universe, man as a source of governing power, arose in Greece; it was Greece that shaped the law of beauty from which came the arts of form, the law of speculative truth from which by ordered observations came the sciences, and the law of liberty from which came the democratic state. This was what the old Greece held in keeping for the world. Alexander was the strong wind that scattered the seed; again, he was the willing hand of the sower."

¶ *Supposing*——?

But there is another side to the picture. Although Alexander and his armies were unconsciously responsible for this widespread diffusion of culture and its

[1] Sir G. Elliot Smith, *Human History* (1930).

taming influence upon men, he was also responsible for extinguishing completely the flame which was already beginning to flicker at Athens. The problem with which we are presented in considering the history of this great general is one which can never fail to interest the student of human affairs. It is this. Supposing, instead of enthroning militarism and annihilating individual liberty among Athenians, he had chosen to concentrate his immense dynamic energy upon fostering the *true* cultural spirit of Greece and propagating it by means of peaceful commerce? Supposing this had been his choice, what might not the result have been for the good of humanity? Some very terrible facts resulting from his militarist career stare us in the face. With the arrival of this selfish, domineering man upon the scene, old Greece began to die; his name afterwards became detested both by Athenians and Macedonians. While militarism spread a light leaven of Greek culture over the face of the world, it killed it surely at its rich source. Nor did the benefits of Alexander's militarism, in the form of wealth and vast territory, take the place of the intense culture that it had stifled at source. Immediately after his death, the lust for power and the greed of his generals asserted themselves. Our old friend Selfishness again. One seized the Persian Empire; another seized Egypt; a third fell upon Macedon. Minor military adventurers and political buccaneers arose on all sides, attempting to emulate the conqueror. Barbarians in the north swarmed down upon the Acropolis at Athens, to be spasmodically driven off. That is the cycle of a dictator's history.

¶ *Toleration Appears*

From an organized little state that had developed a higher consciousness and a soul of its own, Greece changed into an unstable and disorganized rabble. For all that, the culture which had been disseminated over the whole of the ancient world remained predominantly Greek. Egypt under the Ptolemies, successors to Alexander's general of that name, caught a short blaze of the glory of three thousand years before. In the city of Alexandria was founded the first university of the world, the celebrated Museum in which Euclid wrote his *Elements*. Here also worked the fine old engineer Hero, the man who invented the first steam engine. It is difficult for us moderns to imagine the extent of the Greek mind when, in Mathematics alone, to take only one branch of thought and perhaps the most difficult, it is only recently that we have been able to advance beyond it. To quote Elliot Smith again, " Abstract thought is the rarest manifestation of the human mind even in modern times. Every schoolboy and student can make a pretence of abstract thinking by reproducing scraps of wisdom (and folly) acquired from the writings of scholars, or the everyday currency of polite conversation. But when it comes to original observation and real thinking, the influence of the traditions and fashions of the time tends to inhibit abstract thought, and keeps most men's attention fixed on concrete demonstrations." In physics the Museum had a notable exponent in Eratosthenes, who succeeded in calculating the diameter of the world to within fifty miles of what our physicists today have worked it out to be! The Museum library was a publishing and bookselling business, the first in existence. A celebrated librarian named Callimachus devised a method of cutting up the rolls of script to make them more convenient for reference; and so made the first books to resemble our own. Here also began the systematic study of human anatomy. A discipline of science was evolved. *The Scientific Method came into existence.* The list of achievements could be extended, but there is no need to do this. Let it suffice to say that the systematized scholarship at Alexandria, following upon the age of philosophy at Athens, helped in the dissemination of an entirely new spirit throughout the world: one which was to be bludgeoned out of existence for a time, but which came to life again two thousand years later. This was the spirit of intellectual toleration.

§ 6

## THE GOLDEN AGE OF REASON

Culture has been defined by Tylor as " that complex whole which includes knowledge, belief, arts, morals, law, custom, and any other capabilities and habits acquired by a man as a member of society." What was this culture which the wars of Alexander the Great diffused over most of the known world? It cannot be described in a sentence or a paragraph, though I would put it under the broad head of *Right Thinking*. We may differ in our opinions as to whether the Greeks were always right in their philosophy. But to them, above all peoples, we must give credit for an endeavour to achieve *perfect honesty of thought*.

¶ *The Greeks Discuss Everything*

Schools of philosophy or, as they were originally, schools of argument sprang up on all sides. *Men began to discuss everything*, from the constitution of the universe to the meaning of beauty. Metaphysics, the study of ultimate realities, began. With this went the study and discussion of logic, the ideal method in human thought. To the Greeks we owe the beginnings of serious and ordered thought in all the chief branches of human activity. Æsthetics attracted one school, ethics another, politics another; and certain notable schools embraced them all. The conclusions of an Einstein or a Marx could never have been reached; nor could we have modern science without that immense body of spade-work done during a comparatively short period in the different schools of Greek philosophy. This people even attacked psychology, though they did not make much progress in formulating it; nevertheless, they were as far ahead in many branches of psychology as some of our most advanced thinkers of today. Pythagoras began the study of disease and medicine, and Hippocrates drafted a system which was to be the foundation upon which Galen five hundred years later based further advances; the science of healing thus evolved lasted nearly two thousand years. The philosophy of the Empirics began—that which teaches us to pay attention only to what is *useful*—which the English and Americans were to develop so highly. Among a host of schools of thought, yet another group formed itself, the Eclectics, who, without attaching themselves to the whole body of doctrine of any given school, chose what they judged good from each. In the midst of all this scramble after the higher things of life there arose three men who may be added to our list of great characters—to those pioneers who have had their effect upon the development of human nature as a whole: Socrates, Plato, and Aristotle.

## ¶ The Most Honest Human Being

Socrates was the son of a stonemason and a midwife; he was born at Athens about 470 B.C. He is notable in human history as the first great sceptic; as the man who challenged every statement. The chief tenet of his teaching is, like all great precepts, a very simple one: *that the only possible virtue in this life is complete honesty of thought.* His whole life was a quest after truth; there was no belief, no code of laws or morals, no system of government, nor aught else which he did not desire to investigate for the purpose of discovering its ultimate truth. *He would tolerate no belief or hope which would not pass the test of investigation in every aspect and in every detail.* Towards everything he began by holding himself as an unbeliever, capable of being convinced by argument based upon human reason. This is not to say that he did not investigate mysticism and other occult arts; he examined everything that came his way, and accepted or rejected with impartiality and without emotion. Socrates was a living challenge to everything in human thought. His method took the form of question and answer, a dialogue ruthless in its investigatory powers. Such a man inevitably created enemies. He had also many admirers, among them Plato, who immortalized the works of his master in a series of memorable literary efforts. If we think for a moment of the significance of the cardinal maxim of Socrates, that *Virtue is Knowledge*, we can see how it goes to the very root of all that men even still hold dear and have held dear from time immemorial. One half of the world today would hate him and execute him off-hand. Such a man was a grave danger to institutions, to vested interests of religion and government; and, as has always happened in such circumstances in human affairs, a means was found of getting rid of him. Few human beings can tolerate unpleasant truth; a government never. This is a rule which applies throughout the whole of history. The mass of humanity looks backward; it is either the ill-fortune or the ill-luck of a very few to look forward. He who challenges existing institutions courts unpopularity and maybe death itself. In 399 B.C. Socrates was accused of denying the existence of the gods, and of subverting the youth of Athens. There is not the slightest doubt but that he was guilty, in the same way that Christ was undoubtedly guilty of endeavouring to turn the minds of the Jews against their cherished and long-established religious institutions. The grand old Greek was haled before a tribunal and charged with the most serious offences which can be brought against a man—wishing to abolish the gods and to turn the minds of his pupils against the authority of the State. He was found guilty and condemned to death by drinking a cup of poisonous hemlock.

¶ *Plato Defines the Upright Man*

It was not so much during his lifetime as afterwards that the influence of Socrates made itself felt. His pupil, Plato, a man of very different type, did not altogether approve the attitude of quiet disillusionment and doubt adopted by his master. He had been born in the midst of a post-war atmosphere, in which the Greek republic was suffering much social distress and confusion. It was a similar state to that of modern Germany in 1919; there was discord and dissatisfaction and a great yearning everywhere. Hence, much of Plato's work consists of discussions regarding political and social institutions and relations, and the possibility of improving them. He queried whether so much unhappiness and discord could be possible if political and social institutions were as perfect as those who supported them asserted. He had been taught by Socrates that everything— *everything*—must be investigated. At the age of forty he wrote his *Republic*, a magnificent book " drenched in thought " which has had almost as little influence upon subsequent political thought as have the works of the great teachers in the realm of religion. He demonstrated that, difficult as it may be to define uprightness, courage, piety, and what other virtues there may be, the upright, courageous, and therefore happy man, demonstrates in his own person the reality of these abstractions. This alone might 'have sufficed to make Plato a benefactor of the human race; but it is only a part of his labour. He founded with Socrates the Academy of Philosophy which lasted nearly a thousand years—the one which is still the prototype of all such organizations; and he immortalized the thought of Socrates in the celebrated *Dialogues*, which are a guide to the liberal education so desired by men.

We may add yet another name to those of Socrates and Plato : that of Aristotle, whom Goethe called the master-builder among men. To these three men we must attribute the glory of having laid down the basis of practically every philosophic science. Aristotle was the systematizer. Have they been surpassed as philosophers by any three men? We have not yet exhausted the possibilities that their works contain : many of their intuitions have been verified after the lapse of centuries, after a thousand, and in some cases two thousand years.

## ¶ The Ethics of Mercy

Apart from philosophy, the Greeks were responsible for the formulation of a system of government and politics; to which may be added the rhetorical system of Aristotle. They instituted government by parliament, and a system of representation based upon the ballot. They were the first people to introduce humanitarianism into the institution of slavery which they had inherited from Egypt and the East. Human society from the point of view of the orthodox economist begins when the strong man, instead of killing and eating his victim, discovers that he can put him to a much more *profitable* use. And this brings us to the very root of the ethics of the spirit of mercy, which is held up to us as so admirable a thing. Mercy was originally based upon the material interests of the person who granted it : when a prisoner was spared after a battle, it was because his captors thought they could draw more benefit from a use of his service extending over a period of years than they could from the immediate enjoyment of a few human cutlets, probably tough ones at that. Thus, when slavery was first established it marked a great step in human progress! To the institution of slavery we owe much of the law and order which go with property and inheritance, and by means of slavery society was graded into two classes: slave owners (or free) and slaves—in our times governors and governed. Aristotle taught that a servant is an instrument more valuable than any other, although he was probably not the first to discover this fact. The Greeks of his age began to treat their slaves well, realizing that it paid them to do so. In precisely the same way many modern capitalist employers of labour offer excellent conditions to their employees. Such employers practise the enlightened self-interest to which Aristotle first drew attention.

Notwithstanding all that has been said, there are soiled spots on the Greek escutcheon. The Lacedæmonian youths, for example, were trained in the practice of deceiving and butchering slaves, and were from time to time let loose upon them to show their proficiency; once for amusement they murdered three thousand in a night. With regard to rhetoric, the Greeks were not guilty of what is too often to be found in our modern rhetoric: changes in the voice to produce an influence altogether independent of the intellectual worth of that which is uttered—the microphone performances of the dictators, for example.

¶ *Bird's-eye View of " Progress "*

We have now come almost to the end, with one exception—Jesus Christ—of those " Great Codifiers of Morality " among men of the West: Hammurabi, the great Assyrian king; Akhnaton, the Egyptian; Moses and the prophets of Israel, of the Pentateuch, and the Psalms. In the East we found Gautama the Buddha, and Confucius, Lao-Tsu, and Mo-Ti in China. Then in ancient Greece we have seen the challenge to all existing thought, and the real beginnings of the different philosophies, including the science of mathematics, the elements of Euclid, the foundations of physics; the beginnings of the great games and sports, the opera, the drama and parliament, the institution of slavery (which, among the Greeks brought with it the invention of trousers as a sign of degradation). We see after fire and wheel and boat the invention of the bellows, that of the screw and the saw, as well as the beginnings of laughter and mockery as means of criticizing human institutions—we see all these ideas spreading over the world, carried by commercial travellers and barterers. We have seen the invention of money, and of a system of book-keeping and accounts by the early Phœnicians, the forerunners of modern salesmen and trader-capitalists. The *diffusion of culture* has begun. In all these things the thought of the known world was now beginning to run in practically the same channels among great peoples. A part of Europe and a part of Asia had risen from savagery and barbarism to the stages which we call culture and civilization: in Assyria, Babylon, Egypt, Phœnicia, Greece, and a little later in Carthage and Rome, there was a definite growth and decay of culture and civilization. Population increased enormously, and races and nations began to pass through a sort of Spring, Summer, Autumn, and

Winter, like plants or men. Having done so, they left behind them the leaven of a standardized method of thinking which has not greatly altered since then. We shall see later that there have been developments of this thought, and, generally, in intellectual achievements. We have not yet come to the age of modern science, power-politics, finance-capital, advertising, Marxism, Fascism and so forth. But to all intents and purposes, with the combination of Greek thought and other thought in the few hundred years before the beginning of the Christian era we have a world which was thinking almost as it does today: a standardized human nature. From that moment onwards we look only for intellectual changes, and in these there is a great gap. The appearance of Jesus Christ and the diffusion of his teachings made what may be considered to be the final change in human nature, at all events in the whole of Western civilization. We must chronicle the working out of human destiny through a black age of ignorance, thoughtlessness, brutality, and barbarism. First there is retrogression, then stagnation, then a renaissance; and, finally, we shall come to consider the machine age in which we now live.

# Book III: ROMAN MATERIALISM AND INSTITUTIONALIZED CHRISTIANITY

## § 1

## THE HUB OF HISTORY

At a time when the still small world remembered the achievements of Alexander the Great, the Carthaginians—the supreme maritime power—feared that the Greeks might become strong in Sicily, which stood geographically opposite to their city. So they made an agreement with the Romans by which Sicily was given to Carthage, the whole of the rest of Italy to remain in the hands of the Romans. Rome and Carthage were then young, vigorous, and growing communities. The Carthaginians, as we have seen, had in them a strong Phœnician (that is, Semitic) element driving them to trade. The Italians were an agricultural people, living close to the soil, and not caring greatly for trade. It was entirely in the interests of these two people to form an economic alliance, or sign a treaty of perpetual peace. Instead, they decided in 246 B.C. that their differences could best be settled by war. This sort of political stupidity occurs again and again in history. It is based upon two of those fundamental characteristics of human nature: selfishness and pride. Selfishness to acquire wealth and power; pride in the ability to acquire this wealth and power quickly. War in such cases merely hastens (with great loss to both sides) the absorption or economic conquest of one side by the other. By means of an alliance the process could be more comfortably achieved in nine cases out of ten. The inability of Rome and Carthage to reach some sort of economic and political compromise resulted in the Punic War, one of the most bloody in history. It consisted of three main phases, lasting altogether from 264 to 201 B.C. and ending with the supremacy of Rome. The Punic War was the first important economic war in history; and we have not yet left behind the latest phase of economic wars. It decided that the world should be ruled by Romans instead of, perhaps, by Semites; and Rome and Carthage are not unlike two great modern nations or groups of nations.

¶ *Qualities of Racial Success*

From the natural temperament of the Romans (and the systems of government and education which they had evolved) there sprang a people admirably suited to warfare. The freedom of the individual was suppressed in the interests of the State. Early Roman citizens were honest, frugal, pious, and obedient to authority. Neither generosity nor mercy found much place in their character; and they had none of that dissipating, speculative, and cultural spirit of the Greeks. The Roman *paterfamilias* was stern to the utmost degree with his own kith and kin, over whom he had power of life and death; at the time we now consider he did not hesitate to inflict a capital sentence upon a wife or daughter, when he deemed it necessary. Shrewd and grasping in matters of business, cruel in their treatment of slaves, the Romans were a harsh and austere people. A strict discipline permeated their life and institutions; physical bravery and ability to suffer without complaint were considered as the highest virtues. So long as poverty and discipline remained governing factors they were morally clean, if narrow and hard. Politically they were astute, and even at this early period they had a sensible code of laws: their " Twelve Tables " are considered by jurists to be the foundation of most of our modern codes. In regard to usury they were severe: 10 per cent (compared with the English 48 per cent) was the maximum of interest which a lender could expect from a borrower of money, which by modern standards would indicate a weak sense of finance. They could not stand ridicule. A person who wrote libels or lampoons on his neighbours could be deprived of civil rights. This, in itself, would indicate a non-philosophic mind, like that of Benito Mussolini.

The city had lived for three hundred years in a state of perpetual warfare. Steady acquisition of power had produced a love of it and a desire for more. Hence the army was the nation. It was essential for a citizen to have served in ten campaigns before he was eligible for a civil office. The discipline was most severe. Territory won by the sword was used and cultivated, its inhabitants made slaves, their personal wealth confiscated.

¶ *Why Rome Flourished*

Rome won her long Punic Wars against Carthage, and thereby established her supremacy in the Mediterranean. By this she learnt that *war paid*, and so

she turned her bloody sword eastward and northward.
Her well-trained veterans swept all before them and
for the first time wealth from conquest began to
pour into the city as war became more and more
profitable: and so there should be war, WAR, WAR
—in every direction.

We may miss a period.

The population of the city increased steadily and
began to consist of all nationalities: the rich living
in separate houses with their slaves; the poor in
vast tenements in the lower parts, the first slums.
Conquered territories became the legitimate prey of
governors and soldiers: from 73 to 71 B.C. the
exactions of Verres, Governor of Sicily, desolated the
island more than any war had ever done. As a judge,
he sold his decisions. He would steal pictures and
works of art from private houses or temples, and
crucify whoever resisted. On his return to Rome he
was indicted and tried for these depredations. He
was fined, but fled to save his plunder. Noble Mark
Antony coveted the treasures of Verres, and had him
put to death as the easiest method of acquiring them.

The religion of the Romans was the worship of
local deities who could help them in wars, agriculture,
or trade. It was utilitarian: run by the State for
the State. Their literature was negligible, their laws
excellent, in a narrow materialistic sense. Their art
and science were nil, although their architecture and
roadmaking were excellent. This was a cruel,
materialistic, solemn people, whose city was becoming
the hub of human history.

It was during the period of the Punic Wars outlined
above that the Roman military system worked itself

up to an efficiency which was afterwards to enable the great empire to be formed. In every country there are to be found men of adventurous spirit who have no ties, and who are willing to sell themselves for military service—that is, as hired murderers and assassins—to a bidder. The Roman Government conceived the idea of paying its soldiers, and at the same time enlisting them for long periods. A further bribe was held out in an offer of booty. Such is the make-up of human nature that in similar circumstances soldiers can be found anywhere at any time. *Woe to the vanquished, and the spoils to the victors,* although by no means an entirely new idea in history, were moral precepts developed to their highest point after the Roman success in the Punic Wars.

The Empire which followed the Republic was based upon an appeal to the greed of the individual soldier, and an appeal to the collective greed of the whole people. Explorations and conquests were begun in all directions; every point of the compass was to be covered by the Roman legions. Rome turned her face to the world after the Third Punic War, and arrogantly waved her bludgeon in the air. In the course of the next five hundred years the result of this military efficiency was to beat the rest of the world to its knees and thereby to establish a powerful empire. Fascism had begun.

But in the middle period of Rome's greatness there arose in the Roman province of Palestine a set of ideas which were to challenge bludgeon rule and cause the disintegration of the empire founded upon force. A few simple ideas affected the trend of subsequent history; military despotism brought a reaction of peace and a message of pacifism. To begin with this pacifism was fairly successful, but it afterwards resulted, through the strange perversities of human nature, in wars and troubles as terrible as any hitherto experienced.

§ 2

## JESUS AND HIS ETHICAL POETRY

We have seen that from time to time there come into the world men who prove themselves to be Great Codifiers of Morality. Morals are like inventions. Vague ethical ideas remain " in the air " for a time, and then they are captured, sifted, and synthesized by a man of genius, who may advance upon all that has preceded him. The great religions of the world have been formulated by men whose spiritual nature was sensitive to the yearnings and necessities of the contemporary human soul, and were therefore able to capture a *comforting idea*. One must note that the basic religions of the world were founded by men : only in modern times have women endeavoured to compete with them in the formulation of ethical ideas.

When Rome had achieved the state of expansion and development described in the last section, the " religion " of the Western world was in a state of chaos. Egypt and Palestine possessed what may reasonably be called great systems of religion, and of the two it was in Palestine that the truly religious spirit was most highly developed. Here there lived a people with the tradition of the Pentateuch and the Prophets and differing profoundly from Euro-Asiatic antiquity in the conception of the mythical " Golden Age." The Jews have proved their wisdom over other races by fixing it in the *future* instead of in the past. In this they showed a wonderful knowledge of human nature: men are more likely to be influenced in their conduct by what must inevitably happen in the future than by what has gone before and has perhaps become a hazy memory! The people of Israel had made for themselves a Book, which in turn governed them like an irresistible force. They had created the idea of a " sovereign religion," superior to country, blood, man, and laws. Having decided for themselves that paradise was yet to come, their prophet Daniel informed them (vii, 13 et seq.) of the manner in which the forthcoming of the Kingdom of Heaven was to be signalized: the Messiah, a Son of Man, was first to appear—a supernatural being in human form who was to rule over the " Golden Age." Every young Jew was taught these things, and they all looked forward with joyful anticipation to the coming of this Saviour.

¶ *Jesus Abolishes Death*

During the reign of the Roman Emperor Augustus, the child Jesus was born in the Roman province of Judea. A dreamy, imaginative boy, highly sensitive to the religious ideas with which his simple countryside was saturated, he began to believe that he himself was the long-expected Messiah. He possessed the soul of a poet, and gloried in the lyrical poetry of the Psalms of David and the imaginative flights of the old Prophets of Israel: the enchanting dreams which they conjured up in his mind were to him a delight.

He began to live in harmony with the marvellous and the supernatural, and cultivated a close mystical association with the Great Universal God of Israel, whom he regarded as his spiritual father. He was a mystic, not a metaphysician; a poet, not a scientist. Reason or logic found no conscious place in his mind. He placed himself above them and above his fellow-men, deciding the calls of God to be of first importance. Sublime ideals grew within him. The greatest of these was a desire to abolish death spiritually by imparting to those around him a knowledge of the way to salvation. In this manner all men might be saved before the end of the world, which, according to authoritative Prophets, must soon follow the appearance of the Messiah—that is, Jesus himself. He formed a fixed personal resolution to save his contemporaries. Never before or since has man dealt so admirably with the vexed problem of the future, or with more fixed determination or more desperate courage. He began to think only of his work and of humanity. He was a true mystical son of the God of his fathers in Israel: and, as Renan says, " the highest consciousness of God which has existed in the bosom of humanity was that of Jesus." The young prophet wandered up and down his country holding open-air meetings, preaching his poetic doctrine of salvation. It was a religion of the heart, often revolutionary in its principles:

" *Blessed are the poor in spirit ; for theirs is the Kingdom of Heaven. Blessed are they that mourn. . . . Blessed are the meek. . . . Blessed are the merciful. . . Blessed are the pure in heart. . . . Blessed are the peace-makers. . . . Blessed are they which are perse-*

*cuted for righteousness' sake ; for theirs is the Kingdom of Heaven.*" Consider that declaration attributed to him, which probably represents the peak of ethical teaching : " *Ye have heard that it hath been said, Thou shalt love thy neighbour and hate thine enemy. But I say unto you, Love your enemies, bless them that curse you, do good to them that hate you, and pray for them which despitefully use you and persecute you ; that ye may be the children of your Father which is in Heaven. . . . For if ye love them which love you, what reward have ye ? Do not even the publicans the same ? . . . Be ye therefore perfect, even as your Father which is in heaven is perfect.*" Obedience to such precepts has always been rather difficult, as many cannot fully accept them.

Nevertheless, this strange man advanced the general cause of religion in the world as no other has done, for he was a man of action, in the spiritual sense. He lived as he taught, mixing freely with all classes, but making his chief appeal to the poor. He paid little attention to the rich, the learned, the sophisticated, or those influenced by Greek culture. He attacked the existing Jewish religion, which was largely one of ceremonial. Around him gathered a small group of admirers. The small bucolic and proletarian sect thus created was inspired by zeal. It was prepared to work and—most important of all—to suffer for the principles in which its members believed. There was never before in history any question of *suffering* for a religion. The leader, Jesus, often spoke in parables, and in language which, though simple and direct in construction, contains the " eternal truths " of all religions : " *The Kingdom of*

*God is within you,*" was his favourite reply to all who pressed for subtle explanations.

## ¶ *Moralists always Politically Dangerous*

The religion of Jesus is the religion of love. His teaching sprang from the need which the heart of his people felt for consolation during an exceedingly hard period in their history. It was a spiritual reality which was an inevitable reaction against Roman rule. It was a revolt against a state of hypocrisy engendered by the religious formalism of the Jews. Such a man as Jesus was therefore a danger to the authorities of his own race; and in a lesser degree to Roman authorities. As his mission progressed, more and more he attributed to himself a divine nature and referred to himself as the Son of God. His utterances at times reached great flights of extravagance. The priests of the established religion began to consider him a nuisance, and at last, when he uttered the words, " I am able to destroy the temple of God and build it in three days," their opportunity came. The Jews arrested him, tried him for blasphemy, and found him guilty. The penalty was death, but the authority of the Roman governor had to be obtained before an execution. The enemies of Jesus informed Pontius Pilate that the blasphemer had taken upon himself the title of " King of the Jews," which amounted to rank sedition against the Emperor. This statement of the Jewish authorities was inaccurate, but it had its effect. Jesus was crucified, though not before Pilate had tried his utmost to find some excuse for avoiding the extreme penalty. His was a difficult political position,

E

and he merely did his duty in what was an unpleasant and somewhat troublesome case, which he would have liked to ignore.

## ¶ The Religion for " Bottom Dogs " and Slaves

The fidelity of the small band of Jesus's followers, their zeal, the inspiration and consolation of their sublime teaching, and lastly the crucifixion of their beloved Master, all helped in the spread of their gospel. A new spirit was infused into the world by virtue of the life and death of Jesus and the emotional, poetic appeal of his ethics. Nine-tenths of the world have always been poor, and the chief appeal of the new religion was to this great majority of humanity. The new religion was the personal creation of Jesus, and, in its abolition of death, was one of the most startling and original creations of the human mind. Since then hundreds of millions of men and women have lived and worked and suffered for it. No climate but knows it and no land but has felt its influence. Pacifism, self-restraint, love: these were its ideals. Today one-third of the whole world acknowledges Jesus as its spiritual leader, but the chances are in favour of the imprisonment of anybody who attempts to put his teaching strictly into practice.

How can one estimate the effect which this doctrine had upon human nature in the years which followed the death of its founder? One may look at the history of the world before his birth and mission; and one may examine it afterwards. Then, by comparing the former period with the latter, some sort of conclusion may be reached. The reader will have, I hope, already received a rough general idea of the development of human nature, as indicated in the pages which have preceded. In the pages which follow I shall endeavour to indicate its subsequent trend.

I am purposely giving the above account of Jesus and his teaching a very brief form, because the full story is well known. But I trust that the reader will not therefore receive an impression of the unimportance of this story in a consideration of human nature. The teachings of Christ came first as a small ray of light which slowly but steadily spread itself until it entered the innermost recesses of the households of a very large part of our world. The formation of the ideas represented in the doctrines of the Master took a period of perhaps three thousand years. They were the culminating point of all ethical teaching which had come before and, original in the form he gave them and in their culminative energy, separately they had appeared elsewhere: in China, in India, Babylon, Egypt, Greece, and a few of them even in Rome. The mind of the prophet of Nazareth welded them together and imparted new life and a tremendous energy to them. North, south, east, and west went missionaries advertising Christ's Kingdom of Heaven. Tireless preachers with long beards and a fervent glint in their eyes travelled the world. St. Paul and St. Peter expanded Christ's teaching, the former introducing into it much of the doctrines of the advanced Platonists. In the early days the whole movement was Jewish, simple, and direct. Now the new religion began to take to itself many of the essentials, rituals, symbols, and methods of the religions with which it came in contact; and men and women of all creeds and races joined to spread the good news and to lead a new life. To the proletariat of the Roman Empire the message came from heaven; to slaves everywhere it offered freedom beyond the grave. The meek, the humble, the downtrodden were to come into their own; power and riches were a handicap. The equality of men before God was proclaimed. It was good news for all but the powerful.

### § 3

## A SPIRITUAL CHALLENGE TO MATERIALISM

Before the bludgeon wielded by Imperial Rome, the spiritual gauntlet of Christianity was flung. The polytheistic, inclusive, and tolerant paganism of Rome was too weak to offer opposition. Tolerant religions are seldom strong. The monotheistic, exclusive, and extremely intolerant Christianity was a powerful spiritual force. There is a rule of life which applies to human nature as well as to plants or animals, and it is that failure to secure some degree of adaptation involves extinction. The wisdom of St. Paul and St. Peter in modifying the extreme tenets of Jesus and including much Paganism saved the life of the infant sect. The belief of the early Christians that the end of the world was at hand had to be modified immediately, because the world went about its business as usual: God, they declared, had granted a respite of a thousand years. Instead of putting all souls into an eternity of punishment, one out of every million would be spared. And so on.

Roman moralists, if we may judge from their writings, did not take the doctrines of the new teachers seriously, at all events for a long time after the very early period, when they ignored them entirely. Nevertheless, unmistakably powerful ideas were in the minds of those groups of early Christian missionaries and their converts. The doctrine of *love* in its revolutionary form and the memory of the Cross took root in Rome itself and, to quote a French Rationalist who is critical of Christianity,[1] " In the Empire of the world, Jesus succeeded Cæsar."

¶ *Power of the Spiritual in Human Affairs*

Christ's doctrines were taken, distorted, neglected, and often used as a means of inflicting cruelty and oppression. But through them human nature in the West became in many instances more mellowed, more comforted, and more exalted; and stirred to its depths. Jesus and his doctrine was the mirage which attracted the mad rushes of the Crusaders; Jesus was the mystic lover inviting processions of virgins to take the veil. His name provided the motive force of many of the greatest achievements in painting and architecture—we have seen how religious impulse provided the same stimulus in ancient Egypt. The effect of this one man's teaching upon the vagaries of human nature transcends historical measure. The most sublime acts in the history of man may be attributed to the influence of his name; by its perversion the most cruel, the meanest, and the most dastardly acts may also be attributed to it.

[1] See P. L. Couchoud, *The Enigma of Jesus*, for an excellent modern account of the foundation and early history of the Church.—C. D.

It will remain for the historian of a thousand years hence to decide whether the evil of it all has been greater than the good. We are still in the shadow of the Cross, and prejudiced for or against; but I think that the evidence will show that, on the whole, the ideas of Jesus were progressive and effected an improvement in man's nature. The German philosopher Nietzsche has said the most bitter things that can be said against Christianity, and also some of the wisest. He said, for example, that its chief object is to tame wild men, but he points out that in so doing it may sap their virility.

## ¶ Foundation of the Church of Rome

The missionaries who went into the world preaching the new doctrine established churches at Alexandria, Antioch, Thessalonica, Jerusalem, and a very important one at Rome in the centre of the empire. This was about the year A.D. 50. The small organization in Rome consisted of Christianized Jews who came from Palestine or Antioch. It had existed for six or seven years when the apostle Paul wrote his Epistle to the Romans, who probably did not know him, and whom he had never seen. It had been established about ten years when Paul, laden with chains, requested to be landed in Italy and judged by Cæsar's tribunal. Peter, supposing he ever came to Rome, could have reached there only on the eve of his martyrdom. The dissertation by Irenæus regarding the foundation of the Church at Rome by Peter and Paul is now said to have been a fiction.[1] Be

[1] See Henri de la Fosse, *Christianisme*. Also Couchoud, *op. cit.*

this as it may, Rome gloried in having been the scene of a martyrdom of early Christians, and it preserved the tombs of Peter and Paul, thereby acquiring a special importance. It claimed the apostolic origin of its episcopate, and acquired a habit of domination over other Christian churches. It was of the utmost importance for the development and spread of the new doctrine that it should have a central organization armed with authority. It was necessary that a means of inspiring and supporting *Faith* (the ecclesiastical word for credulity) should exist; and faith could not be created without tradition or authority. Rome claimed to have both. One is permitted to doubt if the Christian religion could have been spread so efficiently without the accidents which brought Peter and Paul to Rome, the centre of the Empire and, more important, of the wealth and communications of the known world.

¶ *Truth Unnecessary in Religion, Politics, or Advertising*

The doctrines of Jesus, now with a number of ingenious additions, began to be disseminated to the four points of the compass. The Absolute Truth or otherwise of what was disseminated did not greatly matter. *For something to have a profound effect upon our behaviour, it is a matter of indifference whether it be fact, fiction, truth, half-truth, or merely lies. But it is of the highest importance that we should believe it to be true.* The belief in its truth is the basis of religion, faith-healing, political creed, and advertising. Persuasiveness, coupled with a desire to believe in those who are to be persuaded, is the basis of all propaganda, as when herds of men are caught under the influence of the herd instinct in time of war, in a religious service, or at a political speech.   Faith or ferocity can be created.

It was the duty of the heads of the Christian religion in Rome to persuade the rest of the world that they possessed a certain mystic power, such as is not possessed by other men.   They seized upon a hint thrown out in the teachings of St. Paul to invent a new mystical—that is, intangible and invisible—substance called " grace."   They claimed to possess a knowledge of the theory of grace and the means whereby it might be made available for true believers. The appeal of grace was based upon the selfishness of man and his desire for self-preservation and happiness after death.   The religious man is probably the most selfish of all:  he thinks of his own salvation as being of more importance than that of anybody else.   The most arrogant of all human beings are those who claim to possess knowledge of the means whereby we may achieve happiness during the eternity after death. As regards grace, the theory evolved in the first century may require a little explanation, for its essence is both difficult and important, and concerns us even now.   In the form of religion most familiar to us the theory is this:  There is somewhere—God only knows where—a reservoir of the indefinable substance or quality called " grace."   This reservoir can be tapped only by those who possess the right technical knowledge, which means that, except in rare and very special circumstances, it is available only through a " channel of grace," or in other words an ordained priest.   " Grace " has always been well advertised, and we are given to understand that by means of it the murderer, the adulterer, the cheat, the rascal, the crook, the real-estate agent, or even the profiteer, may achieve blessedness in the hereafter —providing that certain conditions are fulfilled. In all the advertising matter that has been published during the last nineteen hundred years we are told that " grace " may be obtained free—that it is available for the poor as well as for the rich. In practice it is often otherwise. But in every case one condition is essential: that the person who seeks " grace " should *humble* himself before the properly ordained priest. Samuel Butler was right when he epitomized it thus: No gold, no Holy Ghost. And so: No humility, no " grace." For without grace we poor human beings are doomed after death, and for evermore, as Robert Burns put it:

> To weep and wail
> In burnin' lakes,
> Where damned devils roar and yell,
> Chained to their stakes.

This is an unpleasant prospect; and men will do much and pay heavily to avoid it. Some pay regular subscriptions, just as they pay insurance premiums, to keep the " channels of grace " working freely. Large establishments with expert personnel advertise " grace," and send travellers all over the world to extol its virtues. There are different brands of grace, each of which, like a brand of soap or any other commodity, claims to be better than all others. But, as the real test of the efficiency of all brands of grace is in the *hereafter*, and there is no means whereby they may be tested here and now, mankind has often been greatly puzzled to know which one to patronize. There used to be only one brand of grace. Now there are several hundreds, and new ones are being invented every day. This is a pity. Because the advertising of so many has tended not only to make men wonder which one really is the best, but whether any of them is of any use at all. Grace has tended to fall into disgrace.

¶ *A " Corner " in Religion*

It was a monopolistic control of this mystical quality which gave the Church its immense power and wealth. From the early period onwards the Church's whole aim was to achieve power—power over the lives and even the property of man. By psychological exercises and wonderfully elaborate reasoning a scholastic theology began to be evolved. The gospels were relegated to a secondary place, and were to be read only by priests. Roman Christianity took the place of that of Jesus and his apostles; an elaborate organization grew, and the Roman Empire steadily succumbed before its growth, as we shall see later. But here we may conveniently consider the development and expansion of at least one of the pagan ideas seized upon by the early Church, one of considerable importance to human nature. I refer to Hell. With " grace," and almost contemporary with its development and parallel to its development, there was an insistence upon the importance of Hell. Some day an erudite historian must write a full History of the Rise and Fall of the Empire of Hell and its influence upon human nature. Here I can sketch only very briefly the mere outline of that story.

§ 4

# THE SUPERB INFLUENCE OF HELL

Of Heaven very little appears to be known to man, and existing accounts are contradictory. We must accept it as a delightfully vague state or place in which souls are kept in an ecstasy of happiness after death, provided their owners have been good while on earth. Hell is a much more vivid conception. There is much literature about it; a hundredfold more than there is about Heaven, or even about that hazy state of which we hear regarding survival after death, to which neither Heaven nor Hell contributes either pleasure or pain. It is therefore happily possible to offer, out of the mass of learned writings on the subject, a brief account of hellish history, geography, and social conditions, from which some notion may be gathered of the importance of the idea and the effect it has had in forging our natures.

We find the earliest traces of the idea of Hell in the account of Ishtar, Venus of Babylon, who travelled into the land whence no man returns in search of her lover Tammuz. But the Babylonians did not treat this Hell of theirs at all seriously. In Egypt the Sun-God was said to descend into the Underworld, of which there is some account, including the first mention of souls being weighed before Osiris and a calculation made of the punishment to be awarded if found wanting in goodness. (In this we find the germ of a wonderful idea.) The next record of Hell is in Zoroastrianism, founded about a thousand years B.C., but bad souls were merely silently accursed. Indian Brahmins had a special Hell of their own, in which only moderate punishment was inflicted; Buddha was in favour of abolishing all this, and did abolish it during his lifetime. However, the sturdy old idea survived, and in the priestly development of institutionalized Buddhism there is a Hell of quite a useful sort. Every one of these Hells was a pleasant place in comparison with the Hell evolved by the imaginations of the early Christian Fathers. To them must be given the honour of having worked out a subtle and convincing doctrine of the eternity of punishment, not excluding the damnation of infants. With these ideas goes another which to many may seem peculiarly sadistic: the joy felt by the blessed at the sight of the torments of the damned. For this there was sound Biblical authority—" *I also will laugh at your calamity, I will mock when your fear cometh* " (Proverbs i, 26). The great and holy St. Thomas Aquinas writes: " That the saints may enjoy their beatitude and the grace of God more richly, a perfect sight of the punishment of the damned is granted them." Grace has already received some mention.

The list of authorities on Hell could be greatly extended. In every branch of instruction, the Christian teachers who had settled at Rome and were growing daily in power believed it necessary to hold out a threat of the torments of Hell in order to turn men towards goodness. We must always remember that with this threat of Hell there went a promise of a reward in Heaven should the sinner turn to a behaviour exemplary in accordance with the code that was being evolved. Be it noted, however, that the detailed descriptions of the bliss in Heaven always fall far short of those which deal with Hell, which is the basis of religious terrorism.

¶ *Good and Bad Results of Hellish Teaching*

If, as some modern anthropologists assert, man is good by nature, why all these threats of punishments and offers of reward in the hereafter? There is no doubt but that the immediate results of the hell-fire teaching were good, from the point of view of the Christian Church. Large numbers of men became better than they had been before. But the continual threats of hell-fire and brimstone had other profound effects; they caused many to tell lies about their thoughts and feelings; and to become hypocrites. They also created in the authorities of the new religion an indifference to suffering. It would be a terrible accusation to bring against Hell that it very largely explains why man began, about the third century A.D., to be a bigger hypocrite than he had ever been before. Such appears to be the case. The Holy Inquisition of the thirteenth to fifteenth centuries, then the Reformation and sixteenth-century Puritanism, all at first influences for orthodox good, added immeasurably to the development of hypocrisy, until we have it with us today in its many perfected modern forms.

¶ *Hell and Purgatory Useful Institutions*

It may perhaps seem relevant to mention with the fierce doctrine of hell-fire the softening influence of that of Purgatory, a place of temporary and modified suffering, invented by pagans and accepted by the

Roman Church. Souls of those guilty of venial sins may go from Hell to " Purgatory " to be " cleansed "; when clean they may proceed to Heaven. If they are *poor* souls they remain either in Hell or Purgatory, and their friends may pray for them. But if they are *rich* souls—and the proper financial arrangements are made with the Church—they need not remain long in either Hell or Purgatory. The Church sees to that. It is a simple money transaction.

Hell has almost disappeared in the twentieth century. The word is now mostly used as a mere expletive. Once it flourished, and we must never forget that but for it the grand old priests of the Church would never have gained so great a control over the minds of men; a control which was only partly obtained by the ethical value of the Master's teaching. The doctrine of retribution was the keystone of early Christianity, and a great help to the finances of the Church.

§ 5

## FROM EMPIRE AND CHURCH TO CHURCH-EMPIRE

The Roman Empire spread itself over the Western world from Spain to the Caspian Sea, northwards to Britain and southwards to Egypt. It was unlike any Empire hitherto existing elsewhere. Roman law with an army behind it settled disputes in the skin-clad village of Londinium on the River Tamesis, in the fair territory of Hellas, and in the proud city of Memphis. Roman legions marched along cattle-tracks under the sweltering sun of Mauretania and through the frigid passes of the Caucasus Mountains. The progression of the Empire was upward, until about a hundred years after the execution at Golgotha of that then obscure felon Jesus, by order of the representative of a mighty emperor sitting with his mistress a thousand miles away. By then the Christian sect had almost become an *ecclesia militans*, a military church, in spirit. It was prepared to break down all barriers set up by human power; and no compromise was possible. The early Church was socialistic, in so far as it declared all men, even slaves, to be equal before God. While the period before Christ was one of active conquest by the Roman power, that for four centuries afterwards was one in which endeavours were made to conserve and consolidate its gains. The masses now became restless and the policy of " Bread and Circuses " became one of great importance for the well-being of the State. Under the influence of imported ideas, from the East, from Egypt, and from Greece, the hard old family institution weakened. Debauchery, quack religions, " mysticism," extreme wealth and extreme poverty, and loose morals entered into the everyday life of the people. Some of the Emperors were little better morally than the meanest of their subjects; others were worse; not one of them was what we should call a " nice person." Caligula killed his grandmother and forced his father-in-law to cut his own throat. He lived incestuously with all his sisters, one of whom he took from her husband and kept openly as his wife. When once he fell sick, he made a will leaving her the entire Empire. He organized deceits to prove his personal bravery. His head was

bald and the rest of him hairy.   " On which account,"
says Suetonius, " it was reckoned a capital crime for
any person to regard him from above when he passed
in the streets, or so much as to name a goat."   Sometimes he would appear in public dressed like a woman ;
at others habited like a private soldier, but with a
golden beard fixed to his chin, and holding in his hand
a thunderbolt or trident—distinctions of the Gods.
He would dress himself up and pose as Venus.   Sending once in the middle of the night for a few consuls,
he placed them on a stage (he loved the theatre) and
then all of a sudden pirouetted out before them dressed
in a long flowing robe to show his grace, while the band
played an accompaniment.   If any person made the
least noise while the Emperor publicly danced, that
person was dragged out to be beaten and scourged with
his own imperial hand.   But Caligula was not entirely
without a sense of humour : for he despatched a
knight to King Ptolemy in Mauretania, a journey of a
thousand miles by land and sea, bearing a letter with
the words, " Do neither good nor harm to the bearer."
A gladiator named Columbus, who won his combat
with only a slight flesh wound to show for his victory,
had some poison rubbed into the scratch by order of
the Emperor, who afterwards called the poison Colum-
binum.   He took an active part in the circuses, and
was a good driver of the chariot.   He caused his
soldiers to enjoin complete silence the night before a
race, so that the sleep of his favourite horse, Incitatus,
should not be disturbed.   " How I wish," he once
said, " that the Roman people had only one head,
so that I could remove it with a blow."   He was not
the best of monarchs, but there was an imaginative

grandeur about his practice of evil which assures him of his place in a history of human nature.

## ¶ *Persecution evokes Courage*

No longer was there the simple stern code of the Republic. Unbridled cruelty now became common in every grade of society, from the Emperor's entourage downwards. It was a fruitful soil for the new religion, and especially for one which, so to speak, had abolished death and suffering. The activities of the Christians were directed against the cruel attitude towards life. Little by little the missionaries and their followers attracted the attention of the authorities, by their preaching against lust, cruelty, and evil. At first the dislike of those in power for the new preachers was slight, but it grew into a hatred. The celebrated persecutions began, and as they progressed a transcendent courage was evoked by them in the hearts of the persecuted and those liable to be persecuted. From the reign of Nero in A.D. 54 to that of Diocletian (A.D. 280 to 305) those dreadful persecutions grew in volume and intensity until they were proved by the extreme courage of the converts, who were rapidly increasing in numbers, to be quite useless for their purpose. The reason for this was that martyrdom was deemed by the Church to be not merely honourable but a certain way of attaining the salvation of heaven. *Love of death* appeared in the world: an astounding testimony to the limits to which men and women are prepared to go for an inspired ideal. Those who have read the history of Ireland from 1914–21 will appreciate what it means.

Tertullian mentions how in a little Asiatic town the

entire population once flocked to the Roman procon-
sul declaring themselves to be Christians and imploring
him to execute the decree of the Emperor and grant
them the privilege of martyrdom. The bewildered
functionary asked them whether, if they were so
weary of life, there were no precipices or ropes by
which they could end their days; and he put to death
a small number of the suppliants and dismissed the
others. It is difficult for us, who live in an age
when religious enthusiasm has lost its vigour, to
imagine the fervour and courage of those Christians in
the face of so much danger. Surely man is a very
brave creature. The authorities of Rome, with the
aid of their armies and supported by the rabble, made
successive efforts to exterminate them completely.
They did so believing that only in this manner could
they rid the Empire of a grave danger. It was for
precisely the same reason that, a thousand years later,
the flourishing Church instituted the Inquisition—that
is, because the Papacy firmly and honestly believed
that heresy and heretics were undermining its power.
All repressive movements are based on the same set of
reasons—fear or selfishness, or both, with their
subsidiary instincts: selfishness to preserve power or
gain it, and fear lest it be lost. Only a few hundred
years ago the massacres of the Irish by the English
were approved by men who have achieved a reputation for their broad humanity, men such as Edmund
Spenser and John Milton, the former a poet of chivalry,
the latter a poet of deep religious feeling. Against
this we should weigh the military and political measures
taken by the English against the Irish in the years
1920–21, when " Black and Tannery " (as the Irish

humorously called it) caused so much execration to fall upon the fair name of England that some settlement of an age-old question had to be arranged at any cost.

¶ *The Most Important Year of Western History?*

While Rome was steadily declining—the Rome of millions of slaves, of " Bread and Circuses," of vice and weakness in every fibre of the body politic—the Christian religion, now a Church well and truly established, gained more and more converts. The zeal of the converts knew no bounds in proselytizing, for was not their religion " Catholic," universal? In the first three hundred years after the birth of Christ we see an Empire fighting what seemed to it a political or social disease, and without great success. The year 311 was for the West one of the most important, perhaps the most important in its history. It was then that the Empire, represented by its supreme magistrate, the Emperor Galerius, published a Decree which placed the Christian religion on the same footing before the law as the worship of the Gods of Rome. When Constantine, the Emperor at Constantinople (which had now become the seat of government for the Eastern Roman Empire), decided that it was politically expedient for him to become a Christian and to make Christianity the official religion, the fate of the hitherto struggling creed was decided. From about 337 onwards it was no longer a crime to be a Christian; it was *honourable* to be one! What is honourable or dishonourable is a matter of fashion, depending upon the moral code commonly observed at any period. At Rome the words of the Emperor were the moral

code, as the word of Hitler was in Germany, of
Mussolini in Italy, in modern times. From that
point it was but a small move to a direct reversal of
the attitude of mind which officialdom had adopted
hitherto: in human affairs such changes are merely a
question of *power*, often in its crudest form of brute
force. Official lawyers now drew up edicts, the objects
of which were to make it uncomfortable for citizens
of the Roman Empire not to be Christians. *To
differ from the beliefs of the Church was to break the
law.* Those people who had independence of mind
took the place of the persecuted Christians; and
martyrdom changed its form. But the *heretics*, as
these lawbreakers were called, had not an inward
moral feeling of superiority such as the early Christians
had; they had not " the Kingdom of Heaven " on
the horizon of their lives; they had no centralized
force, no general staff, and little ardour or enthusiasm
except of a negative sort. They were able to offer
little resistance, and therefore became the legitimate
targets of their superiors in power. The whole gamut
of oppression started off afresh on a different cycle.
Meetings of the heretics were broken up, organizers
thrown into prison, heavily fined, and their property
confiscated. Their books were sought out to be
burned by the executioners of the State; whoever
concealed one of these works was doomed to capital
punishment. The Emperors helped the Church: the
clergy were exempt from burdensome offices and taxes
and, most important of all, they were permitted to
*receive bequests*. The military power of the Roman
State was behind them, and now they had permission
to acquire property, real and personal. One further

step in the mentality of the leaders of Christianity and we have a Church quietly but steadily taking to its bosom the very materialism which it had succeeded in undermining. A hundred years later (A.D. 440) we have the Papacy. Another hundred years after that we see the Church beginning to dominate the Western world. The marriage of Church and State materially helped both partners.

¶ " *Let us Smash our Enemies* "

Christianity and Empire became one; a Church-Empire, the most powerful human institution which has ever existed, with the longest line of rulers in the whole of history, and an unwritten motto, " *Smash our enemies.*" To describe the influence which this mighty institution has had upon the destinies of millions of men and women is beyond the scope of any writer. From cradle to grave every individual in whole provinces and countries of Europe was to come under its power. It grew into a *political* organization of immense power, wealth, and greed. Behind all this was a set of doctrines which were modifications of Christ's original teachings. By the fourth century the Church at Rome had settled down to the acceptance and practice of a number of its own dogmas. God now consisted of three persons: Father, Son, and Holy Ghost, Three-in-One and One-in-Three, an idea borrowed from the Egyptians, who had taken it from the Assyrians a long time before. For the benefit of women, the mother of Jesus was given an aristocratic title and proclaimed to be the " Mother of God "; another Egyptian idea. Following the Buddhist system of cleansing the mind by a full statement of the iniquities it contains, a system of confession was established; forerunner of the psychoanalysis preached by Freud, Jung, and others, fifteen hundred years later. A series of new and elaborate ceremonies and formulæ was drawn up by the priestly general staff in Rome. Baptism, confirmation, the Eucharist, penance, extreme unction, ordination, and marriage were established as " sacraments " originating in the teaching of Jesus. From birth to the grave the life and fortune of an individual came under the sway of the Church, which claimed omnipotence and infallibility. Purgatory, an invention of Pope Gregory the Great, proved to be extremely lucrative by encouraging payment for masses for the dead. The immediate result of Constantine's conversion was a recrudescence of mythology and a thorough materialization of the Christian cult at Rome, where the supreme authority grew increasingly mundane. The high ideal of Jesus was resuscitated by a few noble men who sought refuge in a monastic life. The men who distinguished themselves by the elaboration of official doctrines were called the Fathers of the Church. They were notable for an immensity of theological learning, coupled with a credulity worthy of any twentieth-century newspaper reader. St. Jerome, a sensuous and passionate man, who produced an excellent translation of the *New Testament*, bolstered up his theology by tall stories of Centaurs and Satyrs who verbally declared the godliness of Jesus. He says, " All Alexandria has seen a live Satyr, who after his death was put in pickle to be brought for exhibition before King Constantine at Antioch."

¶ *A Mindless Period of History*

All mind in the Western world except that represented by the priest ceased functioning. From about A.D. 500 to the twelfth century we find a blank in the development of human intellect in Europe. The middle of this period is reckoned by historians to be the blackest in European history: wars, depredations, sacks of cities, no commerce, little learning except in the monasteries, no science (except that of the Arabs, here and there), no law but that of brute force. Movements of vast hordes from the North; their conversion to Christianity with little or no mollifying effect upon their nature; plunder and rapine; feudal lords stealing land. Everywhere the representative of the Church was either looking on or taking a share in the booty. The Western world was once more in the throes of a struggle for power. The Roman Empire gave the world Roman Law, a highly materialistic system. It passed on to the Church the tradition of a World-Empire, which the Church happily blended with Christ's Universal Kingdom. The Empire showed that, in nine arguments out of ten, force is best. It transmitted the idea of militarism. And, above all, it crystallized the idea of wealth.

§ 6

THE SPORTING SPIRIT OF ROME

We have seen that the Roman Empire was created by the use of the bludgeon; it was based entirely upon the judicious but often violent use of force. It was

Roman statesmen who evolved an idea which for sheer stupidity is unsurpassed in the annals of human nature, one which has unfortunately come down to us and prevails in the world. This inane idea was (and is) that the only means of assuring peace is by armament. The *Pax Romana*, or " Roman Peace," depended entirely upon the sword; but, when the arm behind the sword lost its strength and the brain which guided the arm lost its strength of character and cunning, the much-vaunted peace proved to be an illusion. The Roman mind, with one or two exceptions, *never* rose above the bludgeon. In Rome there was never representative government, and, although a strong political structure and an ingenious system of materialistic law were evolved, they both depended, not upon right, but upon might. The difference between the Greek humanist outlook on life and the cruelly brutal one of the Romans may be seen in their different treatment of the lower classes and criminals. The Greeks used their malefactors as material for medical and surgical research-work—that is, for vivisection; the Romans used them to provide public amusement either as food for wild beasts or as gladiators in the arena. There was a complete absence of science in Rome. Even the science of war made practically no advance and Imperial Roman mentality may best be estimated from a consideration of the public " games " or spectacles, which increased in number and importance until the Empire fell into decline and collapsed.

¶ *Games Preferred to Bread or Money*

The spectacles were originally religious celebrations. They existed under the early Republic, but later, in the time of the Emperor Augustus, they became the chief means whereby the government kept the proletariat contented. " Bread and circuses " went together to hold in a state of political subjection the populace of Imperial Rome. " The Roman people," says a Latin writer, " love most of all two things: bread and games; even distributions of money were less desired than games, for gifts of bread and money pacified only a few, but games *the whole people* ." That oleaginous and smug person, Marcus Aurelius, who has achieved an entirely undeserved reputation for humanity, was in favour of the spectacles. With the exception of Tiberius, all the Emperors approved of them. Aurelian distributed handkerchiefs that had to be waved when a gladiator killed his opponent; Marcus Aurelius did public business from the Royal Box; Nero watched the games from a drunken couch; and several Emperors had a part in the conception of the gigantic circus building, the Colosseum.

¶ *Spirit of the Circus*

The yells of the people at the Circus were recognized by politicians as expressions of popular wishes, and it was at the spectacles that the only liberty of speech existed. Here any man could shout his jibe even at the Emperor. Diocletian, it is recorded, left Rome because he could no longer endure the outspokenness which met him at the circus. For a period of over five hundred years the games pervaded every man's thoughts. " The great spectacle was the spectators," writes Friedländer. " Long rows of rising seats were thronged with a mass of men moved by one passion, almost a mania. Near the close of a race, suspense, anxiety, fury, joy, savagery, burst forth. Their eyes ever fixed on the chariots, they clapped and shrieked with all their lungs, sprang up, bent over, waved handkerchiefs, incited their favourites, stretched out their arms as though they could reach the course, gnashed their teeth, groaned, threatened, exulted, triumphed, or swore. The winning chariot aroused a thunderous applause—and loud curses from the losers—which re-echoed over the deserted streets of Rome, announcing to those who stayed at home the end of the race, and struck the ear of the traveller when Rome had vanished from sight. The races lasted intermittently, except for short pauses at mid-day, from daybreak to sundown; but the people sat there patiently despite sun and rain and never wearied of following their idolized sport with the same passionate attention."

¶ *A Thousand Years of Mass Brutality*

Five centuries after the foundation of Rome the first gladiatorial fights were held; at the end of the fourth century A.D. the Roman amphitheatre was still a centre of attraction. At first there were few combatants, but later the numbers of those who took part, as well as the numbers and style of the spectacles, became more elaborate. Ten thousand men fought in the great shows of Augustus, and the same number took part in the four months' circus given by Trajan after the conquest of Dacia. With the spread of the " Roman Peace " over the world, the captured natives of conquered territories were dragged into the arena and butchered to make a Roman holiday: tattooed savages of Britain, " Nordic " barbarians from the

Rhine and the Danube, Moors, Negroes, Christians, Jews, Franks, Egyptians, Goths, and Samaritans. Gladiators would appear fighting singly or in troupes. Battles were waged in which thousands had to fight to the death, leaving the arena littered with bleeding and battered bodies. Here women often fought— and, under Nero, even women of noble birth—but a wave of sentimentalism in A.D. 200 brought a prohibition of female combats. To the modern globe-trotter who visits Rome I would say that, having first read his eulogistic guide-book to the cultural influence of the Romans, let him contemplate the ruins of the Colosseum which the Flavians built about A.D. 90. Here fought the gladiators recruited from the prisoners-of-war of the nations which came under the cultural influence of their civilized conquerors.

¶ *The Career of Gladiator*

There were many schools for gladiators besides the great imperial one. Often the proprietors of these schools were women, with whom the gladiators were always popular. A lady named Hecatæa of Thasos owned an excellent training establishment and spent many leisure hours with its inmates. Gladiators passed from owner to owner by purchase, sale, or public auction. In this holocaust of debauchery were to be found all types of men, but the most interesting of all were the professional, volunteer gladiators who fought their way to fame and fortune as modern prize-fighters or bull-fighters do. Each volunteer took an oath to the effect that, if he failed in his duty as a fighter, he would suffer himself to be whipped with rods, burnt with fire, and killed with steel.

" How many idle men," exclaims Tertullian, " contract themselves out to the sword for sheer love of combat! " The criminal could fight his way to liberty and the slave to freedom; the poor soldier could gather a fortune in money; the outcast could retrieve his character. Everything possible was done by the Government to add to the spectacular appearance of the fighters in the arena. They were given a splendid equipment, rich and artistic armour, helmets with embossed designs, elaborate shoulder-pieces, belts, breast-plates, and weapons. Their helmets were decorated with feathers and their attire was laced with gold and often set in jewels. The bull-fighters of modern Spain or the prize-fighters, all-in wrestlers, footballers, or film stars of England or America are not more beloved by their crazy mobs than the Roman gladiator was by his.

Great care was taken of the physical well-being of the fighters. The schools were situated in a healthy locality and men were given the best of food. As one writer says, " Fashionable surgeons attended to their wounds and the best physicians supervised the administration of their diet; a special class of slaves was educated for their massage." Even their spiritual welfare was looked after by their masters; to encourage a common worship of the gods of their patrons, the gladiators were permitted to form the equivalent of our Sunday-school groups. They were fattened for the arena, spiritually, mentally, and physically. But among these gladiators there were always large numbers of men who had lost courage and abandoned all hope. This was more especially true among those called *Bestiarii*, or men chosen to fight for their lives with wild beasts. Suicide was common among them, notwithstanding the elaborate precautions taken by their masters to prevent it. Seneca tells us of a man, chosen as a morsel for the beasts, who was being drawn on a chariot to the arena, carefully guarded by the soldiers standing on each side of him. He pretended to be overcome by sleep and, letting his head drop between the spokes of the wheel, so arranged for his neck to be broken. Twenty-nine Saxons who were chosen for the arena strangled one another with their bare hands rather than appear.

We pride ourselves on living in an age of enlightened advertisement, but it is doubtful if any modern advertising king could surpass in ingenuity the well-written copy and the methods employed by the Romans to work up enthusiasm for the spectacles of the Colosseum. Announcements were painted on walls in all parts of the city of Rome, and even on the gravestones. Examples of these have been found in the ruins of Pompeii. A translation of one is given on page 152.

On the evening before a spectacle there was always held the Feast of Gladiators, a free feed at which every imaginable luxury was provided and to which curious members of the public were admitted. Some of the men would eat and drink frugally, to conserve their strength, while others acted upon the motto " *Eat, drink, and be merry, for tomorrow we die* "—from which this phrase originates. The professionals would say good-bye to their families; Christians would hold a prayer-meeting. All would retire early to rest that they might be fresh for the battle. The spectacle would open with a full-dress parade of the fighters round the arena, and they, holding their weapons in the air, would shout as they passed the Royal Box, " Hail, Emperor! We who are about to die, salute thee." Those who appeared for the first time had

---

### GRAND SPECTACLE !

Thirty Pairs of First-class Gladiators !

All Members of the celebrated Quinquennalis

including

### GNAEUS ALLEIUS and NIGIDIUS MAIUS

WITH UNDERSTUDIES TO REPLACE THE DEAD

### WILL FIGHT

in Pompeii

From the 24th to the 26th November

ALSO BAITING OF ANIMALS

### LONG LIVE THE QUINQUENNALIS !

---

then to " run the gauntlet" after which the giver of the spectacle would descend into the arena and examine the sharpness of the weapons. Then there were mock fights, followed by the real thing: fights with sharp weapons and fights by half-naked, armour-less, and mobile men, with net, trident, and dagger against others in visor, shield, and sword. Others with huge square shields and short straight swords

met men heavily armed with small shields and sharp
scimitars.  There were fights between men on horseback  or  between  British  war-chariots  in  which  a
second man concerned himself only with the manage-
ment of the horses.  When a fighter was struck, a
deafening roar went up from the assembled populace,
" *Strike !   Let him have it !* "  If a struck combatant
fell to the ground, the giver of the spectacle had the
right of deciding his fate;  but this decision was almost
invariably  left  to  the  spectators.  The  wounded
man would lay his shield down and lift up a finger of
his left hand as a sign that he prayed for his life.  The
mob signified mercy by lifting up their thumbs;  by
turning them down they decided his death.  " Brave
gladiators  often  rejected  popular  interference  and
made signs that their wounds were slight and that they
could still go on:  such met with pity.  The faint-
hearted aroused the anger of the populace, who thought
it an insult that a gladiator should not wish to die.
Cowards were driven in with whips and hot irons and
goaded  into  fight.  The  mad  crowd  would  shout,
' *Lash him, kill him, burn him !   Why does he die so
sullenly !* ' " [1]  The victor often had to fight an under-
study immediately afterwards.  Between fights the
ground saturated with blood was shovelled over by
boys or slaves and received a sprinkling of fresh sand.
" The victors brandished their palms and the fallen
were taken off by men garbed as Mercury the God of
the Nether World;  others, wearing the mask of the
Etruscan demon Charon, probed them with hot irons
to see if they were shamming death.  Hearses stood
ready in anticipation;  on them the fallen were borne

[1] Friedländer.

into the mortuary through the gate of the Goddess of Death. Any who still showed signs of life were killed." [1] Such was the mentality of the glorious Roman Empire.

¶ *Ingenuity of Circus Managers*

The expansion of the Empire meant the discovery of many wild beasts that had been hitherto entirely unknown to the Roman people. As early as 186 B.C. there was held in Rome an exhibition of animals, and it was not long before the practical Romans decided that to tear a man to pieces by wild beasts would be an admirable and salutary method of inflicting the death sentence. Whatever else may be brought against them, we cannot reasonably say that they were hypocrites: they believed in public executions, and there were no hole-and-corner or secret executions such as take place in civilized countries today. The criminals of Rome, furthermore, had a sporting chance of survival. The public loved to see a good fight in which a man was matched against a lion, a panther, a bear, a leopard, or a pack of hungry wolves. Roman princes were proud of their animal executions. The Imperial Menageries grew to such an extent that they became a costly burden. The problem of feeding the flesh-eating beasts was often acute, but an ingenious and realistic emperor solved it by feeding them with living criminals. Even brutes were trained to be fierce: they were driven on to the great stage with the sound of whips, pricked, hot irons applied, straw dolls thrown in front of them to be angrily tossed; or they were tied together with long ropes to fight like Kilkenny cats. The populace roared with pleasure

[1] Friedländer.

to see animals rend each other's flesh. The condemned men who had to face them were either insufficiently armed or tied to stakes and defenceless. The victims with limbs torn asunder and covered with blood were seen begging, not for mercy, but for death. By way of diversion, criminals would appear in tunics embroidered with gold and purple, wearing crowns; suddenly the garments would burst into flames and the wearers would burn to death. Christians who were condemned to death for alleged complicity in the burning of Rome were either tarred and resined to be used as torches to illuminate other spectacles proceeding in the arena or wrapped in hides to give them a flavour of fresh meat so that the wild dogs or wolves let loose upon them might devour them with greater appetite. A minor scene, which never failed to draw a roar of obscene laughter, was the public castration of a victim in the amphitheatre. There were other scenes of indecency which need not be mentioned here.

## ¶ The Attraction of Torture and Execution

It is all very well for those writers whose custom it is to extol the glory of the Roman Empire to slur over or omit entirely any mention of these spectacles. Some there are who assert that it was a less important aspect of Roman life, one of little importance in a general consideration of Roman history. I do not think so. There is hardly a Latin writer who does not mention the spectacles, and in Latin literature there is only one who makes any pretence to be displeased with the depraving sight; *nowhere* in the whole of the Latin literature of Europe can one find a note of horror at the inhuman delights of the amphitheatre.

F

Where the gladiatorial games are mentioned, they are mentioned with either approval or indifference. All this provides an interesting problem for the social psychologist. There is no doubt but that the gladiatorial games became a habit, and the butchery of fellow-creatures a firmly fixed attitude of mind in imperial Rome. There was also the attraction which has ever existed throughout human history attaching to torture and execution. Again, there was the hypnotic, propagandist effect of vastness and splendour. The gigantic amphitheatre with its Royal Box, its rows of senators and aristocrats, the further rows of priests in their holy vestments; the rows of distinguished strangers, foreign kings, and ambassadors; and behind these almost 100,000 representatives of the public on marble seats rising tier above tier. The colour and glamour of it all! Far away on the top crowded the ragged mob, the subdued, yet fascinated proletariat. This mass of humanity spread itself over the magnificent Colosseum, the impressive architectural lines of which were emphasized by rich and artistic decorations. Around the arena itself fragrant fountains threw jets of perfumed water to cool the air and refresh the perspiring crowd. As a protection against the sun, an awning of unparalleled proportions could be spread over the whole. Rumble of drum and blare of trumpet announcing the beginning of a fight would reduce the immense restless and noisy audience to a state of silent expectation.

¶ *Psychological Effect of Mob on Individual*

The effect of this atmosphere upon a person of sensibility and humanitarian principles is well illustrated by St. Augustine, who tells a convincing story of his friend Alypius, an ardent Christian. This young man was dragged off to be a spectator by a few enthusiastic followers of sport. He declared that, as a Christian, his body might go but not his soul; for he intended to keep his eyes shut and would in reality be absent. He did so, until a deep roar went up from the crowd at some incident of the fight. Struck by a very human curiosity, he opened his eyes. The excitement of the spectacle changed him. He looked on and on, until at last he became fired with passion and the lust for blood. So enthralled was he that he came again and again afterwards with the full enthusiasm of a devotee. Is there among us today a man who could swear he would behave otherwise? The *state of mind* which approved of the public butchery of men existed; he who disapproved would himself have been thrown into the arena. The imagination of many Christians was stirred by the amusements of the Roman holiday; and the process of weaning the Romans from the bloodshed of the arena was slow. In the sixth century the animal fights still existed, though the human combats had come to an end perhaps over a hundred years earlier.

§ 7

## ALLAH VERSUS JEHOVAH

We may leave the vanishing Roman Empire, in which power had moved from the Emperors to the Church. When the Church was already well established, there was born in the year A.D. 570 in far-off Mecca a man who was to have a profound influence in the world, and who was to become for the Arabs a Christ, a supreme leader. Mahomet, founder of Islam, like Jesus of Nazareth, was born in extreme poverty and brought up uneducated. At the age of twenty-five he was unsuccessful in life, but shrewdly retrieved his fortune by marrying the rich widow of a defunct merchant. For fifteen years he settled down to humdrum married life and, in the ordinary way of business, became father of several children. Wells pictures him at the age of forty as something of a loafer: " A rather shy, good-looking individual, sitting about and listening to talk, a poor poet, and an altogether second-rate man." He seems to have become obsessed by the sort of longings for spirituality which overwhelmed Gautama Buddha, Jesus, and the old Jewish prophets. Like them, he appears to have run away into the desert to avoid the insincerity and cynicism which surrounded him in Mecca. There he became a convinced teetotaler. Wandering merchants and vagrant missionaries from Palestine may have dropped remarks which converted him to the idea of a single Deity. He began ecstatically to emit stanzas of imaginative religio-ethical poetry, in which the unity and supremacy of Allah were asserted, as well as a life after death. There would, of course, be a hell for those who did not believe him; and a paradise for those who did. Nothing original about him so far appeared. But time was to work changes.

¶ *Ecstatic Result of Self-hypnosis*

In the manner of delivering his teaching, Mahomet differed greatly from Jesus. He would throw himself into a religious ecstasy and then his words flowed freely. Apparently without effort, he poured forth his sonorous verses; technique never caused him any worries or labours. His half-dreaming, other-worldly mind was in a turmoil; inside him there rumbled a religious volcano, the inspiration of Allah, his God. He went through the common experience of the great mystics: like Joan of Arc later, he saw figures and heard voices and strange noises. Before delivering himself of a section of what was afterwards to be called *The Koran*, he passed through a period of mental and spiritual gestation. His intellect would be in a turmoil, his spirits would become depressed, and his whole being would twitch and dither. He would shake like a man after a drunken debauch, shivering and perspiring by turns. At times he was a man in a trance, his extremities a cadaveric white and his face a piece of carved marble. On recovering consciousness he would quiver all over and the veins of his forehead stand out boldly; then he would begin to sway to and fro. As the paroxysm of ecstatic thought came to its climax he began, slowly at first, to let fall the mighty " Words of Destiny." Steadily the current grew in volume until it poured forth with tremendous power and speed. At this stage he would perspire freely, like a man engaged in heavy labour; and when the section was completed he would fall back exhausted but greatly relieved, like a small woman who is delivered of a big child. The words which he uttered (he said) were not his, but God's. His friends became alarmed. Some said that he was a poetic genius; others shook their heads, charitably declaring that he was merely a little mad. Mahomet stood up against them and began to preach, after the manner of the prophets of Israel, like Confucius, Mo-Ti, Lao-Tsu, Gautama the Buddha, and Jesus, reviling them for their evil ways, their local gods, their immorality. They must turn their faces towards Allah! In the course of this preaching he related the old, old stories of the Jewish prophets, solemnly declaring that they had been revealed to him by no less a person than the angel Djibril (Gabriel) him- (or perhaps her-) self.[1] This evoked satirical jokes in the bosoms of his listeners, and the rumour went about that Mahomet was stealing the thunder of a certain Christian goldsmith of the market-place. Local wags and wits composed rhyming lampoons about him; the poor fellow became a target for ribald louts of his town. But Mahomet triumphed over them all with the aid of that same religious courage which we saw manifested in Jesus; and his words formed the basis of a new religion, its laws embodied in *The Koran*, which means *That which is to be read*. It is the next book in history after Plato's *Republic* and the New Testament in its effect upon human nature. To it many tendencies and movements may be traced.

¶ *Celestial Original of the Koran*

Allah was the author of this work: Mahomet was merely the humble transmitting and publishing medium chosen by him. That is why every section of it is preceded by the explanatory words " *In the Name of Allah the All-merciful and Omnipotent*." Mahomet's own words or thoughts find no place in it. It was intended to be a faithful copy of God's

[1] The sex of angels has never been definitely settled.—C. D.

own laws, of which the Arabic original is carved upon the olive-green tables of translucent magnesium silicate which for ever stand before the sublime throne of the Creator in heaven, where angels " incessantly modulate it by modulations in seven modulatory tones." [1] Those who had listened to the paroxysmic revelations of the prophet himself had put their heads together and learned his words by heart; the Khalif Abu-Bekr acted as editor, having for assistant his good councillor Omar, and wrote everything down. The verses were slightly filed and polished by the scholarly Khalif Otman, and this copy was the *editio princeps* of *The Koran* as we know it. The book long remained in the keeping of the Ommyad Khalifs in their mosque at Damascus, until one day it disappeared mysteriously, " carried off by a messenger from heaven." Mardrus says, " With regards to the style of this work, it is the personal style of God; and as a style is the essence of its creator, it can only be considered divine."

¶ *The Practical Miracles of Mahomedanism*

The religion of Allah was spread with an enthusiasm and rapidity which were a remarkable contrast to the slow growth of other religions. Mahomedanism was final and complete in form, as one might reasonably expect in a religion intended to be a divine and explicit guide to salvation. It was never, like Christianity, stated in contradictory or obscure terms. Hence it had an immediate driving force which far surpassed that of the self-contradictory gospels

[1] *Le Koran.* Traduction littérale et complète des Sourates Essentielles, par J. C. Mardrus. Paris (1928).

preached by our Lord's apostles. It was, further-more, greatly helped by a number of divine miracles which seem to us apposite and to the point, in that they placed Mahomet at the head of a considerable ARMY! After that moment the prophet (who was by no means the fool his people formerly thought him) became a *soldier* of his creed. "Henceforth," says Reade, "we may admire the statesman or the general; the prophet is no more. It will hence be inferred that Mahomet was hypocritical, or at least inconstant. But he was constant throughout his life in the one object which he had in view: the spread of his religion. At Mecca it could best be spread by means of the gentle virtues; he therefore ordered his disciples to abstain from violence which would only do them harm. At Medina he saw that Kaaba idolatry could not be destroyed except by force. He obeyed his conscience both at Mecca and Medina; *for the conscience is merely an organ of the intellect, and is altered, improved, or vitiated, according to the education which it receives and the incidents which act upon it.*" (My italics.)

It is a remarkable fact that religion and sex are often so closely allied to one another that it is some-times difficult to tell where one ends and the other begins. During religious revivals this is abundantly clear to the casual observer; and afterwards to registrars of births. The Christian religion frankly acknowledges the relationship between sexual and religious emotion (because of the grave danger which the former has for the latter) and decrees that sexual proclivities must be suppressed. But, though the spirit may be willing, the flesh is sometimes weak, as our eyes and history tell us. In many religions the priest is not only not permitted to marry, but may not even indulge in the most discreet promiscuity.

¶ *Sex and Sword spread Allah's Gospel*

Mahomet saw the whole problem very clearly and, as he had himself been a married man, he decided upon sexual licence; reserving his prohibition entirely for matters of liquors that intoxicate. At the age of fifty he renewed his youth and began a career in which he distinguished himself as a voluptuary—after which his whole religion took on a more liberal hue; it became more broad-minded and more dynamic. The great achievement of Jesus was to abolish death by the creation of a Kingdom of Heaven in which souls could remain eternally clothed with a vague sort of bliss. Mahomet took this vague bliss and, having analysed it, decided that it was largely sexual. He was fifty at the time; an age of experience in the lives of strong men. The most remarkable feature of Mahomedanism is that which pertains to affairs of sex. We know from a perusal of the *Arabian Nights* that the Arabs were (for that matter they still are) a race in which libidinousness and salacity are racial characteristics. Mahomet himself became a sensualist; he knew the weakness of his fellow-creatures, and did not fail to trade upon it. He preached polygamy and concubinage, and not the least intriguing part of his sublime doctrines is that which promises a " Paradise " in which there shall be an unlimited number of female souls at the disposal of the male souls that are saved. He was a shrewd business man and a good judge of human nature; he taught that this gospel, which offers the bait of a sexual paradise, must be driven home with sword and battle-axe, by conquest, murder, arson and rapine.

¶ *A Brilliant Addition to Theology*

The Arabs had by this time outgrown their old religion, and it was not long before the word of Allah had spread its power over the whole of Arabia. A new ecclesiastical state was formed and ruled by the code of laws embodied in *The Koran*. By far the most momentous of these was to the effect that the gospel of the founder should be disseminated with the aid of the sword—a brilliant addition to theology. The difference between the expansion of Christianity and Mahomedanism was this: that whereas both were based upon rewards and punishment in the hereafter, it was as yet only the Mahomedans who could legitimately spread their light by means of battle: " *We will cast terror into the hearts of those who disbelieve* " was the text of the new preachers. The sword took the place of the Christian Hell; and was far more reasonable. Mahomedanism was, on the whole, a simple, practical, liberal, and easily understandable religion with many highly attractive features. Allah was a generous God. The teachings of the founder were put into practice by his close friend, the scribe Abu-Bekr. This good man had in his heart the complete fullness of the new faith, and so he set himself systematically to subjugate the world to Allah. Military campaigns were begun; among the most instructive in the whole history of humanity. The inspiration of Allah's divine words produced generals who, for military acumen and general cruelty, are worthy to rank with Hannibal, Cæsar, Alexander the Great, Napoleon, Foch, and other great men of similar genius. Egypt, Syria, Armenia, and part of Persia fell before the power of Allah within twenty-five years. During the next century the rest of Persia, Turkestan, the whole of the North of Africa, Portugal, and the greater part of Spain fell under the sway of the successors of the prophet. The new faith satisfied and did good to the races in the area it covered, for the Arabs were then the most enlightened race in the world. Without some easy faith in that dark and unspiritual period the populations of the conquered territories might have degenerated or become devils.

The growth of the empire of Allah continued until the death of the great Haroun al Raschid, in A.D. 809. With his disappearance Islam began to fall into civil war and confusion. Two hundred years later Islamic vigour was renewed by the Turks under the leadership of the rude Seljuk family. It will be understood that the religion of Allah was a serious threat to the power of Jehovah, reposing in his representatives at Rome and throughout Christendom. Bickerings and even wars on a small scale were not uncommon between the followers of Allah and Jehovah. *When one power threatens to engulf another, humanity ripens for war. That is the law of the jungle; and of man.*

¶ *Revolutionary Idea in Education*

Western Europe had by this time degenerated to a condition of rather vigorous barbarism. Feudal lords had established themselves everywhere. In the midst of this general disruption there arose in the north the Frankish chieftain Charles the Great, or Charlemagne, the first German historical personage of whom we have any clear knowledge. He was a remarkable man, renowned for his physical endurance. He conceived the idea of a conquest, based upon the ideal of bringing the Germans together into one great Christian empire. His military feats were such that he has become a legend; even his intellectual achievements and piety marked him as an exemplary character. Although he could neither read nor write, we hear that he thoroughly enjoyed the works of great teachers—the fathers of the Church, for example—which he had read to him, mostly at meal-times. When he had gorged himself with roast pig, he would lean back and close his bright blue eyes. Still masticating, he would sign to a monk to read to him a portion of what would then correspond to a popular modern thriller called *The City of God*; it had been written by the good St. Augustine a few centuries earlier. The century before that in which Charlemagne achieved power is acknowledged to be one of the blackest in human history as regards the general ignorance of the people, and chiefly because of the gross degeneration that had now caught the Church at Rome. But to Charlemagne must be attributed the honour of having preached the necessity for elementary education among the *common people* at large; a revolutionary idea which never went farther. He was successful in his conquests and founded a moderately strong empire in the West, an empire which resuscitated the declining strength of Rome. His empire became disrupted, but left behind it a germ of growth and renewed power of the Papacy. It was this renewed growth which enabled the Papacy to send forth, three hundred years later, its challenge to the power of Islam, causing that astounding series of " religious wars " which, first as the Crusades and later as the religious squabbles of Europe, will be remembered as one of the bitterest and most ruthless periods in the history of humanity. It was responsible, with the Inquisition, for a religious revival of cruelty. It was a general set-back to the spread of humanitarian ideals preached by Buddha and Jesus and by the Greek teachers of antiquity. It almost put an end to Arab science, which promised great things to an unscientific and priest-ridden world.

§ 8

## A RELIGIO-ECONOMIC WAR AND ITS CONSEQUENCES

The Crusades were not the first demonstration of the failure of Christianity to make itself an effective influence for good, or an influence for permanently beneficial change in human nature. But they were the most striking demonstration of both facts. (Here I refer to human nature as a whole, for there is no doubt that the teachings of Christ had good effect upon individuals.) History has few more imposing spectacles to offer than the cut-throat struggle of the two great religions for military supremacy; their dispute for the economic control of the world; and the oceans of blood shed for Cross and Crescent by hosts of armed men. No two symbols ever stood for more. The wearied and corrupt West roused itself and threw itself against the East. For a time nationalism was abandoned and Western hordes united into a single allied community sworn to the destruction of a dangerous opponent. The sublimest virtues of men were mixed with degradation, the wildest savagery, passion, and lust. We see men fighting against famine, climate, and pestilence; we see great examples of bravery, perseverance, and resignation. All for symbols: the Cross and the Crescent. What was the origin of the Crusades? Answer: a superabundance of dominant passions uniting on either side. Religious fervour and the sheer love of adventure and fighting gave birth to this holy economic war; and war is never so sublime, never so heroic, and never so brutal as when it is inspired by religion. One result of the Crusades was to strike a bitter sorrow into the hearts of the generations which followed. But by giving men much military exercise they strengthened the West: and at the same time they caused the East to grow weary. They saved Europe from the Turk; and left us Europeans instead of Eurasians, which we might otherwise have been—possibly to our advantage.

¶ *A Sermon starts a War*

Wars nearly always spring from deeply hidden causes which may never show themselves on the surface. But there must always be *given* a reason for organized slaughter, a spark to set a flame to smouldering fires, a slogan which appeals to the herd. In the case of the Crusades the superficial reason was the intolerance of the Seljuk Turks towards Christian pilgrims who visited the sepulchre of Christ and other holy places in Palestine. Large numbers of these pilgrims returned to Europe with lurid tales of cruelty and insult, not least of which was that one about the patriarch of Jerusalem who was " dragged through the streets by his hair " and thrown into prison to await a heavy ransom. One of these indigent pilgrims, the celebrated Peter the Hermit, a Frenchman born in Amiens, spread the tale with a rude, inflamed eloquence. In the words of Gibbon, " He preached to innumerable crowds in the churches, the streets, the highways; the hermit entered with equal confidence the palace and the cottage; the people were impetuously moved by his call to repentance and to arms. When he painted the suffering of the natives and the pilgrims of Palestine, every heart was melted to compassion; every breast glowed with indignation when he challenged the warriors of the age to defend their brethren and rescue their saviour." After an appeal by the Eastern Emperor Alexius to Pope Urban II for help against the advances and cruelties of the Turks, there was called the Council of Clermont in France. Urban preached a magnificent fighting sermon to the delegates and others assembled, one of such mighty power that there and then thousands were pledged to take part in a holy war. He said in effect: " If you triumph, the East is yours; if you fail—the Kingdom of Heaven "—" the East " being then the synonym for wealth, luxury, and endless sexual raptures. What prospects could be more pleasant and attractive to single adventurers or to healthy married men tired of their wives? Both in physical and

mental condition the people of Christendom were
ripe for war. The right *symbols* and the voice of
*authority* were required to galvanize the crowds into
action. Only *organization* was required. These three
are the essentials of war.

¶ *Influence of Christ in* A.D. 1097

Two mobs of undisciplined rascals swept down the
valley of the Danube towards Constantinople. On
the way they pillaged Hungary and massacred the
Hungarians. Meanwhile, pogroms were initiated
against Rhineland and other Jews for no apparent
reason except that they were Jews and not Christians.
A little later—in 1097—a more ordered body of
soldiers moved into the Holy Land to besiege Antioch
and Jerusalem. The blood of the conquered followers
of Allah the All-powerful ran in the streets, until
the horses wallowed in it. Towards evening on the
15th of July in that year the crowd of fanatical
Christian butchers reached the holy sepulchre sobbing
for excess of pious joy, and knelt offering thanks-
giving to the Lord of Hosts for their memorable
victory. The Arab account states that one hundred
thousand persons were killed on their side, including
the aged of both sexes, and that the Jews were locked
in their synagogue and burned to death. Such was
the fervour of Christianity in the twelfth century of
our Lord. The news of a loss on the Eastern frontier
of the Latin kingdom stirred Europe in a Second
Crusade. St. Bernard was ordered by Pope Eugenius
to preach a plenary indulgence to all who would join
in it. The eloquent Bernard roared from the pulpits
of Christendom, his sermons teaching the moral dis-

grace of allowing a land which had once been recovered from pollution to sink into it again. Soon the cities of Europe once more echoed to the sweet call of war. The Second Crusade was unsuccessful. It weakened the position of Christianity in Palestine, for in 1187 Jerusalem was retaken by the Saracen leader Saladin, after a battle at Tiberias.

## § 9

## THE LAST PHASE OF SIMPLE WARFARE

A Third Crusade—one of revenge—a sort of " return match "—was organized. In this the German Kaiser, the King of France, and the King of England all took part. They met in Normandy in February, A.D. 1188, to consider the position. A priest of the Latin Church appeared and gave an accurate description of the sufferings of the Latins in Syria. So touching were his reflections that the King of France and the Emperor of Germany stood before him with bowed heads, tears welling from their kindly eyes. When the good prelate had finished, they turned towards one another and embraced, vowing that there was no alternative but for them both to go to the Holy Land. An Archbishop handed to each one of them a little Cross.

¶ *Diversion for Crusaders*

The conduct of English pilgrims in these adventures was regulated by a few simple laws springing from the Christian spirit of the English prince. Murder was punished by casting into the water the deceased person, with the murderer bound fast to him. The penalty for bad language and swearing or smut was a fine of one ounce of silver. A thief was tarred and feathered and sent home to his wife. As so often happens among military allies, a squabble between the English and the French caused the religious objects of the war to be forgotten. But the quarrel was patched up and the forces of the Crusaders laid siege to the city of Acre. This famous siege lasted for three long years, and severely tried the patience of the besieging Crusaders. There were, however, diversions. An Arabian author informs us of the happy arrival in the camp of the Christians of three hundred free-and-easy ladies from Cyprus. In the shadow of the camp churches with their pretty wooden steeples (where Mass was celebrated from early morning to night), the women found much favour in the eyes of the bored Crusaders. Scandal spread regarding what took place under canvas.

¶ *How Allies in War hate one Another*

Acre capitulated. On the same day dear, hot-headed Richard of England in a fit of pique ordered the standard of Leopold, Duke of Austria, to be thrown into a ditch—an incident which all but ended the war. How those allied Christians grew to hate one another! It is curious that wars should generate among allies such a detestation of one another that an expressed vow goes up to the effect that next time the allies are to take the place of the enemy, who is not such a bad fellow after all. The hatred of allies for one another is a common phenomenon of all wars. To return—Saladin was engaged in an onslaught on Joppa, and Richard decided to come to the rescue. Part of his troops went by land and the remainder by sea. A contrary wind arose detaining His Majesty's boats for three whole days at Caiaphas, where they had put in. Angry at this delay, the king cried aloud, " O, Lord God, why dost thou detain us here? *Have sense*, I pray thee; and consider the urgency of the case and the devoutness of our wishes! " The old chronicler Geoffrey de Vinsauf (in English Safewine) continues, " No sooner had he prayed thus than God caused a favourable wind to spring up, which wafted his fleet before it into the harbour of Joppa, in the midst of the night of Friday immediately preceding the Saturday on which the besieged forces had agreed to surrender, and when all of them would have been given over to destruction. . . . But their deliverer was already come, his fleet was riding in the harbour and his soldiers were eager to land for their rescue." This sort of thing continued with variations for a further period of over one hundred years.

## ¶ *Influence of the Crusades*

The consequences of the Crusades and their effect upon human nature are so many and so complex that they can be but briefly mentioned here. No wars ever lasted so long, and few wars were more destructive. The most horrible violences of fanaticism were encouraged during that fateful period from A.D. 1096 to A.D. 1291. For one thing, their failure was the beginning of that unpleasant phase in human history known as the Inquisition, during which the papal power, having failed to extend its territory and to bring under its sway the Moslems, turned upon restive Christendom to subdue it more thoroughly. The pastors of the Church were driven, after the use of anathemata, excommunications, interdicts, and other weapons in the storehouse of spiritual artillery, to fall back upon the rack, the thumbscrew, and the heap of burning heretics as an example of its power. The Crusades were the beginnings of modern pogroms against Jews. The practices of prayer, fasting, and alms-giving as institutions may be salubrious to the individual and beneficial to society, capable of soften-ing pride and subduing passions. Against that we must balance the bitterness engendered in the human heart during this series of sanguinary wars which ended in failure and from which sprang the vilest system of torture, mental and physical, of which there is account in the most sombre pages of human history, until we come to modern " Totalitarian " States. Furthermore, whatever may be the virtues of soldiers —and they have many—there are many evils which spring from their freedom from restraints. During three hundred years Latin Christianity lived through a career of murder and plunder of Moslems. The nations of Europe became accustomed and inured to bloodshed on a grand scale. We suffer from this heritage. It is part of our make-up.

Possibly the greatest influence of the Crusades was upon international commerce and the exchange of ideas. Europeans had learnt what the East could give in the way of riches; Venice and other cities prospered by the trade which followed, and the leisure resulting from this wealth contributed to the Renais-sance of Europe. The art of navigation became more perfect, and in a subsequent age was to confer immense material benefits upon Europe. It would appear that the mariner's compass was invented about the period of the First Crusade, no doubt in order that the fleets of the world might more rapidly find their way to the Holy Land. The French navy came into existence about this period. The necessity for transporting large numbers of men brought with it bigger ships, and with them came more masts and the invention of the jib, by which tacking could be done, thereby enabling the mariner to beat against a wind nearly dead ahead: the way for the discovery of America was already being prepared. Gothic architecture, copied from Greek and Arab monuments, sprang up on all sides. Sculpture and painting were cultivated with greater zeal. Men became acquainted with customs and phases of art hitherto unknown in Europe. Finally, those great religious wars were responsible for perfecting primitive weapons and primitive warfare, of which this was the last phase. After that both weapons and war take on what may be called a new orientation: they become more ingenious, more brutal, and more horrible than ever before. The inward spiritual force of man becomes threatened by the power of externals, but as yet he has the latter well in hand.

## Book IV: WAYWARD PROGRESSION OF HUMAN NATURE

### § 1

### A RECIPE FOR THE IMPROVEMENT OF MORALS

WE have seen how the power of a *symbol* moved the whole of Europe to take part in a series of wars which in two centuries left the East and the West almost desolate. Foreign adventures having proved futile, the Church now turned upon its adherents at home and concentrated upon them. The thirteenth century marked the zenith of Church power in the world. By this time the Pope had become " The Vicar of Christ, successor of Peter, of Christ the Lord, God of the Pharaoh, beneath God, above man, less than God, more than man." Catholic Rome was now ruling emperors and kings. The Head of the Church was the final court not merely in matters of faith and morals, but he also controlled the material resources of nations and peoples. The papal Bull *Unam Sanctam Ecclesiam*—" One Holy Church "—affirms that: " *To be submissive to the Roman Pontiff is a condition of salvation for any human creature*," and also that there are, governing this world, two *swords*: the spiritual one in the hand of the Pope, the temporal in the hands of kings. But kings may wield their swords *only* to serve the Church by permission of the Pope. It may seem that I dwell too much upon the influence of the priest on human destiny and human nature. My reply is that there is no influence equal to it in importance before the fifteenth century. Without priests and Church medieval history would be almost a blank.

At this period there began an important social movement based chiefly upon the developments of trade and the growth of business. A " middle-class " of people arose half-way between the ruling aristocrats, feudal lords, the authorities of the Church, and the lower or inferior and ignorant masses of people—the feudal proletariat. There was a great increase in the prosperity of the towns. A communal movement began.

The appearance of this movement is mentioned because from its very beginning, which involved the now powerful religious and moral order, there sprang vehement outbursts of indignation against clerical abuses, and this indignation amounted to a revolt of thinkers. Many began to jeer and many to doubt. The thirteenth century is notable for what we may reasonably call a reawakening of the human mind, a revival in the spirit of man—the first for a period of over a thousand years.

## ¶ Chief Task of the Bishops

" Heresy," as this was called, spread in all directions. There began to be a conscious challenge to the Church power, and for this the Church had to find a remedy or perish. The Church had always opposed movements which were beneficial to the people. It was (and is and ever shall be) antagonistic to any innovation threatening its own well-being.

Innocent III condemned Magna Charta, which has (incorrectly) been called the " Keystone of English Liberty "; and he soundly upbraided the English barons for their challenge to kingly authority. They paid no attention, and he therefore excommunicated them. They cared little about the excommunication; this in itself indicates the new spirit of the age. A number of more serious heresies—that is to say, organized heresies—were viciously stamped out, but dangerous individual heretics often escaped. A heretic in those days was often a person who simply voiced derogatory opinions about the Church and his spiritual pastors and masters. The Fourth Lateran Council in 1215 made it the chief business of bishops to search out heretics and, having judicially found them guilty of heresy, to hand them over to lay authorities for punishment. Before proceeding further it is necessary to emphasize a fact which ought already to be clear enough—namely, that all lay authorities, including even emperors and kings, *were under the heel of the Church*. It has been a favourite excuse of Catholic apologists to say that the iniquities of the Holy Inquisition were perpetrated by secular authorities and that the priesthood concerned itself only with trial in regard to spiritual matters. Such an interpretation of the facts is merely casuistry.

¶ *Heavenly Origin of the Inquisition*

Before the moral sentiment of men had reached its present high state of development, there was a stage of growing pains. Punishment has always been a recognized " cure " for bad behaviour, because many people think it works better than all other cures.

Besides, punishment invariably comes from *above*, from a " superior " to an " inferior " being. As men and women are born in sin—that is, without morals —it has been necessary at all periods of history to inflict pains and penalties in order to impress upon feeble minds and slow wits the difference between right and wrong. The principle is one that has been and still is universally practised. The history of the Holy Inquisition provides a lesson for those who imagine that a moral ideal can be achieved or even preserved without physical suffering. As regards the origin of the Inquisition, the good Jesuit historian Francisco de Macedo [1] informs us as follows :

The Inquisition originated in Heaven. God fulfilled the function of First Inquisitor when He blasted the rebellious angels ; He exercised those functions when He punished Adam and Cain ; and when He obliterated mankind by the flood. He exhorted Moses to act as Inquisitor on His behalf when He punished the Hebrews in the desert by violent deaths, by fire from above, and by engulfing them in the cracks in the earth. God transferred His functions as Inquisitor to St. Peter, who exercised them in striking dead Ananias and Sapphira. Finally the Popes, inheritors and successors after St. Peter, delegated the functions to St. Dominic and members of his order.

What greater authority was necessary ?

¶ *Moral Education of the Spaniards*

A dozen monks of the Dominican Order were chosen for the great work on earth because of their sense of Justice and because they were men whose consciences reacted rapidly to the faintest whiff of " evil " among the erring laity. They constituted the first tribunal

[1] *Schema congregationis sancti officii Romani.* By F. de Macedo. Quoted by Edmond Cazal.

at Narbonne, in 1208.   Their task was to investigate
the state of mind of all men and women who were
suspected of slackness in attending to the calls of the
Church, spiritual or material;   and they were to
arrange for the punishment of such as might not
show an inclination to reform and behave in an
upright manner.   Twenty-five years later the zeal of
these good Christians brought their activities to Spain,
where they were to discover much frailty among
men.   The first *auto da fé* was celebrated with pomp
at Aragon on the 12th of May, 1314:   then and there
the corpses of half a dozen suspected sinners were
publicly incinerated by way of example to the Ara-
gonese, and to make the affair more impressive six
living citizens were set on fire at the same time.
Soon the spiritual education of the Spaniards began
in earnest, but it was not until that exceptionally
holy man Tomás de Torquemada was sent by a
merciful Providence that the Inquisition got into its
full stride.   During the twenty-seven memorable
months when his zeal and devotion reached their
highest point—from February of the Year of Grace
1482 to May in the Year of Grace 1484—two thousand
males and females of the human species were burned
alive in the public fires of Seville.   In the same
historic city seventeen thousand persons were taught
the elements of Christianity by suffering punishments
which ranged from torture to fines, confiscations,
imprisonments, deportations, dismissals from employment, and that benevolent penalty called civil death.
To hasten the work of the tribunals the crude and
rigid rules of evidence used in secular and profane
courts were relaxed;   flexible and more spiritual rules

were applied, which permitted fourth-hand hearsay to be heard by the patient, learned, and devout judges. To be suspect was to suffer punishment. The Inquisition taught the ignorant multitude that the physical discomforts which would follow in the train of sin were so great that Church morality paid.

The strange feature of it is that the Inquisition was *popular*. It was long popular, at all events among the masses of the people, although it was mildly opposed by the more sentimental of the nobility and by many of the higher clergy who still believed in God or mercy. It is a curious example—one of the most striking in history—of suffering approved by the masses. The reason for this is because they firmly believed it was inflicted for their ultimate good. It is an example of how large numbers of people will support monstrous injustice so long as it is done in the name of what propaganda has persuaded them to be their interests.

The psychology of the Inquisition is not difficult to understand. It is based upon that often unconscious experience of the inferior mind which takes pleasure in the mishaps of others. The Roman Church could not tolerate the criticism and derogatory statements attributable to heretics. It suffered from an " inferiority complex," if I may be permitted to use psychological jargon. Having power of governments and armies and catchpoles behind it, every imaginable step was taken to crush its critics. These were subjected to the direst pains and penalties ; and ignorant fanatics found themselves suddenly raised to a plane of importance while they contemplated the burning of the heretics. They received the same kind of thrill as those do who now take part in a lynching; or one similar to that expected by the crowd of Londoners not long ago when numbers of perfectly good citizens held their ears to a prison wall during a hanging, in the hope of hearing the dull thud of the body falling or the official crack of the neck-breaking which is now used to frighten English men and women into virtue. " Ha!—See how superior I am to that wretch," is the thought behind it all. For recent examples of all this one has only to look at the modern states that are governed by the extreme forms of twentieth-century political fanaticism, which has taken the place once occupied by the religious fanaticism of Rome.

## § 2

## THE INFLUENCE OF MERE ACCIDENTS

In the first part of the thirteenth century there lived an English Franciscan monk whose influence was to have an important effect upon our present natures. Roger Bacon was that man. He said that the time had come to test and map out knowledge *by experiment with real things rather than by abstract study*. He foresaw modern science, and prophesied the coming of aeroplanes, motor cars, and ships that would move without oars or sails. It is also claimed that Columbus (over two hundred years later) read the works of Friar Bacon and found in them the idea of a " round " world.

About the time of Roger Bacon, or a little later, the properties of the lens were discovered; from that we get the telescope, the spectroscope, the camera, the cinematograph, and the diffusion of Hollywood culture in the twentieth century. Calculation was speeded up by the use of Arabic instead of Roman numerals. Gunpowder was discovered, and the mariner's compass, which had been little used before, began to be a common instrument of navigators. The whole course of history was altered by those discoveries. The printing press was invented, thereby providing a means of spreading knowledge rapidly. At this period we find a renaissance of learning, the birth of modern invention, the age of discovery, and the beginning of the Westernization of the world—the phase preceding Americanization. Immense progress was made in art and even in letters. It was the age of Leonardo da Vinci: a great artist, engineer, and scientist, one of the new men in whom the greatest qualities of the mind appear in combination. It was the age of Copernicus, Tycho Brahe, and Kepler; the first two being the founders of the science of modern astronomy. Then follows Galileo, the founder of the science of dynamics. To the disgust and dismay of the Church at Rome, Galileo expanded the views of Copernicus to the effect that the earth moves round the sun, and is by no means the centre of the universe, as everyone had fondly and conceitedly supposed hitherto. The Church made him kneel before an assembly of Cardinals and deny the truth of his discoveries. He did so, an old bowed man, but as he rose to his feet he is reported to have muttered to himself the words, " It moves all the same."

Less than four hundred years ago there was no British Empire and no U.S.A. The face of the world was changed, so to speak, by that wonderful invention, the mariner's compass.    It is one of the great examples of how a mere scientific device may affect the destiny of untold millions.    This little instrument became the centre of attraction to merchants, kings, princes, and all others who wished to add to their worldly wealth.    Behind it were the human factors of greed and selfishness, and the combination of the two brought about the exploration and exploitation of the globe by Europeans.    Venice, Genoa, Spain, and Portugal were the countries which first showed most interest in the new instrument.    The voyages of the navigators of that period make some of the most thrilling stories ever written.

¶ *Discovery of America*

Various claims have been advanced for the discovery of America; eighteen different nations compete for the great honour, but the probabilities are in favour of its rediscovery by the Genoese sailor-adventurer and shrewd business man, Cristoforo Colombo.    He was a seaman who was prepared to hire himself for cash to whoever would pay the biggest price, providing a share of the resulting booty and honour also came his way.    He held himself ready for expeditions to go anywhere.    On the 17th of April, 1492, he signed a contract with the Spaniards, by which he was to receive from far-seeing King Ferdinand and Queen Isabella the hereditary titles of admiral and viceroy of all the sea, lands, and islands which he might discover.    On the material side he was to be entitled to reserve for himself one-tenth of all pearls, precious stones, gold, silver, spices, and other articles of merchandise, in whatever manner found, bought, bartered, or gained within his admiralty, the costs of his expedition being first deducted; and he was permitted to contribute an eighth part of the expenses and to receive an eighth part of the profits.

It was purely a business arrangement by a business man with a king and queen who had also an eye to business. The money for it was provided by two Jews—Santangel and Abravanel. An unnecessary glamour has been thrown round the whole affair. Americans should remember that, just as they have become the great trading and business nation of the world, so the very idea of their country germinated in a business contract. On the 3rd of August, 1492, Columbus—as we call him—set sail in three tiny vessels: the *Santa Maria*, commanded by himself, the *Pinta*, commanded by Martin Alonzo Pinzón, and the *Niña*. The expedition was accompanied by a few private adventurers. There were in all 120 persons. The story of that voyage is an epic in itself. Columbus turned his prows towards the west and kept them pointing in that direction. Day after day he sailed the uncharted ocean. On Friday morning, the 12th of October, Columbus saw before him a level island. He landed, threw himself on his knees, kissed the earth, and returned thanks to God with tears of joy for his success; henceforward there would be honourable provision for his declining years. The island they had discovered in the New World was one of the Bahamas, and is now called San Salvador. On the 5th of December they discovered Cuba. On the 16th of January the leader turned his ships towards Spain, and on the 4th of March entered the river Tagus. A fortnight later Columbus returned to the little Spanish port of Palos. His entry into Spain was triumphal, and when he approached the sovereigns to render homage they graciously rose to their feet as if receiving a person of the highest rank. Bending his knees, the rude sailor attempted to kiss their hands, but they hesitated to accept this act of servitude. Instead, they raised him in the most gracious manner and ordered him to be seated in their presence, an act of unprecedented humility on their part. They were thinking of the gold that would come their way by this fellow's achievement.

Soon after the bold enterprises of Columbus, which eclipsed those of their own navigators, the Portuguese despatched their star performer, Magalhães, on a tour of adventure. This man performed the greatest of all feats, for he sailed round the whole world. In the meantime the coast of North America was being explored by English navigators, with the success which we know.

¶ *Chance and Navigation*

Most of the discoveries made concerning North America were the result of pure chance; they were quite unintentional. The Scandinavians admit that their heroes were *blown* to America (if they ever got there at all) by a heavy storm. Columbus was *looking for India* and ran blindly into the West Indies. John Cabot believed he had reached the *empire of the great Khan of Tartary*; it was North America he found. Sebastian Cabot discovered the North-West Passage in his quest for a *route to India*. Even the minor discoveries were the result of chance. The French found Newfoundland *during a cod-fishing enterprise*.

Pineda was *looking for a Strait* and discovered instead the Mississippi. The romantic Coronada set out to discover the *seven golden cities of Cibola* and found instead the gorge of Colorado, the plains of Kansas, and a number of insanitary huts along the coast of New Mexico. Soto looked for *Peru* in North America, but found little new. The English navigator, Drake, found that he had " looped the loop " and circumnavigated the globe while on a piratical, freebooting *cruise in search of Spanish galleons*. Hudson thought to find his way to India by a short cut; instead, he explored the river which bears his name. Thus many of the greatest discoveries in exploration were the result of blind chance; as much credit is due for them as is due to the man who breaks the bank at Monte Carlo. There is every probability that the great inventions (which we have noted in the early parts of this work)—fire, the wheel, the boat, the steering car, and even some still later, such as the mariner's compass and the lens—were also the result of sheer accident. Is it not possible that man's progress in this world—including the development of human nature to that high stage at which we find it today—is it not possible that the advance is based upon a series of wonderful accidents?

¶ *English Genius for the Sea*

We may now profitably glance at England, a country which had hitherto lain on the outer edge of the civilized world and was regarded by intelligent Europeans as a semi-barbarous nation. Britain was a country to which adventurous continentals had often turned in their search for new lands to conquer.

Romans, Saxons, Jutes, and Angles had all had their turn at her. The Normans had settled there in comfort after the battle of Hastings in 1066. There was a link with France, and there were links with the Netherlands: trading links. But the internal history of England (with the possible exception of that short period of Alfred's reign from 871 to 901, when the British navy first came into being) was a very local affair, apparently of no importance to the world at large. It was a most important thing for the English that Southern navigators should have done much of the preliminary work of exploring the seas, opening up new territories in order that British merchants should carry their mission of chivalry and civilization to the four points of the other people's compass. The new routes to the East and to the West showed great possibilities for trade and the spread of culture; for with the English the two always go hand in hand. At that time the British had not yet acquired their " natural " genius for seamanship and navigation; but a certain jealousy of the Southerners began to show itself. The first great English navigator was John Cabot of Bristol, a Genoese; to him may be given the credit for the British part in the discovery of North America. Henceforward the way to wealth lay on the sea. During the sixteenth century the monarchs of England—Henry VII and Henry VIII and the virgin Queen Elizabeth—set about creating naval power. A race in sea armament began. The ships that were made in England were found to be better for long voyages than the older type of ships used by the Southerners. The clash with Spain (hitherto the great naval power of the world) came

in 1588. The Spanish Armada was outmanœuvred
by the 197 English ships which played round and
about the Spanish 132. The English vessels were
easier to work, and they were manned and commanded by very able seamen—men who had already
gained experience by long voyaging and rough dealings
with savages. Furthermore, the Almighty was this
time entirely on the side of the English; for He
caused a wind to blow, one which was any but the
right wind for the manœuvring required by the
Spaniards to gain a satisfactory position in the battle.
The result of this ill wind was the defeat of the great
Armada and the establishment of English sea power.
Things were not going well for the Catholic countries
just then. Cosmic forces were at play, humorously
loading the dice against them, both in the material
and the spiritual sense. Worst of all, the world was
again beginning to think for itself.

§ 3

## THE MACHINE SETS TO WORK

We now come to a phase in human nature which
must be almost as important as those phases which succeeded the discoveries of fire and cereals, the inventions of the wheel, the boat, and even writing itself.
It is the phase in which paper and printing are set to
work. The ultimate effects are impossible to estimate,
but there were certain definite tendencies set in
motion, of which the immediate importance is hardly
in doubt. The first stage of this phase is a popularization of the manufacture of paper. It is not known
who first invented this useful commodity, but we

know that it existed in China in the seventh century of the Christian era; that the Moslems stole the idea from a Mongol prisoner-of-war captured in A.D. 751 at Samarkand; and that in the fourteenth century it had come to Europe through the Arabs and the Greeks and could be made in sufficient quantities for purposes of authorship and the communication or fixation of ideas. It is important to remember this— that paper may fix an idea as well as communicate it. We have already seen how the Chinese mind was " imprisoned " by their writing. Our difficulty is to sort out ideas into those which have been " fixed " on paper, and become almost a part of human nature, from those which are still in a state of flux.

¶ *Sheet-Anchors of Morality*

Johannes Gutenberg, a German scholar of the fifteenth century, was responsible for the invention of printing from movable types, and this simple invention put a light to the torch of the modern world. The invention spread over Europe; it has reached such a stage of perfection in the twentieth century that the printed word is beginning to assume powers formerly vested in priests and kings and great military leaders. At the time of the invention of printing the Bible was the most important book of the West, *The Koran* of the East, and the works of Buddha, Confucius, and Lao-Tsu of the Far East. These contained the moralities which were the great sheet-anchors of human nature. As yet the knowledge contained in them was a vested interest, often of immense material value to rulers, and generally grossly perverted from its original meaning and intention. The "*Love your enemies*" of Jesus became "*Let us smash our enemies*" of the Popes—and remember Urban II's great fighting sermon which started the Crusades. Gutenberg and the admirers of his invention printed the Bible, and copies began to find their way into quarters they had never hitherto penetrated. Then came a period of translation, and the Great Book of the West began to be read by all sorts of people (most of whom had no clear idea of what it was all about), including many who were now confirmed in the suspicions they had been forming regarding its interpretation by those who had " made a corner " in it. It so happened that the invention of printing almost coincided with the revival of Greek learning in the West, and many men were now, like the old Greeks, *discussing everything*. The English reformer, Wycliffe, had already translated the Scriptures into English and spread a number of violently heretical ideas, some of which were taken by a Czech named John Huss and used as a basis for popular teaching. We shall see later the effect of this, but in the meantime the Englishman, Caxton, had gone abroad to take a course of printing craftsmanship and had returned to England in 1477 to found a press. Between that year and 1500, four hundred books were printed in England, and a considerable number of each one issued—" published " to the world. The same sort of thing was happening everywhere. The machine had set to work to diffuse ideas, and there was practically no limit to its work in this respect. Then Tyndale appeared in England. He was a man of great literary genius and indefatigable energy, who brought out a version of the

Bible in a style that immediately found its mark in the hearts of the people who read it. Tyndale was, of course, executed for his work, which was regarded as highly dangerous to all in authority. But the seed was sown, and the authority of the Church was everywhere being challenged. By this time the English (who were never good Roman Catholics) were working out a " liberal " system of parliamentary and legal institutions, and were growing in power. The Church was already a house divided against itself, and there was a growing resentment against the idea of an external sovereignty above that of the King—a foreign sovereignty vested in an Italian sitting at Rome. Furthermore, the English disliked, as they still dislike, rigid systems of morality; they prefer, both as individuals and as a nation, to make their own morals. Yet, it was none of these great tendencies which caused the protests and revolt against Church power, though they provided an excellent atmosphere in which to begin them. King Henry VIII led the revolt to a successful conclusion. Protestantism spread in England, and at Henry's death its adherents were as numerous as the Catholics. A struggle for power began. This meant that whichever side happened at the moment to be in the ascendant would persecute the other party. Protestants sought out, flogged, and executed Catholics; and vice versa. The stake, the execution block, the hangman's noose achieved great popularity. It was a " Golden Age " for State executioners: there were, we are told, seventy-two thousand executions. Sometimes, by way of diversion, a bag of gunpowder would be placed among faggots at the feet of a victim, and cheers

would go up from the English crowd as a limb or a
head was blown sky-high. Bishop Hooper, a Protestant, was so served in the market place of Gloucester
on the 9th of February in the Year of Grace 1555; and
hundreds of others. In 1571 Protestantism was
firmly established in England, and an Act of Parliament bound children above a certain age to receive
the sacrament of Christ in the form prescribed by
Law. Later, a fine of £20 was imposed on all who
failed to go to church.

## ¶ The Germs of Modern Materialism

The Reformation sprang from a general discontent
with the corruption and materialism of Rome—
I use the word materialism in the sense of " a way of
life, opinion, or tendency based entirely on material
interests." In England the teachings of Wycliffe,
the printing-press, and the translation of the Bible
into English were responsible for it. Other countries
affected were France, Germany, Denmark, Prussia,
Sweden, and the Netherlands. Italy was also slightly
affected. The original movement was followed by a
counter-reformation led by the militant Jesuits under
Loyola, a remarkable man of powerful determination
and an amazingly astute knowledge of the hearts of
his fellows. The Jesuits worked by all means in their
power for the re-establishment of Roman authority,
and nearly everywhere with success. They were
great educators and disciplinarians; but their methods
gained them an evil reputation The Scandinavian
countries and a large part of Germany and England
remained unmoved by their efforts. In these countries the reform was consolidated and developed

into a system of Bible-reading in the home. No longer was it found necessary or desirable for biblical interpretation to be the sole preserve of an authoritative Church. Mr. Everyman became his own interpreter. The English Bible became a popular book, a best seller; and the sheet anchor of Anglo-Saxon hypocrisy.

¶ *The Decline of Religious " Conscience "*

The Reformation secularized religious thought, and political thought became secularized at the same time. Religion was no longer the keystone which held together the social edifice. The idea of a spiritual power standing above all others is replaced by economic expediency in the struggle for wealth. And this economic expediency became the arbiter of policy and the criterion of human conduct. " *From a spiritual being, who in order to survive must devote a reasonable attention to economic interests, man seems sometimes to have become an economic animal, who will be prudent, nevertheless, if he takes due precautions to assure his spiritual well-being.*" [1] This marks a distinct change in human nature, for henceforward man develops a dual personality. He begins to dissociate his religious from his secular life. He begins to think of religious duties and observances as something which have nothing whatever to do with his secular existence. And so the " conscience " in human affairs which ruled every act of the Catholic Christians begins to disappear after the Reformation. Henceforward, it is possible for a man who is a member of the reformed religion to devote all his

[1] R. H. Tawney, *Religion and the Rise of Capitalism.*

energy to his material welfare without this interfering with his spiritual ideas, conscience, or other behaviour. The result of the gradual change in the attitude of men began to show itself in the struggle for wealth. It resulted in modern land-grabbing, conquests, slavery, and wars for markets, including the two great World Wars. From it came the modern financial system, with its tyranny and cruelty. All this may, I think, be traced back to the printing-press and to widespread Bible-reading, in which each person developed that form of secular conscience which best suited his worldly interests. We may therefore, mark down the period of two hundred years beginning about 1350 and ending about 1570 as the period in which men's natures showed the most considerable change in modern times. Some may prefer to call it a change of mental attitude rather than an actual change in his nature. But the change is, to my mind, profound.

## § 4

## LIBERTY, EQUALITY, FRATERNITY

We now come to that momentous stage in human affairs: the age of Voltaire, Rousseau, Montesquieu, and other Frenchmen responsible for many changes in the public opinion of Europe and the attitude of Western man towards life. The three men named were responsible on the continent of Europe for instilling into the minds of the masses the pernicious doctrine that they had public *rights* as well as public duties; that religion generally was not what it seemed to be; and that there was such a thing as human reason, which, if only it could be used judiciously, might improve the happiness of mankind. Voltaire is one of the prodigies of all literature. Historian, essayist, pamphleteer, novelist, short-story writer, and philosopher, his influence on the Europe of the eighteenth century was almost freakish. We should not forget that without the printing-press it must have been negligible. The age was one in which men became susceptible to almost any appeal that could be symbolized as " reason." Europeans were becoming tired of the consequences of religion, and by now the printing-press and newspapers were spreading a knowledge of the schisms and sects and squabbles and other frailties that are found in all human doctrines. One of the first works of Voltaire was an appeal for religious toleration. It was so well written that the author became famous immediately, and was everywhere lionized. His satirical wit, brilliant literary style, great sense of irony, and his ability to give a stinging reply to an intellectual opponent soon caused him to be locked up in the Bastille. There he decided that France was not a safe place for him; and so, when released, he went to reside at Ferney on the frontier near Geneva, which could be reached quickly on the first indication of peril. He settled there and began an immense output of works on every conceivable subject; all of them written in his sparkling style, which caused them to be read everywhere. The French of Voltaire is so simple and straightforward that its meaning can be appreciated by a foreign schoolboy who has played with French during three or four years. To the French themselves it is the simplest of the simple; the ideal literary style, rather like the English of the Irishmen Jonathan Swift, Oliver Goldsmith, and George Bernard Shaw. The importance of literary style in such work as Voltaire had undertaken can hardly be over-estimated. For, however good the reasoning, if it were not stated in terms capable of comprehension and even admiration by ordinary men, it could never hope to move masses to action. Voltaire's chief struggle was against the Roman Church, and he dealt it a blow from which it has never since fully recovered. To him it was an infamous institution, and he set up the cry " *Ecrasez l'infâme !* " [1] The French clergy, monks, and nuns, numbered in 1762 over four hundred thousand, with total possessions estimated at two thousand million pounds, producing an annual revenue of about one hundred and forty millions. They were free from taxation, and higher members of the Church possessed all the rights and privileges of the feudal nobility. The Church was the champion of privilege and misgovernment, as in Mexico and Spain in our own times, until attacked by the people. " It was," says Sloane, " the cement of French society to a higher degree than the absolute monarchy."

¶ *Rousseau and Montesquieu*

Almost contemporary with Voltaire was Rousseau, a man of exalted sensibility and active imagination. An early life of misery and suffering made him declare war against the inequalities of society. Relying entirely upon his feelings (which were tinged with much sentimentalism and passion) he attacked nearly all human institutions. A savage, morose, and

[1] " Crush the infamous ! "

speculative man, his appeal was entirely to the sentiments. His style is an exaggerated declamation which, taken in small doses, is stimulating. All Rousseau's teaching was based upon the assumption that *human nature can be moulded by education and environment*. It dismisses heredity and tradition. The way to happiness on this earth, he says in effect, is to have few needs. Unhappiness does not consist in the lack of things, but in an unsatisfied desire for them. Man is not a savage creature, but one that has often grown savage because of the environment of civilization. He is fundamentally a good creature and can, if he but try, make himself and his fellows and descendants perfect by creating good institutions and by developing the goodness that is in him. Happiness should be the end in view of all political and social effort. In other words: constitute man a moral being, and you will make for the excellence of all human nature. Behind all this moralizing was a realistic political doctrine that was to prove far more attractive to men and women: the doctrine of the *sovereignty of the people*, the mild forerunner of what we know as the dictatorship of the proletariat. Such a doctrine challenged all the religious and political dogmas, and was eagerly seized upon for popularization by the followers of the new teacher. Rousseau preached fraternity—almost the same doctrine as that of the Quakers. He firmly believed that man's nature is a thing capable of growth and development; but if it is to be developed in the right direction it must first be thoroughly understood; and if neglected it will grow worse. Harmony based upon the educated will of the mass is what is necessary, he said, for the good of mankind. The emotional teaching of Rousseau was rather vague, apparently inconsistent, and not held together by a very clear logical system of reasoning. This defect was remedied by the third of these great Frenchmen, Montesquieu, in his philosophical work *The Spirit of Laws*, written in 1729. In this work the writer evolved the combination of words—*Liberty, Equality, Fraternity*—that formed the symbol which was to be the battle cry of the Revolution of 1789. He gave first to France the theory of a mixed government, and revealed the principles of a representative system. His work made people think, and, when added to that of Rousseau and Voltaire, was largely responsible for the overthrow of the monarchy, the aristocracy, and the priesthood of France. In every phase of life there were changes during this age. A new architecture, new painting, and a progressive science showed themselves. Literature made astounding progress; natural history for the first time received detailed treatment of a philosophical nature. And yet the King, the Church, and the aristocrats retained their power and continued to grind the faces of the poor. In this atmosphere the French Revolution was born. There is no need to enter into the details of the political squabbles which culminated in the Revolution. Briefly, the monarchy found itself short of money and called a meeting of the nobles, clergy, and Commons in 1789; this body, the " States-General," had been abolished in 1610, when the monarchy became absolute. The gathering gave the common people a means of expressing a long fermenting discontent. The " Third Estate "—the Commons—soon gained control; and the King,

seeing the danger, mobilized troops in the provinces.
This threat of violence sent the whole of France into
open revolution. The monarchy collapsed, and a
government of the people was formed. The King
fled abroad to conspire with aristocrats and monarchies
of other countries; an attempt was made to regain
kingly power. But France showed a mad passion of
" patriotism." A Republic was proclaimed and war
was declared on the aristocrats.

¶ " *Progress* " *based on Cruelty*

The Reign of Terror which followed has been
painted in vivid colours by many writers. But let
us endeavour to look at the aspect of human nature
which especially manifested itself just then. It is
remarkable that there can be no " progress " on this
earth without cruelty. This showed itself in the
architecture of Egypt, built by the labour of hundreds
of thousands of slaves and workmen under the
master's whip. The civilizing influence of Rome was
the result of innumerable wars, and of law based
upon bludgeon rule. The Church of Rome established
itself by the cruel suppression of thought and tried to
conserve its influence by the tortures of the Holy
Inquisition. The Reformation was responsible for
the formation of modern capitalism, of which the first
phase was slavery (to which we shall come soon),
followed by industrialism and finance (to which we
shall come later). Now we see that the French
Revolution, which was largely responsible for the
growth of modern republicanism and democracy, was
achieved by cruelty.

¶ *Dr. Guillotin and his Invention*

A *machine* consisting of men (the outcome of the scientific spirit) began to rule in France. The Constituent Assembly of the people, having declared war upon the aristocrats, looked around for a convenient method of exterminating them. Before that time undesirable persons had been hanged, broken on the wheel, boiled, or incinerated; but the Assembly consisted of a large number of humane-minded men who were unwilling that unnecessary pain should be inflicted. They had misgivings about the various popular methods of official killing, and had well-grounded reasons for believing that they were not as merciful as they might be. Headsmen operating with axe or sword would not be immune from human fallibility; and hanging required far too much skill, and wasted much valuable time—it may take an hour to hang a man to death, as English law admits. In seasons of perplexity in human affairs someone usually comes forward with a remedy which seems to offer a solution of the difficulties. A great philanthropist and humanitarian, Dr. Guillotin, concentrated his intellect upon the problem of how most quickly and most humanely to dispose of the unwanted. He studied old records and read that the Chinese had used an instrument which contained elements of great utility. He found that this machine had been used with success by a highly civilized and, indeed, humane people—the English—in the form of a gibbet at Halifax. The same implement, he discovered, was in contemporaneous use by certain of the more enlightened German States. He consulted the celebrated Charles Henri Sanson, high priest of French executioners, and this quick-witted man showed favour for the machine. A model was built and experiments were made decapitating sheep. The model proved its efficiency. Dr. Guillotin gave a report of the invention which his genius had plagiarized, and the delighted Assembly decided that thenceforward it should be used for executions. Legislation was introduced, and so the mechanical decapitator constructed by Dr. Guillotin was destined to immortalize the good man's name. His machine was so excellent that it is still in use in France for public executions, which are well patronized by the people. They were often so popular that cavalry has been used to keep the crowds of spectators in order.

At first the change was not pleasing to the people. The instrument, it would appear, did not kill, in the sense that hanging kills. It suppressed. It was far too rapid in its action to provide really popular enjoyment. After those early guillotinings the crowds dispersed singing:

> Give us back our wooden gallows;
> Give us back our gallows.

Dr. Guillotin and his friends were hurt to think that they had not scored a success with the mob. How annoying that this swift, hygienic, and polite instrument—the culmination of man's mechanical ingenuity at an opportune moment—should not be immediately appreciated! Never mind. A little patience and——! In the Place de Grave in Paris the guillotine was first set up in France. To this point the executioner came every day, his umbrella under his arm. There he removed his hat and coat, rolled up his sleeves, and set his machine in motion. Soon he developed an artistic pride in the work. As he became more accustomed to the mechanism, speed increased. It was found, to the delight of those in power, that if an isolated guillotining was æsthetically unsatisfying, a day's work at it could provide excellent entertainment for the mob. Think of the thrills— each one depending upon the character and reputation of the person to be decapitated, and therefore different from the last. It was ideal.

When the extermination of the aristrocrats began in earnest, the " Widow " (as the guillotine was familiarly called) became the centre of social attraction. In the midst of a wave of fanaticism, to the cry of " *Liberty, Equality, Fraternity*," the rhythmic music of the rising and falling blade rendered a sweet accompaniment. Aristocrats were brought to it in carts. Later the machine was moved to the Place du Trône, where prisoners had their heads swiftly removed in batches.

Gradually, we are informed, the Quartier Saint-Honoré wearied of the spectacle that was presented day after day. The carts of condemned completely ruined business at certain hours. When a procession approached, the shops had to be shut and the streets abandoned to the mob. First hawkers would appear, circulating the freshly-printed list of victims, whereupon the bystanders gathered into groups and posted themselves before the house-fronts, shouting ribaldries or singing revolutionary choruses. The upper windows were filled with onlookers. Suddenly the cry went up, " Here they come! " The lines of the

Grand Avenue of the Tuileries were strangely broken by the spectacle of the guillotine, while the soil surrounding it was always saturated with blood to such a degree that the footprints of those who crossed the square could be traced to a considerable distance— as far as the pavement of the Rue de Bourgogne— and this, it seems, was not regarded as an attraction by the inhabitants of the district. A hole measuring " about six cubic feet " was dug underneath the platform to take the blood, and also the water with which the engine was frequently washed. But this trench was quickly filled and began to poison the surrounding air to such an extent that the authorities, in the interests of public health, decided to fill it up and make another deep enough to absorb the blood. Between the 6th of April, 1793, and the 29th of July, 1795, Dr. Guillotin's great machine had severed two thousand eight hundred and thirty-one heads, and the inspiration behind this activity was the cause of *Liberty*, *Equality*, and *Fraternity*, which had been preached by those two humanitarians, Rousseau and Montesquieu. Danton excused himself for it all by saying: " The Revolutionary Tribunal! I ask forgiveness for it from God and men." Saint-Just wisely remarked: " *The experience of the Terror dulled the sense of crime, as strong liquors dull the palate.*"

An impetus was given to the use of the mind; the guillotine sharpened the wits of men. In England, in 1796, William Godwin published his book *Political Justice*, the pioneering work on Anarchism. The resultant " Gospel of Democracy " reached far outside the borders of France, although there was little immediate Liberty or Equality and still less Fraternity.

Nevertheless, the idea caught on in many countries, and those which were not prepared to put it into practice were forced in time to render lip service to it. Aristocrats everywhere grew less domineering, and the priest for a while ceased from interfering in political matters.

## § 5

## GOD IS GOD, BUT BUSINESS IS BUSINESS

We have seen that the most profound change in human nature produced by the vagaries of religion during the Reformation and afterwards was a division of the mind of man into two separate compartments. The spiritual life was now a thing which he no longer intermixed with common and sordid affairs of every-day, as he had done hitherto from time immemorial. The division between the two was not at first sharp: the change was a gradual one from the domination of human nature by God and priest during seven days of the week to that stage when one day was considered sufficient. The date at which this great change took place was between 1550 and 1750; for historical convenience we may put it down as about 1650. From that time the Western world began to act on the principle that, whereas the worship of God and a strict observance of religious morality may be excellent things, they need not interfere greatly with the general tenor of one's way, provided always one solemnizes religion in certain seasons or on occasion. " God is God, but, after all, Business is Business," was the feeling that was steadily growing among trading peoples. I propose to demonstrate the truth of this by dealing summarily with the history of the slave trade—a phase of history which also illustrates a few further truths.

¶ *Christianity and Slavery*

Slavery has existed from the beginning of man's records. It has existed because of the great conveniences and facilities it offers to the happiness of certain human beings and communities; it still exists in a surprisingly large number of places; and will probably continue to exist somewhere for a very long time. By slavery I do not mean the " wage-slavery " which in modern capitalist States has taken the place of actual ownership, but that system by which the slave-owner possesses the slave against the world, as he might possess a horse or a cow, and by which he can sell his slave or make him work in return for food and shelter, just as he can make a horse or donkey work, or sell him or her to the highest bidder and make profitable commerce when this course seems the more lucrative. In real slavery the owner has also the right to recapture his slave, and may call upon the State to help him. One might imagine that Christianity ought to have put an end to the vast system of slavery which contributed to the comfort and wealth of the Roman Empire. But there was not a word in early Christian literature to encourage the manumission of slaves : St. Paul had recognized the position of the master; and that was good enough. Nor do we find any condemnation of the institution anywhere in the writings of the Fathers. The Church itself owned slaves, and we find that the Council of Toledo in A.D. 597 stigmatized as *robbers* those who set free the slaves of the Church without giving an equivalent. The Council of Epaeone, A.D. 517, prohibited abbots from emancipating the slaves of their monasteries. Slaves were bequeathed to the Church by will, or given as an act of piety; and seldom if ever was a gift refused. The Church, too, held its own slaves to the very end. Voltaire estimated that in his day the Church still possessed between fifty and sixty thousand of them.[1]

¶ *The first Big Business*

The modern capitalist world, with an eye to business on a scale that was lacking among our pagan and barbarian forbears, made the slave trade into Big Business—the first really Big Business in the world. It was the Christian peoples of Europe and America who first fully appreciated the cash value of human cattle and the compound profits that could, with a minimum of care, be drawn from a commerce of buying and selling members of races inferior in war and culture. With the Greeks and Romans the slave was, on the whole, well treated and often had more personal freedom than the modern industrialist will give his employees in working hours. Roman law provided for the freeing of slaves, many of whom reached high and responsible positions in society; indeed, there was little stigma attaching to being a Greek or Roman slave, for such a position nearly always resulted from capture in battle or otherwise as a prize of war. The benevolence of Greeks and Romans towards their slaves seems nauseating sentimentalism when we

[1] Chapman Cohen, *Christianity and Slavery*.

compare the sterner and saner attitude adopted by civilized modern Europe and America. For us the slave became a commodity which brought cash. Out of slavery grew business on a scale which laid the foundations of the wealth of England, U.S.A., and, to a lesser degree, other countries, because they did not possess our commercial acumen.

¶ *Progress through Bloodshed*

Notwithstanding the wealth that was being drawn to England by the pursuit of slave-trading and slavery, it was a decision of a British Court of Law which first sent through the world the moral influence which ended in the emancipation of great masses of slaves. It took this moral influence sixty-two years to ripen in England, for it was not until 1834 that slavery was abolished by law throughout the British Empire. America tends, they say, to be slower than Europe in an appreciation of the finer shades of morality where morality touches the pocket, as it did in this slave question; and a terrible war was necessary to enforce it. Twenty-eight years later, after a bitter struggle, and about an issue which now seems to us to be in a moral sense ridiculously simple, Abraham Lincoln achieved fame by giving negroes in the States their freedom. Seldom in human history had there been a greater gesture, when we consider the material interests which it flaunted. Lincoln paid the almost inevitable penalty which follows those who attempt to free either the body or the mind of old and lucrative shackles. On the 15th of April, 1865, he was despatched from further pernicious educational activities by the bullet of an assassin. Had Lincoln and his spirit lived, it is doubtful if American prosperity could have advanced so rapidly; but the soul of a nation might have been preserved.

The period between Lincoln and the League of Nations' decision of 1925 favouring the abolition of slavery " in all its forms " is notable for struggles by backward races in all parts of the world to achieve their freedom. America was not last in the race. In Putomayo, where man treated his fellow-man worse than he has ever treated brute beasts, and in the Congo, where, under Belgian supervision, about *five million* negroes disappeared as a result of the unparalleled cruelty of profiteering taskmasters, we have almost contemporary record of the degradation to which commercialized human nature is capable of descending in the twentieth century. In 1924 the Maharaja of Nepal denounced in his neighbourhood an institution which, though shorn of Western refinements, was but a form of slavery. And so the struggle for *Liberty, Equality, Fraternity*, still continues. It may come as a surprise to many that, notwithstanding the work of the three great emancipators, Wilberforce, Lincoln, and the Maharaja of Nepal, slavery and slave-trading with all its amenities still exist in parts of Abyssinia, Algeria, China, Egypt, Eritrea, the Far East, the Hedjaz, Kufra, Liberia, Morocco, South Morocco, Rio de Oro, East Sahara, West Sahara, Somaliland, French and Italian Sudan, and South Tripoli. It is practised openly in several Mahomedan States in Asia, the Arabian Peninsula, and the Hedjaz. In a veiled form it still exists in so many places that a list would merely bore the reader, who may remember a recent Sierra Leone scandal.

## ¶ *Value of Money*

It is a maxim of modern capitalism to pay the minimum of cost consistent with maintaining the efficiency of an article or a piece of work. This principle has remained unchanged in the whole history of the race. He who pays more than is necessary is regarded by his fellow-men and women as an imbecile; and he who gets the best result with the minimum of expenditure is regarded as a genius. By employing slaves dominant human beings have been able to obtain services for the bare cost of physical support, and in countries rich in agricultural produce the cost of nutriment is very low, almost negligible in some cases. Add to this a healthy climate, and human effort is obtainable with hardly any expenditure; for clothing and shelter are then requisite only in certain seasons of the year. No further details are necessary to explain the origin of slavery, except that slave owners must always have behind them law and a military or some other force strong enough to keep slaves in order or to exterminate them should rebellion or other unfortunate contingencies necessitate this most regrettable loss. Men and women who have failed to perfect their powers of resistance, whether these powers be psychological or military, have always fallen victims to their more powerful neighbours; hence slavery, ancient and modern. All this is the ABC of human nature, and although the manner of application and the customs that go with it may have changed on the surface, it is still true in most parts of the world. Selfishness and greed again are the driving impulses of the conquerors.

To the modern phase of slavery, which itself was part and parcel of the " God is God, but Business is Business " idea and to the French " *Liberty, Equality, Fraternity* " movement, we may trace those great differences between human nature as it is today and as it was a thousand years ago. We find now a cynical business morality which (especially in America) is often closely escorted by pseudo-religion. Alongside of this we find that there are innumerable humanitarian impulses, which spring from the soul's reaction against the cruelties of the slave trade and its legitimate child, modern industrialism. Cruelty disappears gradually from the individual, who holds his head in the air and becomes ashamed to beat a naughty child or ill-treat a dog. But nations still go to war on trivial excuses, prompted by commercial greed; and then we see the vilest qualities of human nature mobilized by an appeal to our baser feelings and stimulated by poster and cinema, sermon and pamphlet, book and newspaper. The machine exerts its mighty power and then—poor humanity goes back to the jungle.

§ 6

## WAR AND THE IDEALISM OF NAPOLEON

We come now to a man who may almost be called a modern Codifier of Morality, one whose nature differed from that of his great predecessors, but whose effect upon the world has been great and whose idealism is still with us, although in a slightly modified and improved form. In the year 1769 there was born in Corsica an important child, Napoleon Buonaparte.

A clever, hot-tempered, and autocratic boy, with a prodigious memory and a bent for mathematics, his qualities and ambitions turned towards a military career. Young Napoleon had read Rousseau and other writers of the revolutionary period and, like many great men, his early ideas ran to extremes. Glancing at Europe, he saw the Holy Roman Empire tottering, while France was becoming a great political Power. He conceived a magnificent idea: to replace the old Roman Empire with one whose headquarters he would establish in Paris.

About this time there was a reaction against the doctrines and general activities of the revolutionaries. The young artillery officer had the good luck to be in Paris at a moment when the Royalists and aristocrats in 1795 made their last attempt to snatch power from the Revolutionary Government. The services of Napoleon were enlisted by the Government, and there is no doubt but that his military skill was the means of saving the Republic. Delighted with the ability of the brilliant young officer, members of the Government arranged that he should be given promotion, so in 1796 he was appointed to the command of the army which had been created to make an attack upon Northern Italy. He wrote home that he intended to exact twenty million francs from the Italians, and, like the old Roman generals, he held before his soldiers the prospects of honour, glory, and loot. In his imagination he saw himself the leader of a French campaign which would make the French the most powerful nation in the world. He won his first war brilliantly, and imposed a peace which had in it vigorous germs of further wars. He then persuaded the Government to allow him to attempt the capture of Egypt; in this he succeeded, but after he had landed, his fleet was destroyed by the British at the memorable battle of the Nile. He was thus completely isolated. The Turks gathered against him, but he defeated them at Jaffa and butchered the prisoners taken by his army. By another of those strokes of chance (by which so many military campaigns are won) the cutting off and isolation of Napoleon prevented the people at home from knowing what was happening. Affairs were not going well in Paris. There was a severe financial crisis. Meanwhile, Napoleon slipped through the British fleet and landed in France. He was the " strong man " who was required at the moment. A conspiracy placed the Corsican in the chief executive position. A new constitution was drawn up and submitted to the country. It was couched in terms favourable to Napoleon, and when the nation accepted it, France had completely placed herself in his hands. Five years later he was crowned Emperor by the Pope.

¶ *Napoleon Converted to Religion*

Napoleon was a close student of human nature, and he had formed in his mind the lowest possible estimate of it. He saw that man can be happy with religion, so he made a cunning pact with Rome. He would restore the authority of the priest in the parishes, and so make the people more manageable; for he believed that there is nothing better than religion to keep the masses quiet, so long as it is on your side. The Emperor became a Christian teacher. " It is my wish," he said, " to re-establish foreign Christian missions, for missionaries may be very useful to me as spies in all the lands they visit, in Asia, Africa, and America. They will be protected by the sanctity of their dress, which will serve to conceal their political and commercial investigations. The head of the missionary establishment shall be in Paris and not in Rome." In matters of education he was also astute. Realizing that the great educative scheme (drafted by the revolutionary Condorcet in the Age of Reason to provide for a system of free education for the entire nation) would tend to develop the minds of men, and perhaps even make them think, the course before him was clear. Elementary education must be completely neglected or encouraged as little as political expediency would permit. With regard to women he found education entirely unnecessary; their job was knitting. In a Code of Laws he fixed the status of the workers and peasants as well as that of the women: all of them were placed on a basis which would leave them entirely at his disposal—for war or for peace.

The English navy caused the downfall of Napoleon, first by an indirect influence, and afterwards by a direct one. It treated as contraband of war all articles of foreign commerce attempting to enter the French Empire or belonging to Napoleon's allies. The selfish Russians, in the face of this threat to their trade, broke their alliance with France in 1807. Five years later Napoleon entered Russia with an army of six hundred thousand. After one great defeat the Russians refused to fight a pitched battle, but instead they devastated their country before the invader, removed all supplies of food, and proceeded to harass the

French army from all sides. They repeated the tactics of Fabius in the Punic War. When the French reached Moscow in the middle of summer, their spirit was broken; after the one battle they had lost as many men as their enemies. The Russians, rather than permit the French a comfortable occupation of their capital, resolved to burn it; much of the city was destroyed and still in conflagration when the French arrived. Napoleon decided to retreat, and made his way back to France, arriving with scarcely more than twenty thousand men. Over half a million souls of French nationality, and perhaps half as many again of Russian, not to speak of the material damage to property, perished as the result of Napoleon's fit of pique with the Tsar for having broken an unprofitable alliance. This is an excellent example of how the mere splenetic whim of a man with power may control to the point of death the destiny of hosts of his fellow-creatures.

France, though weary and disappointed with the Russian adventure, had not entirely lost confidence in her Empire. A new army was created from what remained. It was necessary, because the English, with their genius for diplomacy, had begun to organize alliances against the Napoleonic threat to their existence. The moment was ripe for such alliances, and they quickly came. In 1814 Austrians, Prussians, Russians, and Swedes crossed the Rhine; from the south came British and Spanish troops to join them. Napoleon was defeated and abdicated. The victories restored the old monarchy in the person of Louis XVIII, and Napoleon was exiled to Elba in the Mediterranean, where he was permitted to retain his imperial title. But this strong-minded man was not prepared to sit down under defeat. In less than a year he escaped, and was trumpeting to the French his promises of Liberty and Freedom—always an excellent slogan. He promised to renounce adventurous wars and to rule constitutionally. Such was his influence over the French mind, which was still smarting from defeats, that the public was once more prepared to support the skilful military adventurer. Napoleon raised an army from the exhausted country. This last rather miserable force was just defeated by the British and Prussians at the battle of Waterloo in 1815. Its leader was exiled to the little island of St. Helena, and remained there trying to live down a bad conscience, until he died in 1821.

¶ *Always Deliver some Goods*

The life and career of Napoleon in themselves provide the student of human nature with ample material for a treatise. The first lesson they emphasize is the practicability of the doctrines of Machiavelli and the idea that what counts for most in the overcoming and governance of nations is brute force. Also, that if you wish to rule men and to be supreme you must keep them from thinking too much; or give them something unimportant to think about. You must provide them with something—religion will do very well— which will satisfy the spiritual side of their nature; and you must provide them with bread and circuses. (Here the reader should compare these political tactics with those of Kemal Attatürk, Adolf Hitler, Benito Mussolini, and other modern Dictators.) It is necessary to create the illusion of a possession of some great ability or power in the " leader " such as is not possessed by ordinary people, and it is necessary to do this *continuously* by means of propaganda. It is also necessary at times to " deliver the goods." Much more may be promised than can possibly be delivered; for it is only those hostile in spirit who remember unfulfilled promises of a ruler or politician. He is forgiven many sins if he delivers something or other and takes care to work in the right atmosphere, which itself can often be created. Napoleon had amazing powers of organization and he laid the basis of modern propaganda; for which see Book I, to refresh the memory as to the meaning of propaganda in war-time.

If we are to sum up Napoleon's greatest contribution to human progress, we may say that it was towards the perfection of the science (or art, I never know which it is) of war—that is to say, he laid the foundations for really thorough-going slaughter, as we now understand it. After him we look, in time of war, for the organization of the entire resources of each nation. After him we regard as quite natural that modern spirit in which every able-bodied man must be prepared to throw his bomb and every woman to make it. Every female must be prepared to make clothes, poison gas, high explosives, ammunition, or other supplies for the males who are fighting. Or she must lend her tender care in nursing them when they are wounded, and use her influence to send them back to be targets for bullet and shell and shrapnel and flame-throwers, etc., etc., until such moment as they are stuck by a bayonet, blown to smithereens, or rendered a burden to themselves, their friends, and their country.

¶ *War and Human Nature*

To discuss the effects of modern war upon the development of human nature is a task which must be left to posterity. If we take the mere slaughter itself, the mind and heart recoil in dismay. The loss of life occasioned affords an excellent standard whereby to measure both human wickedness and human greatness. It shows to what extent desire to do evil or enthusiasm in support of a " cause " may counterbalance the instinct of self-preservation. Then consider the wounded—and those who are not actually wounded, but whose nature has undergone a complete change. Of eight thousand defenders left in Port Arthur at the time of its capitulation, for example, no less than two thousand were found to be suffering from neurasthenia; and there is no doubt that a certain proportion of them never fully recovered their normal capacity for work. But this is not all. Men who have been fighting for a long time become so accustomed to adventure that they find it difficult to readapt themselves to ordinary life. Richet says that we may estimate at approximately three million the number of French lives sacrificed for the gratification of the insensate pride of Napoleon. Fröhlich, who gives a detailed and reasoned statement, estimates the figure at 5,925,084. In the American Civil War, the dead numbered not far short of a million men, and in our own 1914–18 World War there were ten million dead, according to Westergaard; seven million killed and three million who perished by disease. The world accepts war as inevitable; and makes its preparations accordingly. It is a disease of man for which no cure has yet been found. Treaties and pacts are signed from time to time to put off the evil day. Sooner or later it comes. Then we all of us go back to the jungle, and he or she who will not move with the herd must be prepared to be crushed or (if the herd so wishes) exterminated. The idealism of Napoleon was, like the idealism of Buddha or Jesus or the other Great Codifiers of Morality, by no means original. But in it he crystallized a host of hitherto vague moral ideas and transmitted them to us in a form easy of assimilation. The spiritual receptivity of the human soul has done the rest.

## § 7

## THE AGE OF PROGRESS

Nations now begin to hate each other more thoroughly than ever; the bogy of the modern world has come into existence. It was not until the end of the eighteenth century and the beginning of the nineteenth that the work of Roger Bacon (and his namesake, Francis Bacon Lord Verulam), made its influence on the intellectual development of mankind thoroughly felt. The Renaissance had swept across the world a thirst for knowledge, and the French revolutionary thinkers made men concentrate upon the use of " pure reason." In 1795, when the Terror had almost expended itself in France, the Englishman, James Watt, made the first practical steam engine. It was used for driving machinery, and the first engine so employed was installed in a mill at Nottingham in the same year. The first locomotive appeared in 1804; in 1830 Stephenson's " Rocket " was put on rails between Liverpool and Manchester to race along

H

at over forty miles an hour. The printing-press of the fifteenth century had shown how a machine could change human nature. But here was something different, with a power external to man behind it. Great *external power*—something extraneous: this was to be the new and terrible factor in forming our nature. From the moment of its discovery there began a quest for more and still more power, and this quest ever continues. Faraday's discovery of electromagnetic rotation in 1821 added immeasurably to this external power, and the internal-combustion engine of the latter part of the nineteenth century still further. A great era of mechanical invention began, and new machines appeared in every direction; machines which would tend to eliminate the personal factor from the making of articles for trade.

¶ *The New Code of Ethics*

It is unnecessary to go into details of the application of electricity to the telegraph, to the telephone, and wireless. Nor is it necessary to mention the thousand and one advances in mechanical powers that took place during the nineteenth century. The prophecy of Aristotle that machines would abolish slavery showed signs of fulfilling itself. As it happened, slavery was being abolished for other reasons. Now a new and equally unpleasant form of slavery showed itself. Men became slaves to machines, and to industrial capitalism. In England, France, Germany, and in the United States, factories sprang up on all sides, but this industrial movement was quicker in England than elsewhere. New types of human beings were created. A new type of *Homo sapiens* appeared:

the man who used his money to employ large numbers of other men in the production of goods by machinery. These goods were eagerly bought by the rest of the world, and England began to be a moneyed nation, *a new code of ethics springing from financial power*. Human power was being substituted everywhere by machine power, and the drudgery of human labour was not required so much. What was now needed was men with a little mechanical aptitude and a little intelligence who could be trusted diligently to look after the simple operations of the producing machinery. A slightly higher standard of intelligence and education was required of these machine-minders; but not too much, for that would be dangerous. The second half of the nineteenth century showed an extraordinary advance in the elementary education of the masses throughout most of Western civilization. The printing-press, now with power behind it, the increase in wealth, and a general feeling that education was a good thing, caused working classes to thirst after what knowledge existed.

¶ *Socialism Appears*

The characteristic of the industrial revolution which resulted from the mechanical revolution was in the creation of large masses of men who were driven into factories by the necessity for earning a living. Wage-slavery and machine-slavery took the place of the other old form, which was now in its last phase. Slums arose in the neighbourhood of factories, mines and workshops. Those men who, in the beginning of the nineteenth century, had received favours from Heaven in the form of wealth from slave-trading and other profitable activities, now put their wealth at the disposal of the factory system because it promised to create still more wealth. Greed and cupidity increased enormously among the already rich. An English cotton manufacturer named Robert Owen saw the demoralization and degradation that were fast spreading among the workers in the factories. " Bad and unwise as American slavery was," he says, " the white slavery of the manufacturers of England was at this unrestrained period far worse than that of the slaves whom I afterwards saw in the West Indies and the United States; and in many respects, as regards health, food, and clothing, the latter were much better provided for than the oppressed and degraded workpeople in the manufactories of Great Britain." There was with Robert Owen a number of other men who wanted social " uplift " for the wage-slaves and a change in the system which created wage-slavery. This movement was the germ of modern Socialism, the force that emerged as Communism to combat extreme Capitalism, resulting from the causes already outlined: the Reformation, the wealth created by slave-trading, plunder, conquest, and the mechanical and industrial revolution. About this time—that is to say, in the eighteen thirties—the agitation of Socialists caused an inquiry to be made into the factory system. Its report states that, among other things, the manufacturers employed children down to those of five years of age for working days of fourteen to sixteen hours, exclusive of meals and intervals. Many of the manufacturers employed overseers to flog and ill-treat the infants with a view to speeding up their energy and output. In England there were many scenes similar to those previously common in America. A Scottish Presbyterian manufacturer on horseback chased a runaway bad boy sixteen years old, forcing him to return to his work as fast as the horse trotted, while the good Presbyterian beat him soundly the whole way with a whip. Although wealth was pouring into Britain at that period, the greed of the capitalists was merely being whetted. A higher output was required. That good old driving force of human nature—selfishness—into which we inquired in the first pages of this book, showed itself to be stronger than ever. The enlightenment and philosophic perceptions of a few employers were turned upon the important problem of how to increase output still further, and so a system of night shifts was invented; two sets of operatives were employed, each numerous enough to fill the whole mill; one set worked by day and the other by night. The nervous system of the working classes was steadily undermined by all this drive, for about *two thirds* of the employees were young persons and children.

¶ *The Wealth-is-Power Idea*

In such circumstances as this the human being invariably has recourse to some form of psychological compensation. The Reformation had killed the Catholic Church (or almost killed it) in England, and the new religions were pale reflections of the old, and had few sensual attractions. Workers therefore began to find compensation in alcohol and vice. With each new invention that came along work became more and more simplified, and here and there, with the installation of new devices, large numbers of men were thrown into unemployment. To add still further to the complexities of the situation, the population of now unnecessary creatures steadily increased. Masses were toiling for wages representing bare subsistence, and at the same time the riches of capitalist manufacturers steadily increased. Land-owning aristocracy was replaced by capitalist aristocracy. Morals and manners based upon the sublime ownership of real property began to go, and the process which started in England spread itself throughout the world, in some countries more quickly than others. Everywhere the phenomena of the first phase were the same: in each country those with wealth did their utmost to increase it by compelling the workers to labour for long hours at the lowest possible wages. The internal history of all countries that have been affected by industrialism— that is to say, the principal countries of the world— is since that day a struggle between employers and their workpeople, and it is based purely and simply upon the selfishness of both parties. The workers are selfish in wishing to live comfortably; the others are selfish in wishing to pile up wealth for the sake of the material comforts it gives and because of the power with which it provides them over those who do not possess it. *Wealth-is-power* was the basis of the new ethic.

## ¶ *The New Framework for Human Affairs*

Towards the end of the nineteenth century there was an interesting development in the history of invention; the internal-combustion engine came on the market. The chief advantage of this over the steam engine is that it reduces weight enormously. It developed at last to such a pitch of lightness and efficiency as to bring flying within the bounds of practical achievement. There is no doubt but that the nineteenth century saw an entire change in the attitude of man towards the world and the universe. Hitherto, he had lived close to the soil, and was to all intents and purposes little in advance of the Roman, the Greek, the Egyptian, or the agricultural and pastoral man of prehistoric times.

The nineteenth century saw many lesser changes in the behaviour of human beings towards one another; they reflect minor and superficial changes in a man's nature.

Now nearly everybody was semi-educated, which they thought was better than not being educated. In Protestant countries everybody settled down to the fixed idea that the advances in science and material wealth meant that God had definitely taken their side against the Roman Catholics. Human nature became sure of itself, certain that all problems spiritual had long been solved and that the material ones were panning out satisfactorily. And, with all this the world had not yet lost its pleasing old simplicity, its old politeness, or its old credulity. Did not Miss Mackay see a mermaid in 1809? And did not the Rev. Dr. Philip write in the *Gentleman's Magazine* of July, 1822:

I have today seen a mermaid now exhibiting in this town. The head is almost the size of that of a baboon. . . . The ears, nose, lips, chin, breasts, nipples, fingers, and nails, resemble those of a human figure. The appearance of the teeth affords sufficient evidence that it is full-grown. The canine teeth resemble those of a full-grown dog; all the others resembling those of a human subject. . . . The resemblance to the human species ceases immediately under the mammæ . . . below the vertex of the head it resembles a large fish of the salmon species.

The smugness, credulity, and greed of that age were such that one bold fellow offered to let the world know of a discovery of his which would, no doubt, have made many fortunes. An advertisement appeared offering the secret of perpetual motion for the sum of £300,000. This was the romantic age of Joanna Southcott, who ushered in the Millennium, offered to chain down the devil for a thousand years and to save the faithful (exactly 144,000 all told); she was, she said, "*The Bride, the Lamb's wife, the woman clothed with the sun.*" She announced that at the age of sixty-four she would bear a son, the second Messiah. Thousands believed her. On nearing that age she shut herself up, and when, on the testimony of women and doctors, she was found to be pregnant with a living child, the doubters began to look solemnly at each other. She showed all the symptoms of gestation. Money was raised for this most important accouchement. The crib alone cost £200 and a silver cup was got ready with the words "*Hail, Messiah, Prince of Salem!*" engraved upon it. At last, when the normal period had elasped, she fell into the conventional pains and movements which precede the delivery of a new human being. But no child came. Joanna died. A *post-mortem* examination showed that she had suffered merely from an excess of wind.

¶ *The Century of " ISMS " and " OLOGIES "*

Against religious eccentricities there arose a characteristic growth of the nineteenth century: Secularism, under the leadership of Holyoake in England and of Ingersoll in America. The teachings of the Secularists were a revised version of those of Voltaire, and they provided many vigorous germs to help in the decay of religion in England; their effect in America has so far not been great. This nineteenth century is the century of " ISMS ": Socialism, Secularism, Vegetarianism, Utilitarianism, Spiritualism, Fenianism, Salvationism, Nihilism, Æstheticism, Fabianism, Liberalism, Radicalism, Capitalism, Communism, Anarchism, Mesmerism; and a host of others, not to mention another host, almost as great, of " OLOGIES." The two " ISMS " of foremost importance to the subsequent trend of events were Socialism and Finance-Capitalism. There are as many definitions of Socialism as there are disciples. George Bernard Shaw, for instance, bases his Socialism upon equality of income. He says, in effect, " Let all men and women have the same income and all our troubles will vanish." There was a time when Socialism was a force to be regarded as a revolutionary one, but its place has been taken by militant Communism. Western civilization seems to have taken the Socialistic ideas most consistent with the preservation of wealth and industrialism, and used them in the education of masses for machine-minding or other productive work. A European Socialist is now often a hypocritical capitalist, especially in England. Of all the brands of Socialism which came into existence during the nineteenth century, none was to have so much influence as that of the German, Karl Marx, whose powerful book became the Bible of modern Communists. His slogan was, " Workers of the world, unite "—that is, against Capitalism. Marx's book *Capital* was largely responsible for the growth of international thought among workers in different countries during this period. There was an exchange of the thought representing the interests of wage-slaves. Such a thing had never before taken place. It was to result in Bolshevik Russia in the twentieth century, one of the most powerful and, so far as one can judge, one of the most far-reaching movements in history.

We see in the nineteenth century the triumph of nationality. It was now that the nations of Europe, following the example of France, developed their nationalism to a great intensity. Meanwhile the two most momentous events of modern times took place: the expansion of England into the British Empire, and the strengthening of the Union in America after the Civil War of 1861–65. For the results of the latter we have the modern United States; and the words United States are the modern equivalent for supreme efficiency in business and finance. Here a new idealism came into being, based upon wealth. The word " Success " took on a new meaning. The most successful man is he who collects the largest quantity of worldly wealth; the most successful nation is that which has most gold. Land is no longer of so much importance; its place has been taken by machine-made wealth. With this idealism, having wealth as its goal, there grew a strong quasi-religious sentimentalism, which is its psychological compensation. This sentimentalism showed itself in a thousand welfare schemes and movements of a highly humanitarian and genuinely beneficial nature. The standard of comfort of the ordinary human being, as a result of the search for wealth with its parallel creed of humane sentimentalism, stands higher in the United States of America than in any other country in the whole of human history. America has contributed most towards raising the standard of living of the modern human being.

¶ *Man Decides that he is a Kind of Ape*

I will mention only three further notable and characteristic achievements of the nineteenth century, where one could mention a thousand. The first of these was the publication of Charles Darwin's *Origin of Species* in 1859, the book which stated a theory of life-development by natural selection—that is, by the strong overcoming the weak and the subsequent " survival of the fittest." Another idea propounded by Darwin was to the effect that man is related to the great apes, and this was regarded as highly ingenious and original. The second of these three achievements of the nineteenth century was the proclamation in 1870 of the Infallibility of the Pope in matters of faith and morals, a matter which had long been in abeyance and doubt, but was thus settled for ever. The third was a mechanical invention of the great English executioner, Mr. Marwood, for the more efficient hanging of criminals. It is rather surprising and pitiful that it came so late, for in his time there were only a few crimes involving the Death Penalty, as against the hundred and fifty of a century earlier. Mr. Marwood proved himself to be a master of the hangman's great art. He it was who introduced the humanitarian long drop, which, he claimed, instead of asphyxiating his clients, simply broke their necks. This method is still used in England, though nobody knows if it lives up to the claims made for it, because the new hypocrisy insists upon secret executions. The great inventor was fond of saying of his predecessor in regard to the State-killing of undesirables, " Whereas he *hanged* them, I *execute* them." Those words succinctly and metaphorically express the progress of the century in every direction. Perhaps I should also mention that the science of official killing was not without advances in other countries, for a few years after the establishment in Boston, U.S.A., of the first branch of the Society for the Prevention of Cruelty to Animals, the State of New York, taking advantage of a means to popularize electric power, decided to kill its criminals by electrocution.

What with war, invention, industrialism, the abolition of the bad old slavery and its substitution by capitalist wage-slavery, the ISMS and OLOGIES of later years, the inculcation of white culture into black races during the scramble for Africa, and the transformation of man the agriculturist into man the machine-minder over an important part of the globe, there was a great change in human nature in this period. It all pointed in one direction: the superficial standardization of human nature, much of which may be directly attributable to the influence of the machine, which already seemed to take a grip on the " souls " of men and women in many parts of the Western world.

# BOOK V: HUMAN NATURE TODAY AND TOMORROW

## § 1

## ETERNAL FRAILTIES OF HUMAN NATURE

HUMAN nature has as many varieties and shades as there are men and women. Nevertheless, there are such things as trends and tendencies, and one must somehow grapple with them. Clearly the nineteenth century was the one which contained the greatest possibilities for change in the world, for had there not been two great revolutions?—the industrial and the mechanical. It was yet a little early for the machine to have any great standardizing effects; but the germs were there, and already in the first days of the twentieth century the disease had begun to show itself on all sides. The invention of the linotype printing machine gave an immediate impetus to newspaper production, and men of genius—the late Lord Northcliffe, for example—were not slow to take advantage of it. Elementary Education Acts in England and their equivalent in other parts of the world were producing a more enlightened person—one who could read news items and simply written articles on matters that were not too intellectual: crime, sport, sex, and so forth. The circulation of newspapers, books, novelettes, and periodicals for these new readers increased enormously. Writers were wanted who could write to a formula. So began the widespread provision of a standardized mental pabulum. Great news agencies collected news to fit the formula, and the resultant concoction was telegraphed to strings of newspapers in all parts of the world. Wireless telegraphy, which appeared a little later, and broadcasting, its latest phase, have added to a standardizing process; while the cinematograph adds to it still further.

In the United States there was an astounding material growth during the nineteenth and twentieth centuries. The sea-machine (in the form of ships that could carry many times as many passengers as the old ones and at a far greater speed) assisted another—and the last—of those great nomadic movements of humanity which regularly occur in history. Once again nomad man appears; and there is a new canalization. Hundreds of thousands of people cross the Atlantic to found a new country and be born again. The abolition of slavery, the sublimation of a number of French ideas (which came from the " Age of Reason "), and the continuation of strong puritanical ideas among the English who had early settled in America, as well as the hard struggle of pioneering days, were producing a new type of human being: the American citizen. Racially he might be of any origin. But in the new atmosphere, which differed entirely from the old one (it was a harsh, crude, but healthy, atmosphere), he abandoned old ideas and wholeheartedly agreed with and adopted those of the land in which he had settled. Those who did not conform paid the usual penalty in such cases: they were eliminated. Those best fitted survived, and only those survived who were inspired by the ideal of achieving Success in the new surroundings. It was during that period of settlement and tremendous struggle for existence that the grand American ideal of SUCCESS arose. It was to be the godhead of a new Trinity: SUCCESS, PROSPERITY, OPTIMISM.

¶ *Freud Discovers the Unconscious " Cesspool "*

The beginning of the twentieth century was the end of that very compact and clean-cut phase of English history which we call Victorianism. After it comes a period in which solidity begins to disappear from the old ideas and the old morality, both of which were replaced by new and nebulous ones. It is a period of Socialistic growth, of experiment, and of inquiry. Human nature began to be the subject of intense investigation, and many weird facts were unearthed concerning it. Sigmund Freud, for example, was pursuing investigations into human psychology which were to culminate in a sensational book, *The Interpretation of Dreams*. It was first received by European publics with something akin to horror; but in a decade it had changed the ideas of educationists and psychiatrists in all parts of the world. Freud proved beyond reasonable doubt that the hidden part of the human mind is little better than a cesspool—a thing which had been suspected by many unscientific people before him.

¶ *A Few Vagaries of Human Nature*

During the period of investigation into human nature which followed Darwin's and Freud's investigations, the information collected from all sorts of sources proved the variegation of humanity and what a queer creature man is. The facts also indicated that there can be such a thing as a great *cultural* change in human nature, though not a great *biological* one. Information appeared regarding the origin and development of the religious spirit and in regard to the origin and growth of religious symbols. In the quest after this information men of science have provided us with veritable encyclopædias of the vagaries of mankind. The works of Frazer and Westermarck alone prove that there is no limit to man's simplicity, credulity, absurdity, and caprice. We read of such occurrences as men worshipping turkey buzzards; of using a rabbit to stop rain or to retard the movement of the sun. We read of the Ajumba hunter who abjectly apologizes to the hippopotamus he has killed, and of people guilty of a crime coolly transferring it to a goat. In modern times— that is to say, in the time of our great-great-grandfathers—a stray anthropoid ape was arrested in England on suspicion; it was court-martialled as a foreign spy and, I believe, duly executed. We read of men whose religion is the worship of each other, and of others who set nets to catch escaped souls. We discover Brazilian Indians who devour the hearts of courageous foes in order to acquire some of their bravery. Of people who solemnly debated how best to embark upon a campaign for an amelioration in the character of their gods. Of others who decided that an elongated head was an indication of beauty, and who therefore spent their whole lives in a process of elongating it artificially. And of another part of the world where women one year believe that big hats are beautiful and the next believe that they are ugly. Of one race which believes that long hair in men or the wearing of soft black hats is a clear indication of unspeakable habits. We read of human souls being stored in bottles and boxes, and of a tribe which practises sham burials in order to deceive Satan. Another race transfers its sin to weeds; another disposes of wrong by eating it; another eats a mixture of cooked flour and water believing that it will cure sin. We find that the aborigines of Australia had an excellent method for controlling the movements of the sun, and that certain Arabs preserve their nail-parings for a religious purpose, and that another race drinks fermented grape-juice to cleanse their spirit. One people finds that fever can always be transferred to a bald-headed widow; another can tie the soul in a bandage, and so prevent it from running away. We read of childless women who crawl into a certain hollow rock which possesses the magical property of impregnating them during the night; of a people who believe in the beneficial properties and virtue of mutual vituperation; of others who once a year expel all the evil of their tribe by means of a ritual. We read of a man who, two thousand years or so after the disappearance of the tribes of Israel, discovers them in the Middle West of America. And of a race in which the wife's adultery is supposed to bring bad luck upon her absent husband; of another in which sexual crimes disturb the whole course of nature; of another which uses an instrument which creates a big noise to make people courageous; of another which believes that by emitting groans they induce piety. Another race arranges for its priests to fertilize their women by a religious ceremony which is effective only if the priests be in full health and strength. We discover that for a long time Alaskan Islanders mistook Russians for cuttlefish. There is one race among whom the eating of almonds will cause virgins to conceive; another in which continence is practised to improve crops; another in which only whores may serve God; another which regards all their ancestors as mischievous beings; another which speaks with bated breath and the highest respect of all wild animals; another which religiously preserves the tribal prepuces; and another in which the men decorate their codpieces, to draw public attention to them. This race uses an iron chain to promote the growth of beards; that one soundly flogs girls the moment they attain the age of puberty; the other one transfers ill-feeling to a banana.

One race respects the ghosts of men, but wages war against the ghosts of women; and another takes the chief's soul and bottles it the moment he dies. One race believes that fornication is bad for prosperity; another believes that it is good, but not for the crops. One race believes that reading will cause wind; another that the moon can be persuaded to impregnate barren females; and another forms a brotherhood with trees by sucking their sap. On one side of the world there is a race which believes that the poisonous juice of a certain fruit is bad for themselves, and forbids its use, but that it is an excellent thing for another race on the other side of the earth. In this race the kings become boa-constrictors after death; that one uses the bandicoot for rain-making. A race in one part of the world has no word for chastity and cannot understand what it can mean; another race knows what it means but regards it as something evil and to be avoided if possible. One race considers it bad luck for parents to have children resembling themselves; another that fatigue can be transferred to sticks and stones. In one part of the world a tree is married to a mango; another whole nation worships gnats. Some races there are who believe that by imitating the grunts of a wild boar they will prevent sore feet; others that by crawling under a bramble they can cure boils; others that a brass ring worn on the finger will cure pains in the hip-joints. One race chooses its kings only from among the best singers; another has an admirable method for supplying an internally diseased man with a new set of bowels. In one tribe there are people who acquire wisdom by eating the brains of the dead; in another corpulency is regarded as a mark of aristocratic birth; and in another it is looked upon as a sign of vulgarity. A priest of this race declares that pointed toes are an offence to the god of the tribe; a priest of that race provides eternal punishment for women who wear their hair short or who expose their knees.

The list could be extended indefinitely, for the libraries of the world are packed with records of human vagaries, absurdities, and stupidities. No race or individual is free from them, now or at any other time in history. The astounding feature of all this is that they exist and persist in the midst of civilization. There are so many of them around us that one can only conclude that men will never become really standardized, in spite of machines. We smile when we read of the simplicities of savage and barbarous races. But are not the practices, customs, and beliefs prevalent among the most enlightened races on a par with the vagaries of human nature recorded by the anthropologists? If we merely follow our daily newspapers carefully, we shall find everyday occurrences far stranger than those to be found among primitive or half-developed peoples. I have beside me a popular monthly magazine containing advertisements for methods to produce beautiful eyes, perfect noses, methods to make thick lips thin, to banish corpulency, thinness, bad complexion, or protruding ears; methods to reshape the body or to achieve popularity or sex-appeal, or fascination or charm. Patent medicine charlatanism is *vieux jeu*. Hoaxes occur on all sides—commercial and financial hoaxes, scientific and religious hoaxes, and a host of others.

## ¶ Our Obsessions and Eccentricities

There is no need to enter into details of the obsessions and delusions from which thousands of people suffer. Many of them are so typical that they have been classified and are to be found in every text-book dealing with neurosis. There is scarcely a human being who has not an obsession of some sort, occasionally developed to the stage when it can be regarded only as a disease. There are people who dread open spaces and others in whom confinement in a closed space produces a sort of helpless lunacy. There are some who fear being in high places; and others who dislike low-lying places. There are obsessions for drink; and for drugs, such as tobacco. There are people who have a mania for collecting things and others who desire to count everything. There is a fairly common fear of the colour red (which some psychologists declare to be an indication of self-reproach or shame of some kind). And there is among literary men the common (unconscious) impulse to repeat themselves. Such things are of the very warp and woof of human nature in every country at every period. The 1914 and 1939 World Wars intensified them and made them, with insanity generally, increasingly common among us. We may expect the next great war to leave behind it none but lunatics or neurasthenics.

Eccentricities and abnormalities are by no means confined to half-wits or simpletons. Indeed, it is among men of genius that we find them exemplified in the highest degree. Respect for the law of libel prevents me from mentioning what I know to be the strange behaviour at times of many contemporary men of genius. But we all know that Dostoevsky's behaviour and manner of life were such that, had he not been recognized as a man of genius, he might have been put away in an asylum for the insane. His imagination would sometimes create for him a great fear of nothing which he could define; and then his days and nights were spent in misery. Michael Angelo suffered from a mad and melancholy humour; Benvenuto Cellini suffered from hallucinations; Beethoven undoubtedly bordered upon insanity. Schumann had suicidal impulses, while Donizetti suffered from moral insensibility—his was a sort of Jekyll and Hyde personality. According to his biographer Jeaffreson, Lord Byron was tortured by hallucinations; though one hardly doubts this. Charles Lamb was confined for six weeks in a mad-house during the period in which he wrote most of his sonnets. William Blake, Jonathan Swift, and the poets Cowper and Southey were all, not merely unbalanced, but suffering from definite brain disease; and everybody knows of the neurosis from which Edgar Allen Poe suffered. Napoleon suffered from that morbid excitability of the motor centres, which is characteristic of insanity. Wellington and Peter the Great of Russia both suffered from epileptic fits. Charles V, one of the greatest kings of the sixteenth century, was born of insane parents, and suffered from scrofula and melancholia. His stammering was so bad that it was with great difficulty he could make himself understood at all. That political genius Cardinal Richelieu was also an epileptic; Moreau reports that on one occasion the Cardinal suffered so greatly from mental disturbances that he believed himself to be a horse, and galloped about neighing and jumping. The English statesman, Pitt the Elder, was a victim of both gout and true mental aberration. Newton confessed, in regard to a very odd letter he had written (one which would nowadays justify his friends in having him mentally examined), that he had done it under the influence of a " distemper " which seized his head and kept him awake for five nights together. The German philosopher Kant became a complete imbecile in his old age. Descartes was convinced that he was followed about by an Invisible Being who begged him for the sake of humanity to continue his researches. Auguste Comte, the French philosopher, was locked up for two years, a raving lunatic, during which period he put the finishing touches to his Positivist philosophy. The English economist, John Stuart Mill, was insane for a part of the year 1826, after which he began his book on logic. Rousseau developed into a maniac, finally suspecting that there was a conspiracy of heaven against him. The number of men of genius who suffered from delusions of their own grandeur or divinity is a very large one. Hegel would begin his lectures with the words, " With Christ, I may say that I myself *am truth*." Hallucinations were the mainspring of many great religious achievements such as those of Ignatius Loyola, the founder of the Jesuits, and of Joan of Arc, who was kissed by certain angels. She declared that she felt they " had a good odour."

§ 2

## MANNERS AND MORALS OF THE MODERNS

Let us glance at the morals and manners of our contemporaries and mentally compare them with those of past generations of men and women. We have already seen how Protestantism following the Reformation introduced the sharp distinction between a man's private life and his religion. In every country which is not Roman Catholic, and even in some of the Catholic countries, the new system of morality has reached an intensified form. In Catholic Ireland, Southern Germany, Northern Italy, Northern and Eastern Spain, and other places where Catholicism has come into close contact with Protestantism or Industrialism, one can see that Catholics are becoming unconsciously followers of the new idea—because of its great commercial convenience. Throughout the whole of Western civilization religion now occupies a less important position than formerly in the affairs of men. It still has a strong appeal, but its restraining moral influence is disappearing and is now considerable only among women and children. The man who introduces religion in any form into his everyday life is ostracized—not as an evil or untouchable person, but simply as a confounded nuisance whose presence is disturbing. In England religion or politics are taboo in bars, public houses, or social gatherings. Organized forms and practices of religion are on the wane, except for social or business purposes, and there is far less expression of the true religious spirit than there is among savage or primitive peoples. Irreligion is the mark of highly civilized man in every phase of history. This is not to say that modern morality is better or worse than that which went before. But modern morality is based on motives rather than dogma; in practice it depends upon the expediency of the moment. There has undoubtedly been a great passing of deliberate and wanton cruelty, except in time of war. In some cases it has merely been transferred from beast to man, in that gladiatorial fights, animal combats (or their more modern counterparts, blood-sports such as cock-fighting, fox-hunting, and badger-baiting) may be regarded as barbarous, but the soul-killing results of machine-minding and factory life, or life in coal mines, do not seem greatly to matter. When at least they do appear to matter, powerful social movements or revolutions are required before improvements can be effected.

¶ *Modern Man Easily Turned into a Beast*

Organized cruelty on a vast scale takes the place of individual acts of cruelty. In twentieth-century warfare we see men banded together and trained with the avowed purpose of inflicting the most cruel injuries imaginable upon their fellow-men. It is considered to be quite the correct and proper thing to turn men into beasts and (speaking as an ex-instructor in poison-gas, bombing, and bayonet-fighting during the 1914–18 War) I can assure the reader that it took about a couple of months to achieve this desirable end. Brigadier-General Crozier of the British Army, who gave much study to matters of warfare, says:

I, for my part, do what I can to alter completely the outlook, bearing, and mentality of over a thousand men in as short a time as possible—for the blood-lust is taught for purposes of war in bayonet-fighting itself and by doping the minds of all with propagandic poison. The German atrocities (many of which I doubt in secret)—the employment of gas in action, the violation of Frenchwomen, and the " official murder " of Nurse Cavell all help to bring out the brute-like bestiality which is so necessary for victory. The process of " seeing red," which has to be carefully cultivated if the effect is to be lasting, is elaborately grafted into the make-up of even the meek and mild through the instrumentality of martial music, drums, Irish pipes, bands, and marching songs. Sacred and artistic music is forbidden, save at church, and even then the note of combat is struck. The Christian Churches are the finest blood-lust creators we have and of them we made free use.

That shows how superficial civilization really is.

In spite of these occasional and often artificially created lapses into savagery, there was in twenty centuries a general levelling-up and spreading-out of happiness resulting from a growth in the humanitarian spirit; and this tendency is not on the decline. We no longer regard the lunatic as a person to be beaten unmercifully in order that an " evil spirit " may be driven out; nor do we chain up in dungeons the mentally infirm. So long as they are harmless they may walk about freely, as we all know from daily personal encounters. No longer is a wife regarded as chattel; her status has recently—that is, within the last half century—been raised above that of the domestic pig and frying-pan. In the year 1927 a gold-digger in Johannesburg sold his wife for the sum of ten pounds and a motor lorry, a transaction which was pleaded as a defence and set off to an action for the return of the lorry. It was not a successful defence; fifty years ago it might have been. In England, State pensions are now paid to the aged whose income is below a certain figure. This money is paid, not as charity, but as a right. Before 1908 old people who suffered from poverty were left to die as best they could; and there was no hub-bub about it. A great advance in social legislation took place in England in 1949, with State insurance to provide health and unemployment benefits for the whole population.

¶ *Industrial Cruelty to Children*

A peculiar form of modern cruelty is the employment of child labour. In England this has all but disappeared, but not so in the U.S.A., where industrialism is more highly developed. In 1927 the American Child Labour Committee reported that:

The tendency to employ children has not materially lessened since 1920, when, according to the U.S. Census, there were more than 552,000 working, not including those on home farms. On the contrary, there are indications of an increase. Economists say the restriction of immigration and the rapid development of industrial activity will undoubtedly add to this tendency. The harmfulness of child labour has not been clearly understood, or, if understood, has been disregarded. Recent legalistic discussion has to some extent obscured the facts both as to the number of child workers and to the effects of this labour. Many thousands of children who ought to be at school are at work, and many thousands are at work under conditions that must be condemned. Stricter regulation of child labour, coupled with better provision for education and recreation, remains a social necessity, and therefore the immediate concern of every citizen of every State. There is a grave danger of false complacency growing out of a belief that the job is finished. It isn't.

The report goes on to say that seven States permit children to go to work at fourteen without evidence of ability to read; eighteen States do not make physical fitness for work a condition of employment; twelve States allow children at fourteen to work nine to eleven hours a day; twenty-two States allow children at fourteen to run elevators; nineteen States have no laws prohibiting children of fourteen from working on dangerous machinery; seventeen States allow children of fourteen to oil, wipe, or clean machinery in motion; thirty-five States allow children at fourteen to work on scaffolding; twenty-eight States have no laws prohibiting children of fourteen from working in the immediate neighbourhood of explosives. And this is in the enlightened U.S.A.! It all seems a horrid nightmare. These are merely facets of modern industrial morality, and they are to be found in greater or less degrees in every capitalist country. *Modern industrialism is such that we cannot afford to sneer at the morality of any race or people under the sun.*

¶ *Wealth and Crime*

Perhaps one of the most interesting features of modern American life is the amazing increase in crime. This has been called " The National Dishonour." The annual murder rate in the U.S.A. increased 350 per cent from 1900 to 1930. Most of the crimes committed in the United States are committed by persons born in Europe or by their immediate descendants. In other words, while in every European country there is less lawlessness than there is in the United States, the chief contributors to lawlessness in the United States have been immigrants from European countries. In many of the larger cities of America there is a political and sometimes a financial partnership between the underworld and the very officials who are sworn to protect the lives and property of law-abiding citizens. The causes of this great increase in crime lie much deeper than the influence of the World Wars or Prohibition. There has been a steady increase in crime and disrespect for law for fifty years. First and foremost among the causes is the *increase in individual wealth*, " which has made for wastefulness, extravagance, and display, and tempted the weak to the acquisition of easy money, which has brought in the conscious part of the economical and political and social life of the nation many thousands of a new generation who have heretofore hidden in poverty. They have *caught the spirit* of the sordid game, and being participants, they have less confidence in their own judgments and easily follow the examples of others." Another cause is the " stupid increase in the number of laws, which by the force of multiplicity alone have increased the sum total of crimes." Next in importance is the " stupendous growth " of physical conveniences, such as automobiles, automatic pistols, machine-guns, smoke-screens, and aeroplanes. " The inefficiency of the judicial system " and the " business of amassing wealth and devoting to frivolity the leisure thus gained " are also blamed.[1]

Another reason given for the prevalence of crime is the insufficiency of the police force. The relative necessity for keeping citizens in order may be gathered from the numbers of police per head of the population : *in America, where there is most crime, the necessity for law and order is considered to be less than in Europe.* Probably the greatest cause of murder in the U.S.A. is the fashion of carrying revolvers. There is an almost complete absence of restriction in the sale of fire-arms and ammunition. Crime became a business, and the Chicago Crime Commission said :

Organized crime has adopted and promoted all those elements of weakness in democratic government which develop, particularly in a large city, the evils of petty politics. One price paid always in some measure and in some way for a democratic form of government is privilege or advantage traded and dealt in to secure votes and the personal advantage accruing from securing political office. Whether the appeal is to one class of voters or to a single gang leader for the support he may give, the condition to be dealt with should be frankly acknowledged and intelligently handled.

The period referred to is the late 1920's. Gangster crime was afterwards largely " cleaned up," but crime in general, especially juvenile crime, was increasing in the U.S.A. and in Britain up to 1948. In Britain, this was attributable to the Second World War, during

[1] From the Report of Bar Association's commission. Reported by the *Manchester Guardian*.

which the moral code received serious shocks from which it may never recover.

## ¶ *Lynchings and Rape*

Lawlessness in the United States is further exemplified in lynchings, of which there is a recurrence every year and sometimes an epidemic, although there has been some decrease since the great year 1926, when there were thirty-four recorded cases. Lynching is a survival from the days, after the liberation of slaves, when the white population set about driving the negro out of politics. It is a custom which has disappeared from the whole world with the exception of America. The excuse usually made for lynching a negro is that he has been guilty of rape. One can seldom get at the truth in regard to this, but I quote from the best authority I can find.

During the thirty-year period, 1889–1918, less than one-fifth of the coloured men done to death by lynching mobs were even accused of " the usual crime," and in that period fifty-fifty coloured and eleven white women were lynched. It should be borne in mind that the mob's accusation is not by any means equivalent to conviction or even to an indictment for crime by a regularly constituted jury. In fact, in a number of cases in which investigators were sent to the scene of lynchings by the National Association for the Advancement of Coloured People, their reports showed that, not only had the victim's guilt not been proved, but that he was actually innocent of the crime charged. To take a recent five-year period, that of 1914–18, the number of negroes lynched in the United States, exclusive of those killed at East St. Louis in the riot, was 264. In only twenty-eight cases, or slightly more than one-tenth of the lynchings, was rape assigned as the cause. If we compare these figures with the record for New York County, which is only a part of New York City, we find that in this one county, in the single year 1917, there were 230 persons indicted for rape, of whom thirty-seven were indicted for rape in the first degree.   That is, in just a part of New York City, nine more persons were indicted for rape in the first degree than there were negroes lynched throughout the entire United States in a five-year period.   Not one of the thirty-seven persons indicted in New York was a negro.[1]

I have no means of checking the accuracy of these statements, but, as they appeared in a publication read by those best able to contradict them, and no contradictions appeared, one must assume their truth. Lynching provides an excellent example of the effect of example and suggestion upon a crowd of otherwise decent citizens.   It is an example of how far seemingly peaceful modern people will go in giving expression to hate the moment they are aroused.   And it is a striking example of the fact that the reasons and actions which arouse frenzy in a crowd need not necessarily be either moral or based upon truth.   It is sufficient for the crowd to *believe that they are true.*   The " atmosphere " does the rest.   This applies to the actions of crowds in every country, and in every country their madness is precisely of the same nature.   Lynching is merely a local mannerism or fashion in certain States of America.   Happily, it tends to decrease, though instances recurred every year until this writing.

¶ *European Heritage of Cruelty*

Modern civilized man (*Homo sapiens*) is at times far more savage than any animal to be found in any jungle. I may perhaps mention one case, to show how a silly little incident may lead to a great riot.   In the spring of 1921 at Tulsa, Oklahoma, a careless and no doubt

[1] " *Lynching*," by James Weldon Johnson in the *Current History* Magazine, January, 1924.

impertinent negro—a mere spirited boy—had stumbled as he entered the elevator (*Ang.* lift) of an hotel. In an instinctive effort to regain his balance he caught the arm of a young white lady who was " operating the elevator," whereupon the girl screamed loudly. A sensation-seeking newspaper reporter who happened to be near wrote what journalists call a " good story " of a " Negro's attempt to assault White Girl." In the newspaper office this " scoop " was further embroidered and embellished; stunning headlines were added, and the story was duly published. That started the fun. The " boys " got busy. A white mob collected to lynch the " negro," and a coloured mob assembled to defend his life. All signs of law and order vanished, together with the influence of three thousand years of culture. Mob spirit rose to great heights, and a conflict raged until the death roll numbered one hundred. A considerable portion of the city was wiped out. Similar epidemics, I find, have occurred within more recent years in East St. Louis, Omaha, and Chicago; and there have been other murderous outbreaks of less consequence elsewhere. I trust that the facts which I have quoted will convince the reader of one thing: *that among the most civilized races the spirit of savagery and cruelty is by no means dead.* Instances of modern cruelty could be quoted from every civilized country. The birth and growing-pains of Hitler's régime in Germany showed appalling cruelty. The Civil War in Spain is not likely to be soon forgotten. The revolutionary and post-revolutionary period in Russia fills our minds with terror. Under the Fascist rule in Italy there were innumerable brutalities; the English effort to subdue the Irish before the settlement of 1921 indicated the presence of the old spirit. All that is required—now as in the past—to set flame to the passions of man is a " cause." It is rather curious that the " causes " nowadays productive of most cruelty are always publicized as for the benefit of mankind. In capital punishment, which still survives in many countries, we find an example of violence " righteously " used by States for the benefit of their citizens. If killing be of any use whatever in dealing with crime—which many experts doubt—it is a standing example of how a brutal old law can survive. And it sets a bad fashion in morality.

¶ *Great Physical Courage of Modern Man*

Protestantism introduced the " God is God, but Business is Business " idea and finally put the hallmark on this facet of morality during the golden age of slave-trading; then nineteenth-century industrialism intensified feeling that God must be kept in his place. And when we come to the twentieth century we find the influence of the Supreme Being so far reduced that he is becoming a polite term of reference. The fear of God, which was formerly the beginning of wisdom, has almost disappeared from the world. An English preacher, Dr. Dale, of Birmingham, stated even some years ago, " *No man now fears God.*" The steady elimination of fear generally is another interesting feature of the modern world. The general philosophic outlook of mankind has been so changed by two World Wars that far fewer people regard the fear of death as something that need seriously disturb them. The terrors of Hell have vanished. Further-

I

more, fear is playing a small and decreasing role in penology. A hundred years ago the hangman's noose was the cure-all for crimes. At present there is serious discussion in all countries where capital punishment exists as to whether it is of any use whatever in dealing with the few crimes for which it is retained. Fear of parents has also practically disappeared: the birch-rod no longer has its former honourable place in the average household. The old idea of morality was " punish the wrongdoer "— child or adult—and there was considered to be no great need to argue about right or wrong, because might was always right. Parents now reason with their children, and the process frequently ends in an argument in which the child wins. The result is a good-humoured disrespect for parental authority. One school of thought believes that the new morality is undermining the hitherto strong, resolute, and daring character of men; that the present generation is a flaccid one, with none of the old courage that " sprang from religion." Such a view as this is based upon a complete ignorance of history, a lack of common sense, and an absence of the power of observation. There was probably no time in history in which both the physique and intelligence of Western man were greater than they are today; and there was no time when men have more widely demonstrated, beyond a shadow of a doubt, their great courage and tremendous vitality. Some peoples may be exhausted after the strain of war. But what does the loss of twenty or thirty million men matter biologically in a world consisting of two thousand millions, and in which the population is steadily increasing? War losses and the psychological effects of war are quickly retrieved. The physical, mental, and spiritual reactions afterwards merely represent human nature having a rest after an exhausting activity. In much less than two generations the biological effects have disappeared completely, but certain psychological effects remain a little longer, and a few may even be intensified. Of these I think the most important is that part of the human psyche which governs the quality of courage, and this, I think, is strengthened. I believe that Western man (that is to say, the type we find in Western European and American civilization) is in every way a braver creature than any that has ever before existed on this earth. Looking through the pages of world history, I doubt if one will find any phase in which man more resolutely faced more terrifying or devastating creations than the modern engines and explosives of war which millions faced in World Wars I and II. There is no need for me to illustrate this fact by quoting incidents, nor any need for me to enter into the history of our wars. This generation has been made familiar with the whole business. Every book that is published on the subject of modern war merely adds further evidence to support what I wish to emphasize: the great courage obviously to be found in all classes of society and in a diversity of nations and races.

¶ *Bolsheviks try to abolish God*

In spite of the fact that the influence of God in human affairs is declining, masses of people everywhere continue the devout worship of the Supreme Being. This is especially true of Catholic countries and the

U.S.A. The great wave of post 1914–18 war prosperity in that country was reflected in a wave of church-building everywhere and by all denominations. When American civilization has crumbled to the dust, there will remain (for the Russo-Chinese archæologist of five hundred years hence) so many ruins of churches that he will say to himself: " These Americans were either a very religious race or perhaps, like the English, they were a nation of hypocrites." It is also in America that toleration grew less as Catholicism grew stronger, and this in itself indicated that the spirit of religion had not yet disappeared. In Europe religion reached the phase at which few people took it seriously, and hence there is great toleration; though not where Catholicism became allied to the State. But matters have sometimes gone beyond mere toleration. By far the most interesting phase of modern religion was the attempt by the Russian Government to abolish deism entirely. In the Federation of Soviet Republics the law provides that every citizen is at liberty to practise any religion or none at all. It is, however, the definite belief of the Bolshevik leaders that religion is not a good thing for human nature, and they began an intensive campaign of propaganda to educate millions of peasants and workers to this belief. Accusations were brought against the Soviet Government that in their enthusiasm to propagate Atheism members of Christian and other creeds suffered persecution. It is inconceivable, in view of the whole history of human nature, that there should be any profoundly revolutionary idea which does not involve cruelty or even persecution in some form or other, though the modest claim is made that under the Soviet régime there is more toleration than there was under the Tsar. We must content ourselves with the one important fact which emerges beyond doubt even at this stage. For the first time in history, a powerful government definitely set itself the immense task of preventing God from interfering in the affairs of men. If they succeed, they will have effected a complete revolution in human mentality. There is as yet no evidence that they have succeeded.

¶ *Cultural Influence of the Cinema*

The cinema is the modern attraction which everywhere seems to take the place of church-going in countries where this practice is admittedly declining. There is now no city in the world without its cinemas, and bigger and better ones appear in all directions. The screen is one of the factors which goes to the shaping of human nature in its latest phase, though it is a little early to say exactly how and where this shaping process is taking place, not to mention its ultimate effects upon the nature of man, and especially upon his morals and his manners. As usual, the experts disagree. Some say that the influence is good. Those who favour the Church influence or who obtain a livelihood as professional moralists righteously maintain the contrary. In Europe nobody worries about it one way or the other (except in countries where political censorship exists), but in the U.S.A., where more money is at stake on both sides, the pros and cons of cinematograph morality are matters of considerable financial importance, and are therefore subjects of deep study. The Rev. Clifford Gray

Twombly, D.D. (Rector of St. James's Church, Lancaster, Pennsylvania), estimated that of the twenty million people who in 1929 daily went to films in America, 75 per cent were under twenty-four years of age, and, he says, " more than 30 per cent of the films, or about one in every three, are striking at the very basic cornerstone of American life, for they are tending to destroy the sanctity of marriage and of the family, and are making light of personal purity. They are subtly and insidiously and intentionally sensual." Dr. Twombly estimated that ten million children of school age daily attend cinemas. They contemplate the behaviour of their elders and no doubt are influenced by the astounding sexual and other tergiversations of cinematograph heroes and heroines, villains and villainesses. " One needs to do no more," comments the Rev. Twombly, " than scan the billboards or read the movie-showhouse announcements in the press to be certain that the vile is emphasized and the suggestive played up above all other forms of attraction. That the cinema industry has become one of the largest in the United States under these conditions would seem to justify the judgment of the producers in feeding out so great a proportion of filth."

Replying to this in a scientific paper (read to the policewomen of San Francisco), a representative of the film industry gave an imposing array of facts to show that, *but for the films*, crime might reach really serious dimensions in America. He said that a study of six hundred and twenty " feature " pictures produced (in America) during 1928 showed that actually 33·7 per cent contained *no villain* and *no crime*; in 17·5 per cent the villain was *killed*; in 33·8 per cent the villain was *imprisoned*; in 4·4 per cent he was *reformed*; and in the remainder of the pictures he was *punished by the hero*. The lecturer, warming to his subject, went on to say that, in the thirty-eight " underworld " pictures of the preceding year the villain was *killed* in fourteen instances, *arrested* in nineteen cases, and *reformed* in five. " *Such is the iron-clad moral of the movies*," he declared, " *that not once does the guilty escape punishment*." (My italics.)

By 1948 films had become a little more serious, but the capacity for producing films of doubtful morality remained.

## § 3

## WORLD WARS, HUMANITY IN CRISIS, ATOMIC POWER

That peoples, nations, and systems rise and fall is recognized by every modern historian, but the reasons for their rise and fall have not yet been satisfactorily explained in terms sufficiently clear to be a reliable guide to the future. The destiny of man continues to be an unanswered question. Fashions in interpretation come and go, as systems come and go. The simplest interpretation seems to be nearest the truth: that the most efficiently selfish peoples succeed and survive best, and that even these decline from the moment their alertness slackens. And it seems always and inevitably to slacken as a result of over-success or weariness; and not necessarily immediately or quickly but inevitably. The successful people, nation, or civilization reaches a peak point at which it remains for a short or a long period, after which the collective

activity succumbs to the strain of reaching and maintaining it, and thenceforward there is decline: at
first on the surface and then more profoundly by the
collective activity, which is no longer creative but
disintegrative, no longer strong and forceful but
whimsical and baroque, no longer of clear, straight
lines but wobbly and oscillating. Once this stage
has been reached recovery becomes impossible; the
end may be a quiet " fade out " or a catastrophic
collapse.

The new science of geopolitics has been combined
with religio-mystical speculation in recent attempts to
explain in terms of rationalism the whys and wherefores
of all this, but like other attempts in the past they do
not take us much further.  Human nature remains
something of a mystery, the only certainty about it
being that man remains as he always was: a tragic
being struggling to define himself and his existence
and, from such definitions as he may succeed in
formulating, always attempting to work out a plan
which will make life easier and more comfortable and
better for the mass.[1]   In this sense the present period—
the middle of the twentieth century—though in many
respects threatening and promising little in the
immediate future, contains the germs of great advances,
of which the benefits can be reaped only by the
generations to come. Meanwhile, the world has
become an unpleasant place to live in for millions of
people. The social revolution of the twentieth
century progressed with growing pains felt everywhere,
all of which represented a crisis for humanity which

---

[1] See *The Proper Study of Mankind*, by Stuart Chase (Harpers,
New York, 1948).

showed itself in various forms in various countries—
in war, neuroses, struggles, and frustrations, but
nearly always in suffering.

## ¶ *The Second World War*

This is not the place for an account of the Second
World War (1939–45), the memory of which will
be fresh in the minds of most readers. Little need
be said about it, more than to record that for cruelty
and horrors, for " man's inhumanity to man," it
exceeded all records in human history. But, in all
its horrors, some were worse than others. Perhaps
the worst of all were these two: (1) the use by Germany of the lethal chamber for the mass-killing of
political and racial enemies, the total number of
humans thus destroyed in cold blood being estimated
in hundreds of thousands; (2) the use by the U.S.A.
of the atomic bomb, which will be dealt with later.
This was for the political purpose of assuring the
surrender of Japan to America before the armies of
the U.S.S.R. could inflict an inevitable military
defeat on Japanese forces in China and thus cause
Japan to capitulate to them. In both cases the
political end justified the means. Everything said
on pages 39–45 about the madness and cruelty of
humanity in the First World War, and the generaliza-
tions drawn from it (with the exception of the references to Abyssinia, the Spanish War, and the Second
World War, all of it was written in 1929), applied to
the Second World War and, if there should be a
Third, will apply to it also. For, so far as we can
judge from the teachings of history, there is a con-
stantly recurring extreme of madness which seizes

mankind in the mass and shows itself in the form of death and destruction, in mutual extermination, in hatred and in all the abominations with which our generation is familiar. The number of casualties in dead, in wounded, and in terms of suffering generally was many times greater in the Second than in the First World War. With the increase in the efficiency of his weapons, man showed himself by the middle of the twentieth century to be either indifferent or unaware that such destructiveness can become suicidal.

## ¶ War—a Bad Human Habit

Because of the general tendency of mankind to forget, to obliterate from memory by an unconscious though powerful process all that is unpleasant or disturbing, most people are left with the idea that peace is " normal " and war " abnormal." Those who are responsible for wars—ruling classes and castes—encourage this idea. The First World War was called " the war to end war," and during and after the Second World War much play was made by statesmen with the term " peace-loving peoples." In Block's book, *The Future of War*, the author shows that in the past 2,500 years the world has enjoyed peace during only one year in twelve; and that from 1878 to 1910 (the last year of peace) there were only four years without fighting. As a rule, most peoples like to have themselves regarded, and indeed to regard themselves, as " peace-loving "; but it is regrettably true that mankind has a long record of bellicosity. Statesmen and their propagandists are wont to indulge in all sorts of sophistry to convince their people when involved in war that it is a " defensive " war. A

refinement is the " preventive " war as propounded
in the U.S.A. after the end of the Second World War,
the thesis being that, if the U.S.A. made proper use
of the atomic bomb against the U.S.S.R. while the
latter had not yet got it, Russia might be quickly
knocked out and thus the Third World War would be
" prevented." A whole school of political, military,
and religious thought in the U.S.A.—the religious
thought being chiefly though not exclusively Roman
Catholic—became attached to this idea. Every
modern war becomes to those with an interest in it
either " defensive " or " preventive." Christian
Churches, instead of condemning such horrors as the
atomic bomb, fail mankind in their humanitarian duty
and agree to its use for " defensive " or " preventive "
purposes, the military truth being that the atomic
bomb is a weapon of aggression for use when mass-
destruction is the military objective. The Roman
Catholic Church did not condemn the atomic bomb
and, as it claims to be God's exclusively representative
body on earth, the implication is that God approves
of the atomic bomb; as presumably He will also
approve of the still greater horrors being hatched in
the form of bacterial warfare and what not. This
helps to explain why so many people in the modern
world disapproved of God as propounded by his
official representatives. Many think more highly of
Him.

The term " peace-loving peoples " deserves scrutiny,
since it implies a claim that is world-wide. In his
*Study of War* covering the years 1480–1941, Prof.
Quincy Wright of Chicago University provides a
statistical conspectus of the wars in which the principal

peoples of the world have been engaged during this period. Here is a small statistical item from it:

| | | | |
|---|---|---|---|
| Great Britain . | 78 wars | France . | . 71 wars |
| Spain . . | 64 „ | Russia . | . 61 „ |

The U.S.A. War Department credits the U.S.A. with 110 wars with Indians and 13 other wars in 150 years—a total of 123. This gives the U.S.A. the place of honour as the country with the highest record for bellicosity, taking into account its comparatively short history. Britain comes next, then France. Germany is low on the list with a mere 23 wars in the period 1480–1941; China still lower with only 11; and, surprisingly, Japan holds the lowest record with 9. I use the word " surprisingly " because we have been taught otherwise. The usual reply to such a statement is that " anything can be proved by statistics," for, although it shows beyond much doubt that the battle-record of some peoples is glorious, such a record is inconsistent with the claim of those same peoples to be " peace-loving." While it is unsafe to draw hasty or too many conclusions from such a sharp perspective, we are all quite prepared to condemn this or that race of dog as " quarrelsome " or " too much given to fighting," precisely because we have observed that, rightly or wrongly, it is always getting into " trouble " with other dogs. The truth seems to be that man is easily led into war, but would be peaceful if given a chance.

¶ *Power-States' Struggle for the World*

In his gloomy work *The Decline of the West* the German philosopher-historian Oswald Spengler gives reasons why he believes that " Western man " approaches the end of his tether and is apparently doomed to sink to an inferior position in the world. The interpretation of history known as dialectical materialism—initiated and propounded by Karl Marx, developed and clarified by Lenin, and further refined by Stalin and others—in contrast to Spenglerism provides both an analysis and a programme. The analysis can be summed up very roughly to the effect that the system of Capitalism contains within itself the germs of its own destruction, that after flowering it " declines " and must inevitably fall, but that before falling it may very well make a supreme final fighting effort to save itself by a war in which it hopes to destroy the greatest threat to its existence: the system based on the Marxist programme. This is known as Communism and was put into practice by the men of the Russian Revolution of 1918 and resulted in the Soviet Union which, from the chaos of its problematical and speculative beginnings, rose steadily in strength until, at the end of the Second World War, it had become a World Power second only to the U.S.A. Rival capitalist empires were responsible for the First and Second World Wars; the Third would be a struggle between surviving Capitalism and the anti-Capitalist camp as represented by the Soviet Union and its friends. Whichever system survived the Third World War would rule the world. Although not now expressing itself so plainly, each side in its own way followed the German slogan of pre-1914 days: " World Power or Downfall."

Whether or not this interpretation is correct, it resolved itself into a struggle for power, a struggle between all-powerful States using the masses to assure the perpetuation of their ideology. On both sides powerful new social classes arose around the Power-State and regarded themselves as society, or at least as a representation of society. Their principal mission was to manage by command. Their means was based on force as the final arbiter. New tyrannies arose, not tyrannies in the old sense, but tyrannies in which complacent or helpless masses were managed and did what they were told. One might conclude from this both great wickedness and great weakness on the part of human nature, but it would be a mistake to assume a totality of either the one or of the other. A breaking-point is reached at which human nature rebels against restraint, even when that restraint is claimed to be for the collective benefit. The cry for liberty goes up, the cry for a new social order based on the freedom of the individual, the abandonment of rule of law based on force, the cry for self-realization based on mutual help in mutual interests. Thus, the struggle for liberty, having survived all struggles, may survive the struggle for the world and be helped by it. Until that day comes, the outlook for the individual cannot be bright—the only brightness possible for the individual in the greater part of the mid-century world being dependent on his complete acceptance of the dictates of the Power-State. All these factors contributed to the " World Crisis," the " Crisis of the Individual," both being a crisis in human relationships, but hardly a crisis in human nature.

¶ *Human Gullibility*

Many " advanced " or " progressive " people in the middle of the twentieth century prided themselves on having lost, through the hard experience of life, most of their illusions and what they regarded as their fathers' susceptibility to deceit and gullibility. It is, in fact, the rarest thing imaginable to find a human being who is not in some way gullible or easy to deceive. Every one of us is biologically only too ready to accept as truth that which we wish to believe, because it is in some way flattering to our egoism, bolsters up pride-in-self, or warns us against something which we are prepared to believe is a danger or a threat to our existence. Propagandists take full advantage of this fundamental quality in human nature and, during and after the Second World War, a sort of official " science of suggestion " showed itself, in which often successful attempts were made to "mould public opinion " in the way demanded by rulers. All of this was based on the old principle that it does not matter greatly whether something is true—all the better if it is; just unfortunate if it is not—but on the expediency, desirability, and practicability of " creating a myth " and that, once the " myth " is created, it can be extremely difficult to eliminate it from the minds of men.

The " myths " of the second quarter of the twentieth century were chiefly those springing from -ISMS and ideologies, beginning with Socialism, continuing in Communism, with reactions against these two in Italian Fascism and German National Socialism. There was also the vague ideology of Social Democracy which attempted to compromise between Socialism-Communism on the Left and Nazi-Fascism on the Right and thus provide the " middle course " to satisfy large numbers of men and women. In the

Second World War the combined forces of Communism and Social Democracy defeated in the field those of Fascism and Nazism, but did not eradicate their ideology, though this was shaken. From the resultant position arose the " Struggle of Ideologies " of the mid-twentieth century, with the division of the world into two groups or *blocs* of human beings, each of which believed that it was " right " and the other " wrong," each maintaining its position by propaganda on an unprecedented scale, each meanwhile beginning a race of armaments and preparations of fiendish weapons to be used one day in a war of mutual destruction which, if it should come, would kill off a considerable percentage of mankind, put an end to Western civilization, and quite possibly leave large areas of the world so contaminated by poisons as to be uninhabitable for years afterwards.

Never in history was the irrationality of man so completely demonstrated as in this " Struggle of Ideologies," the most remarkable feature of which was its intensification immediately after the end of the awful Second World War, that being the worst war hitherto known to humanity. From the point of view of the Social-Democratic group or *bloc* of nations the menace was Russian " Communism "; from the point of view of Russian " Communism " the menace was " Capitalist Imperialism " led by the U.S.A. with the atomic bomb. The peril in which millions of human lives were placed, and the implications in the vast threat to humanity caused by the preparations made on each side in this struggle for power, were certainly not lost on those millions. This fact, by a curious paradox, was not without its comforts. The dangers of war were these: first, that never in human history had there been any such armaments race, nor indeed any considerable armaments race, which did not end in war; and second, that the nature of Capitalist Imperialism was such that if it reached a crisis within itself (partly due to Communist competition for the world) the only " solution " could be war. On this reasoning, to say the least, the prospects for humanity were gloomy, and we might well ask where does one find the comfort. The answer is that we must attribute some weight to what has been proverbially called " the first law of nature ": self-preservation.

Men on both sides of the " Two Worlds " fence must sooner or later realize that in such a war as an " ideological " Third World War would be, the winner might end by being as badly off as, or perhaps worse than, the loser. The comparatively small nucleus of people whose type, from the dawn of history, has made use of war to decide policy, if they survived at all, would be left with a useless, dangerous, and vicious world. A stalemate result would not leave a different world. Finally, in this sort of war, the chances would be that those responsible for it would themselves not survive its ravages, whatever the result. Hence, although it can with truth be argued that, although man has not always permitted risk of death and annihilation to prevent him from embarking on foolish enterprises, one may hope that the threat of world-wide destruction—by the new weapons such as the atomic bomb and bacteria launched from supersonic aeroplanes and rockets, and other horrors that may be employed—will compel even the most ferocious

K

and short-sighted leaders to take thought of self-
preservation and the perpetuation of the race. Thus
a simple factor of biology may make man decide in
favour of peace. If this does not, human history
shows us that if we rely upon the "morality" of
rulers to avoid war, we shall be relying upon something
which has invariably failed.

¶ *Factors in the Ideological Struggle*

What rulers describe as the "preparation" or
"moulding" of public opinion is an essential preliminary to war: a will to fight and resist must be
created—and at any cost. Organizations are created
for the dissemination of every sort of story, news
item, comment, or fable, which will do one of two
things: show "our side" in the most favourable
light and the "other side" as consisting of devils
incarnate who, sooner or later, must be faced in battle
and destroyed. Churches join in the process, and the
working slogan, not always publicized, is that "the
end justifies the means." Hence we have the appalling
phenomenon of a horrific weapon of mass-destruction
such as the atomic bomb justified from the pulpits
of Christendom for purposes of "defensive war,"
the propounders of this doctrine relying on human
gullibility being such that it can be counted upon not
to realize that every war can be justified as a "defensive" war. The average human being is only too
ready to form an opinion without evidence or to dis-
tort evidence to support a frame of mind that is
willing to believe anything good about his own side
and anything evil about the enemy. The names of
those who can find something to be said in favour of

the enemy or some flaws in the propaganda of his side are black-listed; these " suspect " people are often debarred from official employment, and witch-hunts and persecution become the order of the day. In these circumstances, many men and women in the Social-Democratic countries who had once been Communists gave up their Communism, and some washed themselves clean of suspicion by becoming members of the Roman Catholic Church, which, because of the Pope's uncompromising attitude and declarations after the end of World War II in the " Christian Crusade against Atheistic Communism and in Defence of Western Civilization against the Aggressions of Soviet Russia," was considered to be one of the safest alibis.

Witch-hunting and persecution showed itself at its worst in the U.S.A., where an official committee was set up to investigate " un-American " activities. At one of its meetings in 1949 an ex-Communist named Chambers appeared and gave his testimony of reform. Doubts about the value of the evidence of an ideologically " reformed " man were dealt with by a member of the committee, United States Attorney F. Edward Hébert, who asked Chambers: " Isn't it a fact that there are many saints in heaven who were not always saints? " To which Chambers replied: " I believe so." Hébert then assured him: " We would not take their sainthood away from them after they have become saints and repented, not saying, you understand, that you are a saint, now mind you ". Chambers could only reply: " I am not a saint, indeed." It must also be recorded that the Committee for un-American Activities, although it provided great copy for the sensational Press and caused widespread misgivings in the minds of those who believed in freedom, at times came near to being the laughing-stock not only of the U.S.A. but of the civilized world. But it was a useful indicator of official thinking and of official preparation of the national mind for war. In this ideological struggle regimes and governments took over and expanded the spying and counter-spying personnel, the ' security ' and ' secret ' services of their predecessors, constituting in civilized countries vast corps to watch the politically doubtful and to keep track of the power-state's enemies at home and abroad. According to the *United Nations World* expenditure per annum on this espionage and counter-espionage by 1949 was as follows: U.S.S.R.—£27,500,000; U.S.A.—£20,000,000; Great Britain—£14,000,000.

¶ *Wars Create Reasons for New Wars*

That the danger to Capitalist Imperialism was real enough can be gathered from simple statistics. The most important political consequence of the First World War was the Russian Revolution and with it the creation of a Communist State embracing 180,000,000 people. A basic consequence of the Second World War was the addition of a further 100,000,000 Communists and the rapid advance towards Communism in China, with its 400,000,000 potential Communists. The political consequences of a Third World War are unpredictable, but one sure thing at the end of 1949 was that the Communist advance in parts of Europe, in Asia, Africa, Latin America, and elsewhere had begun to show itself on a scale the developments of which it would be unsafe to predict. From originally small groups, the doctrines of the new religion of Communism spread to whole countries and, by the end of 1949, whole continents were becoming aware of them. The fact that the British, Dutch, French, and other colonizing people, whom millions of " natives " had grown to regard as exploiters, were now joining the Americans in a *bloc* with open hostility to the Soviet Union and its satellite countries, and that Communist doctrines as expounded to those " natives " promised freedom from the known exploiters, began to have the easily predictable result that " reds," in the ideological sense, could be created under skins of all colours. The new " liberating " doctrines and the disciplined fervour of the preachers had a potent appeal to under-dogs everywhere.

This was another incalculable factor in the " Struggle for the World." This struggle involved possible changes in human nature which cannot be estimated during the period of flux and turmoil, and may not be possible to estimate for many years after that struggle has ended. The tendency everywhere was to move away from individualism towards regimentation with the Power-State controlling the destinies of millions; the decline in human freedoms as hitherto understood; the growth of " Police States," controls, an increase in material efficiency, the collapse of the old morality and the disappearance of all that pre-1914 " social security " which enabled the peoples of Western civilization to plan their lives within a frame which seemed solid but has now completely disappeared except in the memories of nostalgics. The changes in outlook, mentality, approach to life, and in human behaviour after the Second World War showed themselves to be deeper than any ever known. This is the outstanding fact which emerges from any long-term perspective of human history. A new " myth of life " was in course of creation by the middle of the twentieth century, one which challenged the old myths. In the creation of this new myth, the passions were everywhere as lively as they had ever been in the creation of the old, and here human nature showed no change whatsoever. In this turmoil what might seem to be the most desirable aim in life got lost, obscured, or continued to be propounded by a few helpless people who were usually dismissed as impractical " Utopian " idealists. That aim might be simply defined as follows: good behaviour by human beings one to another, with mutual aid for mutual benefits; and good relations between peoples, based on a determination that, however any problem is to be solved, there is one way of solving it which must *never* be used in any circumstances—namely, war. Such is human nature that it seemed as if something in the nature of a world catastrophe would be required before men could agree on so simple and desirable a programme.

¶ *Organized Religion and War*

When religion is organized and the organization develops into an authoritarian Church, the true spirit of religion tends to become absorbed by political ecclesiasticism with a greed for power in various forms. These show themselves as Absolutism in mental domination, a quest for material wealth and property, efforts to gain influence on governments, and influence over everything secular.  In this process ecclesiastics trade on what has been and still is widely regarded as humanity's fundamental need for spiritual consolation. The spiritual power thus achieved by the organized Church is applied to non-spiritual or secular purposes. The outstanding example of this process is the institutionalized Christianity of the Roman Catholic Church, to which references have been made in an earlier part of this book.  Attention has been well distracted from the political part played during the twentieth century by this powerful Church.  Yet it is a subject of considerable importance, in as much as the Church, as represented by its Supreme Pontiff the Pope, with its centre at the Vatican and its hierarchies throughout the world, has always interested itself and continues to interest itself in the most destructive aspect of human nature—war—and always with the interests of the Church in mind rather than those of humanity at large.

The chief interests of the Roman Catholic Church are (1) *religious*, which amount to theocratic monopoly and (2) *political*, represented by power over secular rulers.  The Church regards itself as a *societas perfecta* independent of all temporal rulers; and not merely international but supra-national.  It regards the advancement and defence of its interests and rights as taking priority over all else everywhere and at all times, under widely differing régimes in very different circumstances and, today, in a rapidly changing society. The greatest problem with which it has to deal is the reconciliation of its moral leadership with its interests. This presents the Church with a permanent dilemma, and accounts for the fact that there are often differences of opinion among unchallengeably sincere Catholics. But the Church, of which the Pope is Absolute Ruler whose decision is final, shows great flexibility and ingenuity in maintaining the broad and essential unity of its adherents and, in regard to war or war-in-preparation, changes in circumstances can modify its attitude in practice though not in principles. A war can be " just " or " unjust " and is so *in accordance with its effects on the " rights " and interests of the Church*. Hence it may be thought worthy of either the " moral " support or the " moral " condemnation of the Church; or the Vatican can proclaim its " neutrality." The Vatican itself used to go to war and have its own armies in the field to fight for its interests; but that has ended and now the battles must be fought by others. Large-scale war can be dangerous for Church interests, and for this reason neutrality is often preferred, as it was in the two World Wars. But when a situation arises such as that which arose after the Second World War, in which the whole world became divided into two *blocs* preparing for war, with the prospect of the winner being left to " rule the world," all such dialectics are resolved into a consideration of the problem of which winner would be best for surviving Vatican interests after such a conflict; or what would be the best policy for the Vatican, having in mind the possibility of an ultimate stalemate in the war. Such a problem might appear to present great difficulties to the Church, but the main principle had been long established; the ultimate goal of the Church itself has been and is world domination. The dream of all Popes is to see the world as a new Holy Roman Empire, with the Pope as its Absolute Ruler. Only non-progressive forces can help towards that goal. *Any* form of democracy is inimical and a danger. And in our times Communism is the greatest danger of all.

Bearing in mind what has been said above—that to the Vatican its own interests come first—it is not difficult to understand why, for example, when Mussolini with his Fascist doctrines appeared, the Pope declared that here was " a gift from Providence "— although the Duce was a self-declared atheist, having written a book with the title *God Does Not Exist*. The English Cardinal Hinsley, in 1935, said that if Fascism in Italy went under, " God's cause goes under with it." In Hitler's Germany, the pagan *Führer* was supported by the Church. During his rise to power the Catholic Centre Party tipped the balance in his favour and backed him to the end. During the Second World War the Catholic bishops in Germany held a Conference at Fulda, the decisions of which were not permitted to be published, though one of them was officially reported as a promise by the Church that " after the completion of the final German victory, special ceremonies of gratitude to the German troops and of loyalty to Hitler will be announced," reminding one of Pope Leo XIII's insistence, in a conversation with Kaiser Wilhelm II reported in the latter's *Memoirs*, that " Germany must become the sword of the Catholic Church." Hitler, Mussolini, and the Vatican helped General Franco to overthrow liberal-democratic government in Spain and to establish a brutal Falangist-Fascist régime more repressive than any ever known in the Peninsula. After the Second World War the Pope

K 2

showed great energy in a campaign against Communism in general and in openly declared hostility towards the Soviet régime, one in which the world's 300,000,000 Roman Catholics were told where their duty lay and irrespective of the interests of the particular country in which they might reside—thus creating " Fifth Columns " and " Trojan Horses " within many frontiers. Whatever the political discretion of the Vatican might be—and the Vatican is usually discreet —it was frequently abandoned by hierarchies, bishops, and individual priests, who proceeded to fan the flames of hostility towards the " enemy of the Church " and thereby help governments to " mould public opinion " in preparation for the final struggle. This campaign, which at times in certain countries such as Franco's Spain and even on occasion in the U.S.A. (now the greatest Vatican material interest, with its wealth, power, and 25,000,000 Catholics), reached record-making levels of mendacity, and demonstrated more clearly than it had ever been shown before the application of organized religion to problems of mankind involving mass-destruction and suffering. The interests of the Church took precedence of all such considerations; and its spiritual mission was largely replaced by one of Vatican politics.

¶ *Atomic Power*

Physicists have long been aware of the incalculably vast resources in atomic energy which might be obtainable through changes within the atomic nucleus, yet the cost of producing and exploiting such energy on a practical scale was deemed to be prohibitive in time of peace. The Second World War, into which the resources of the civilized world were thrown regardless of cost, saw the manufacture in the U.S.A. of the first atomic bomb, one with an appallingly destructive explosive force coming from a chain reaction based on nuclear fission. The mechanics of exploding so monstrous a creation in such a way that it could be used militarily presented problems which the war-time ingenuity of experts duly solved; and all that remained was to use the bomb to best effect. The American air force first used an atomic bomb on Hiroshima on August 6, 1945, a date which marked the beginning of a new period in history known as the " Atomic Age," " characterized," *The American Modern Library Dictionary* says, " by atomic energy as a *military, political,* and *industrial factor* "—this being the order of its importance in American judgment, though not in that of other countries. The decision to use the bomb was made, it is said, in defiance of the protests of many of the scientists who had worked on the project; and it was essentially a political decision. The main effects of such a bomb would be known to its users; a brilliant flash, an explosion " equal to that of 20,000 tons of T.N.T.," the creation of great heat and gamma-ray radiation. In terms of human destruction, the Hiroshima bomb killed not less than 60,000 men, women, and children; it maimed or otherwise injured about 100,000 more; it virtually destroyed by blast or fire a great seaport of 250,000 people; and it left behind it an aftermath of old and new diseases and all forms of human suffering, the ultimate effect of which on survivors or their offspring cannot for a long time be medically or otherwise classified or even imagined. This horror was the result of research by scientists of many nationalities, including Japanese, and of a final-stage collaboration almost entirely Anglo-American. The decision to use it was, so far as the world knows, exclusively American; and this responsibility was accepted. No advance warning was given to the Japanese. The victims were nearly all civilians.

Eye-witness accounts of the bombing and its results will be found in John Hersey's *Hiroshima* [1] and there is no need to dwell on them here. One important point should be noted: the American action at Hiroshima was an apt illustration of the depths to which human nature can sink, and represented perhaps the cruellest single wartime action by a State against a civilian population in the whole history of mankind. It would be unjust to regard it as having received the approval of the population of the U.S.A., for it was widely criticized and condemned; but the ethical arguments against the use of atomic bombs have so far counted for nothing. Hersey comments: " The crux of the matter is whether total war in its present form is justifiable, even when it serves a just purpose. Does it not have material and spiritual evil as its consequences which far exceed whatever good might result? When will our moralists give us a clear answer to this question? " Such decisions as that to use the bomb are the work of rulers; and war is not regarded by rulers as an " immoral " activity. From 1945 onwards the U.S.A. continued to make atomic bombs and pile them up for war. How many other

---

[1] Published by Alfred Knopf in the U.S.A. and Penguin Books in England. (The total of *deaths* was later said to be between 210,000 and 240,000.—C.D.)

countries were making them or trying to make them in 1949 was a well-kept secret. The American bomb as used at Hiroshima, with uranium or plutonium as its base, is not the only type possible. The science correspondent of *The Nation* (New York, 28/10/48) reported :

> From time to time, there has been talk of an atomic superbomb a thousand times more powerful than the " ordinary " uranium or plutonium bomb. I refer to the deuterium (heavy-hydrogen) bomb, which does not now exist but probably will be produced some day in the not-too-distant future. . . .
>
> A deuterium bomb can be made much larger than one of the present A-bombs, which have a very limited size range. Below a certain critical size, fission bombs cannot be made to explode ; above it, they cannot be prevented from going off. The only size limits imposed on the deuterium bomb are the lift and range capacities of its carrier, plane or rocket, and the amount of material that can be made to react in the millionths of a second within which nuclear reactions take place. The bomb will explode only when the smaller uranium or plutonium trigger is fired. Responsible physicists have stated privately that two more years of work on a war-time scale by the Manhattan District could have made the deuterium bomb an actuality. Moreover, current research on heavy hydrogen, a substance of special importance to theoretical as well as applied nuclear physics, is advancing the date of actual demonstrations.

That bigger and better bombs were being prepared need not be doubted ; that man will one day solve the problem of making such horrors expeditiously and possibly at no great cost need not be doubted. It seems to be a quality of human nature that when the problem is one of destruction, human ingenuity seldom fails. Nor does man fail to do his worst when he goes to war. As for defence against atomic bombs, the scientists may speak for themselves. The

Emergency Committee of Atomic Scientists in the U.S.A. issued in 1946 the following statement:

1. Atomic bombs can now be made cheaply and in great number. They will become more destructive.
2. There is no military defence against atomic bombs and none is to be expected.
3. Other nations can rediscover our secret processes by themselves.
4. Preparedness against atomic war is futile, and if attempted will ruin the structure of our social order.
5. If war breaks out, atomic bombs will be used and they will surely destroy our civilization.
6. There is no solution to this problem except international control of atomic energy and, ultimately, the elimination of war.

In April, 1948, the Emergency Committee added: " Every scientific development in the intervening seventeen months has supported the accuracy of this statement."

¶ *The Spectre of Malthus : More Men Less Food*

In the nineteenth century, the English political economist Thomas Malthus wrote an essay in which he outlined his famous theory to the effect that the increase in food production does not keep pace with increase in population. The position by the middle of the twentieth century was that world population had increased from the 400,000,000 of three hundred years ago to some 2,000,000,000, and continued to increase at the rate of about one per cent per annum. Thus, in about forty years, the population of the world will reach about 3,000,000,000, and in eighty years time it will be doubled. In the past, newly-discovered or newly-developed lands helped to provide the food required by the increasing population. Today there are no new lands to discover, and such have been the effects of a greedy, short-sighted, get-rich-quick mechanized civilization that vast fertile regions which hitherto produced great quantities of food have been gravely and perhaps irreparably injured. In the U.S.A. for example, the *daily* loss of surface through soil erosion was estimated in 1948 to be the equivalent of 200 farms of 45 acres each. Sir John Boyd Orr, one of the world's leading experts on the subject, wrote: " The rising tide of population and the falling reservoir of food-producing resources are a more serious problem for human society than the conflict of human ideologies " (*Observer*, 9/1/49). Experts were of opinion that science could be applied so as to increase food production faster than the population increase, but only on condition that the nations call a world truce and co-operate in a World Food Plan. The threat of hunger is a powerful one and seldom fails to affect human nature. We have already seen (page 280) that the destructiveness of modern weapons threatens to obliterate or at least ruin mankind if there should be a Third World War, and that an impulse for self-preservation may come to the rescue. We now see that the threat to man's continued existence is twofold: from his own weapons and from food shortage. It may well be that *dire expediency in the interests of self-preservation* will do what morality and religion have failed to do: compel men to behave as sensible human beings and not as hopeless, suicidal lunatics. In his masterly book *Mutual Aid*, the Russian writer Kropotkin fifty years ago challenged the Darwinian concept of the " survival of the fittest " with a theory that only by peaceful co-operation could social groups flourish. Such was the world situation in mid-twentieth century that increasing numbers of people began to realize somewhat vaguely that, unless war could be abolished and unless human beings put into practice some such principles of " mutual aid " as those enunciated by Kropotkin, mankind was doomed.

¶ *Neuroses of the West*

In the U.S.A. and, to a far lesser degree in European countries, the circumstances of life, the insecurity of existence, the fears engendered by the development of the atomic bomb, the " cold " stage of the " ideological war," all these factors and no doubt others contributed towards the increase and intensification of various forms of neuroses, until by 1949 it was estimated that in the U.S.A. about 40 per cent of the population was neurotic. Of all the available hospital beds in that country, 41 per cent were occupied by mental patients. There was a steady increase in alcoholism and in the demand for all sorts of means of mental " escape," from " escapist literature " to astrological prognosis. Crime increased in both Britain and the U.S.A., and Church leaders everywhere spoke of the shattering of the moral code. Not altogether new theories of human nature were expounded and exploited. The psychiatrist increased in importance until among the well-to-do in the U.S.A. it became almost as common to consult the psychiatrist as to consult the dentist. " Self-examination " became a sort of game in which individuals tried to " analyse " their personality and character. To this end, one professor got out a " test " consisting of eight photographs of people characteristic of the ugly tendencies which are to some degree latent in large numbers of human beings. The types represented in the photographs were: the *hysteric* or emotionally unstable; the *katatonic* or " split mind "; the *sadist* or person who likes to inflict pain; the *epileptic*, who suffers from fits ; the *depressive*, who gets very miserable and enjoys it; the *paranoic*, who suffers from delusions; the *manic*, who is given to violent outbursts; and the *homosexual*. The patient is asked to select from the photographs the two types he likes best and the two he likes least. The pictures exclude good types, but on the patient's selection a " diagnosis " of character is made; and everybody comes out of it badly, as might be expected. The fact that this silly and dangerous fraud had a nation-wide vogue in the late 1940's was in itself an indication of neurosis. Less extreme forms of mental sickness showed themselves in western Europe. By 1949 the suicide rate in Britain had increased to 6,000 per annum; nearly one-half of those discharged from the Forces during the War suffered from neuroses; and a group test among engineering workers showed that, of those absent from work through illness, one quarter were mentally sick. Anxiety neuroses became common in all grades of society in the West. The only certainty of life was its uncertainty and insecurity in an armaments race which menaced the peace of the world.

On the more serious side, a speaker at the 1948 meeting of the American Association for the Advancement of Science tried to answer the question: " What hope is there for man? " This was Dr. Brock Chisholm, Canadian psychiatrist and chairman of the United Nations World Health Organization. In his view our crisis was simply a crisis made acute by our long and steady refusal to recognize the primitive behaviour which is at the root of " our method of competitive survival." *If man goes on behaving as he always has behaved*, we are doomed. In a very short time " we shall have to recognize that the guides we use to human behaviour are uncertain charts, obsolete bearings resting on premises as naïve as a flat world, old folk-tales, the loyalties and magic we learned in our childhood." He emphasized that psychiatrists and social scientists " are not altogether ignorant of the techniques of human co-operation." These techniques, he argued, were not to be regarded as merely helpful aids to politics and diplomacy, which are themselves based on ridiculous and childish antagonisms. They are new and fundamental and must be taught to governments and their agents. We must begin to see that these scientists of emotions are " serious students of reality " and enlist their help as experts in human relations.

Many individual human beings experience and live down neurosis, but few are the better for it. Whether this applies to a widespread neurosis, we do not know. The picture of the world which emerges from what has been said above may to some readers appear unnecessarily pessimistic. But it is based on human nature as shown by human behaviour up to the time these lines are written. If the writer is permitted to express a hope which is also a belief, it is that the strong instinct for self-preservation will come to the rescue of humanity if and when the danger is well and widely known. The biological need for continuity must assert itself sooner or later; and it is stronger than governments or systems.

## § 4

## CONCERNING CHANGE IN HUMAN NATURE

The question, " Does human nature change? " will, I hope, have answered itself by this time. *Human Nature does change*; often for the worse. History is not too short for certain changes to be perceptible, and it may be instructive to attempt to draw up a rough schedule of how and in what manner changes occur, one which will indicate whether they are superficial or fundamental. To understand the nature of these changes it is necessary to appreciate the fact that man is *an animal* with social propensities, and an intelligence developed to an extent which we do not find in any other form of nature. Let us then consider those qualities of man which are to be found among all highly developed animals—that is to say, those qualities which are subject to the laws of biology. Such qualities spring from fundamental instincts and emotions pertaining to the existence, the preservation, and the perpetuation of the species— for example, hunger and sex. In these there has been hardly any change in the half a million years in which human beings are supposed to have existed on this earth. In circumstances of extreme hunger and privation one cannot be sure that the most civilized man will not kill and eat his dearest friend. There are many recent instances of widespread cannibalism in famine areas in China; there are recorded isolated instances of cannibalism at sea among Englishmen during the Victorian era, and there has been a rumour of a recent case having occurred in an exploring expedition whose members consisted of an old and highly cultured European race. When driven by hunger, man will eat almost anything and will do anything for food: law, morality, manners, and all influences of heredity and environment are driven out. The sublime law of biology—the law of jungle and ocean—takes their place. It is the promptings of this law which make so many " criminals " in civilized countries. In regard to hunger, then, there has been no fundamental change. Nor is there in matters of sex any great change, though there are a host of changes in the moral code and in the manners governing it at different periods of history and in different races. Rape is no longer considered polite by men and women, though they both object to it in principle far less than they care to admit. In regard to fear, another fundamental instinct based always upon the desire for life, there is a slight change due to the steady disappearance from the world of a dread of Invisible and Intangible Things, and the fear of the consequences of death. Man now *seems to be* a braver being than he has ever been before, although one is not too certain of this when one thinks of his struggle against the monsters of the prehistoric world and those of the jungle during the incalculably long hunting period, when his character and nature were mostly formed. It is doubtful if there has been any change in the range of man's intellect, though one cannot yet be sure. In regard to combativeness, there are considerable changes; although some people may consider that they are superficial. The original physical struggle for existence during the period when man was still a hunted animal has been replaced by (or sublimated in) a sort of commercial combativeness and ruthlessness exemplified in life under modern finance and industry. The gregarious instinct is another of the fundamentals that has undergone a change, in that it has become intensified. Although the world is still for the most part engaged in agriculture, there are now whole areas in which 90 per cent of the population consists of city dwellers; and when human beings have dwelt for a couple of generations in a city they lose desire for bucolic life. It is doubtful if the human powers of imagination have changed greatly in two thousand years. The powers are the same, but behind them they have an immense cultural structure providing endless stimulating and suggestive ideas. I have already referred to the seeming inevitability of inventions. To this may be added that each new invention provides material for many others. Who could imagine in the early nineteenth century that Faraday's experiments in electricity would lead towards the American financial and commercial conquest of half the world? For American industrial efficiency and wealth are based upon electric power and the internal-combustion engine, and the highly efficient use of them in dealing with the immense natural resources ready to hand. Those immense natural resources were discovered as a result of Columbus's leisure reading, together with the appearance in the world of those two amazing inventions, the mariner's compass and the jib for tacking against the wind.

¶ *The Intelligence of " Average Man "*

In the whole history of human nature there have been at least two attempts to reduce to scientific terms the intelligence of a large number of men. During the First World War the American Army authorities collected data of which the object was to discover the intelligence, if any, of about 1,800,000 men, of whom 41,000 were officers. Nearly 30 per cent were found to be unable to read or understand newspapers or write letters home. The whole army was eventually divided into the following categories: (A) Men of *Very Superior* intelligence, such as those with ability to make a good record at a university; of these there were no less than 4½ per cent. (B) Men of *Superior* intelligence; that is, men capable of average work at a college or public school; of these there were 9 per cent. (c +) 16½ per cent were of *High Average* intelligence, and included some men with a capacity for " leadership." (c) About 25 per cent were of *Average* intelligence, who made " excellent privates " (mental age fourteen). (c −) About 20 per cent were of *Low Average* intelligence—only moderate privates—(mental age twelve). (D) About 15 per cent were of *Inferior* intelligence, slow to learn but " fair soldiers," though unable to understand written directions. (D − & E) About 10 per cent were of

*Very Inferior* intelligence (mental age of from three to ten years). Fielding comments: "Assuming that the drafted men were a fair sample of the mental development of our [*i.e.* American] 100,000,000 population, it means that 45,000,000 or nearly one-half of the whole population have the mental capacity of a normal twelve-year-old child, and that only thirteen and one-half per cent possess superior intelligence." The same probably applies throughout Western civilization, to judge from the general social history of recent years. A similar intelligence survey based on a much greater number of conscripted Americans in the Second World War gave more or less the same result.

We cannot well estimate the intelligence of our prehistoric ancestors, apart from such guidance as may be obtained from the brain capacity of the skulls that have been found in various places. But we do know that the brain capacity of the Cro-Magnon woman far exceeded that of the average twentieth-century man. The skull which informs us of this had been smashed by a heavy blow from a bludgeon, perhaps some fifty thousand years ago (and probably during a domestic argument). It is therefore a little difficult to say whether we have more intelligence, though there is evidence which points to slight improvement. In this respect also we may, therefore, give man the benefit of the doubt and say that human nature has changed for the better. I am well aware that there is a powerful group of anthropologists and sociologists opposed to this conclusion, but I do not care to admit that they are right and that man is now lower in intelligence than he used to be.

¶ *Influence of the Cultural Structure*

Whether there is any great advance in human energy, I do not know. A casual glance at the great feats of endurance of the past makes one doubtful, and one is also doubtful of the pellet-philosophy of modern chemists who think that a pill can be made to contain the equal in energy-production of a good healthy meal. Is there any modern feat of endurance which surpasses the marches of Alexander the Great across half of Asia? Or Hannibal's feat in crossing the Alps? Or the building of the Pyramids? Or the voyages of the navigators, or those wars of the Middle Ages in which men fought terrific hand-to-hand combats while carrying armour and equipment of appalling weights? The answer may be that in our own times there have been feats of energy and endurance which at least rival all these. The march of a Japanese army in Asia, the attempts to scale Mt. Everest, the defence of the Alcazar in the Spanish Civil War of 1936—here are but a few examples of what modern man can do. One thing seems to be certain, and it is that the modern collectivist use of mobilized energy surpasses anything known to history. It is this mobilized and controlled energy, harnessed to machine power, which has in course of a hundred years provided a means of rapidly changing whole cultural edifices: this may best be illustrated by the case of Japan. The cultural edifice of Western man has itself now become an external influence which is at present engaged in remaking and re-shaping the superficial facets of his nature, those which change from age to age, and may even change considerably in the nation or individual during a lifetime. Thus, the Western world is being divided into two categories of people: those who are slaves to the machines and those who come under machine-made or machine-magnified influence in some form or other. The tending of machinery is even producing a new type of man. In the old days, a craftsman made his product from start to finish and in it expressed his originality, personality, and dignity. In so doing he fulfilled a psychological yearning. Now the tendency is for a worker to spend all his very short period of maturity and fitness in doing a single operation which, after a week or so, requires no mental effort whatever. The machine knows no fatigue in the natural sense of the word. It sets the pace of human labour in a ruthlessly exacting manner. Science has been called in to estimate nicely how much a machine-minder can stand; the vigilance of employers takes care that he uses up to the very last ounce his powers of endurance. Tension, monotony, and noise unite to turn what might have been a fair example of *Homo sapiens* into a creature that is neither a good machine nor yet fully human, for it cannot develop intelligence, imagination, dignity, or personality. Such is the position over large areas as we enter the Atomic Age, but whether this will change it we cannot tell.

¶ *Standardized Man*

The man who is half a machine is now common to most parts of the " civilized " world; the man who is one quarter machine is to be found in every grade of society, and the man who does not come under the standardizing influence of machine-discipline in some form or other is as rare as a white blackbird. Every phase of capitalist civilization is coming under the sway of machinery and the ruthless commercial greed that is behind it. The higher artistic faculties and latent powers of creation are eliminated in all directions; they survive only among courageous rebels, who tend to be overwhelmed or to develop into freaks. Later cultural achievements of the modern world are the invention of the Talking Film, Broadcasting, and Television, and of such machines as that which enables a telegraph operator to set up type at the rate of sixty or more words a minute in one or more printing factories or newspaper offices situated at great distances. Ideas are valuable only when they are strikingly original and as near to absolute truth and absolute honesty as is humanly possible; and they must tend towards the happiness and comfort, not of a few, but of all men. Hence the utilization of this machine, of the Radio, the Films, and others of a similar nature by the commercially, financially, or politically powerful can end in the mental and moral degradation and enslavement of huge conglomerations of people, many of whom are already more than half standardized.

A writer in the English Press drew attention to a phase of standardization which has, apparently, been overlooked by the anthropologists. It is one which must have unconsciously occurred to many people who visit the cinemas and see machine-made heroes and heroines. I mean the standardization of the human race. Ideas and motor-cars, buildings and tea-cakes, music and literature, ice-cream carts and petrol pumps, clothing, haircuts, and film stars are, we know, already much of a muchness everywhere, not only in the U.S.A., but also in the more highly civilized parts of Europe such as England. But faces? One might have thought that they would be the last things to resist standardization. Apparently it is not so. The observer I have mentioned says:

The third generation of European immigrants seen in American public schools tends towards a uniformity of face and feature suggesting the work of a Heavenly Henry Ford. I have seen children of Italians, Swedes, Germans, and Greeks sitting side by side looking almost alike and talking exactly the same. Impressive thought! One day America may have one single face. This will be not at all like the marvellous long face of Lincoln, thought-worn and tender; it will be a round, fattish face, with a jolly smile flashing on and off like electric light. It will be a Middle-Western face, and it will have few lines but quite a number of creases. It will be very pleasant and good-natured, but, oh! so redundant.

¶ *Lessons of History*

No lessons are simpler than those of history and none receive less serious consideration by the human being. One thing may yet save Western civilization from standardization and Robotization, and that is the preservation of languages and dialects and the encouragement of individual absurdities, bizarreries, grotesqueness, mysteries, superstitions, and beliefs, the cultivation of such originalities as those recorded in our own times in the Press regarding the solemnization of a marriage under water and the refusal of an English bargee to permit his children to read or go to the cinema, because he did not believe in such silly, new-fangled ideas as newspapers and films. The human mind must be kept free at any cost. We must, indeed, as Rousseau recommended long ago, " get back to nature " and to the " Golden Age " of ancient mythologists and modern anthropologists; to minding a cabbage patch and tending pigs and sheep. One must cultivate one's garden, as Voltaire said. It is only in this way that human nature can avoid being transformed into a standardized efficiency resembling that of termite ants—those terrible insects which have organized themselves to such a pitch that their whole life seems to us a horrible nightmare.

## § 5

### THE FUTURE OF HUMAN NATURE?

What of the future of human nature? My answer must be that it will go on and on and on and on—more or less as before. Manners and morals will change and cultural structures will change, but man and woman will never profoundly alter their natures. By profoundly I mean *biologically*. That there will be great discoveries and advances in such sciences as biochemistry, nobody doubts. It may one day be possible for a man sitting at a wireless machine to cause physical reactions of a foreseen and even deliberately calculated nature in thousands of people who have previously been doped (in the right manner) through the water supply. Such achievements as that will not be beyond science. But they are freakish possibilities, and there are already hundreds of such possibilities in the minds of imaginative scientists at this very moment. The mass of humanity jogs along more or less the same in spite of them all, though they are a great comfort in time of war. Man will probably become a fitter animal—death-rates will be reduced, the span of life lengthened, and birth control will counterbalance the extra numbers of useful and useless human beings which science will preserve for us. This may, in the course of four or five hundred years, raise the intelligence of " average " man from the mental age of fourteen to, say, fifteen, or perhaps a little less. It is not upon science that the immediate future of humanity depends so much as upon politicians, and they are a breed which, without doubt, grows steadily worse. Bernard Shaw says, " Government presents only one problem—the discovery of a trustworthy anthropometric method," and Plato long ago recommended a system which would have " philosopher-kings " in charge of affairs. But would the trustworthy anthropometric method (supposing such a method could be devised, which seems to me beyond human capacity) eliminate the bad qualities to be found in the make-up of all good men? By " bad " I mean those unsuitable for the direction or conduct of human affairs. Biology cannot be altered by mere measurement. Man is happiest, or so it seems, when his existence is most orderly and peacefully monotonous, and when all his problems, physical and spiritual, are solved without too much irritating effort of the intellect.

We live in an age when affairs of the spirit are said to be in a bad way, and with every prospect of growing steadily worse. The germ of efficiency and " Success " has bitten two great sections of the world: first America, and now Russia—the latter in a different and less selfish sense. The most significant possibilities for the future of human nature are to be found in Soviet Russia.    Suppression and cruelty resulted in the Bolshevik revolution; and Russia has passed through its " Terror " and is going through an " Age of Reason " and compromise.  But it is an " Age of Reason " with science and English and American and German industrialist experience behind it from which to learn.   Hence Russia, to judge from such evidence as is available, promises one day to leave every other country behind in efficiency.  The Russian mind is a blend of the oriental with occidental, and at its best it is a mystical mind of immense range and of more devastating logic than the French mind. It has now (as a result of Tsarist rule and the reaction thereto) a high social consciousness.  This social consciousness is being grafted upon a mass of over two hundred millions of people by means of propaganda on a scale before which all previous propaganda pales.  The object of it all is to teach individual man that he must use his individuality for the benefit of the mass.  The welfare of the mass has taken the place of God and Heaven.  " Bliss " and " Grace " are achieved by work for the earthly community.

This doctrine has reached in a very few years a power which almost justifies one calling Russian Communism a mystical religion—one with all the drive of any of the old religions.  The material strength of Soviet Russia expanded at a rate for which there is no parallel in the history of any other race or nation on this earth.  It is expanding, and its ideas are being disseminated at such a rate that a rival creed—Fascism— was created by those who fear it.  While Russian Sovietism represents an advance upon Capitalism in the interests of the masses, Fascism represents the fear-ridden creed of a decaying Capitalism which wishes to re-assert itself before it succumbs to progressive ideas.   As these lines are written, the world is engaged in taking sides in the Struggle of Ideologies, and there may yet be another war in which the old, the halt, the maimed, the blind, and the young will be poisoned, bombed, shelled, and burned with the same cynicism as that of a tiger tearing its prey to pieces. If it comes, the West as we know it will go under.   A new civilization will arise.   And a new cycle of history will have begun.

But will all that change human nature?   A little— perhaps.   The fundamentals as outlined in this book will remain.   The superstructure of the new culture may be an improvement upon all cultural superstructures that we have known.   It may mean restarting from almost zero.

The world may be saved from desolation if man will recognize that war is atavism—a return to barbarism; and that a militant and disinterested campaign in favour of peace any cost is necessary.

Meanwhile the " average " man will jog along somehow, perpetuating human stupidity and goodness as before.   Nations will come and go.   Some men and women will be beautiful flowers; others rank weeds; others monkey-puzzles.   And so on.   Men will live their three-score-years-and-ten, if they are lucky; they will sleep one-third of this period and be immature or ageing for one-half of it, leaving about twenty-five years of full life—as before.   There will always be joy and sorrow—sometimes more of one and sometimes more of the other—in the lives of men and women.   Eating, drinking, sleeping, and breeding will ever remain the most important functions of human life. The rest is all mere extrinsic, superficial ornamentation—which may be either simple or elaborate, often depending upon the vagaries of weather and climate and physical surroundings, which are themselves governed by planetary movements and forces over which we can never hope to have control. Scientists may show us a method of ectogenesis or parthenogenesis: but men and women will persist with a superstitious prejudice in favour of the old, old system of procreation. In that lies the future of human nature. In that lies the assurance that it will be as variegated as ever; that future generations of men and women will laugh and weep; that they will fight and hate and love one another just as we do.

The generations to come will have the heritage we leave them, and this is the only thing of which we can be really certain.